BEETHOVEN HERO

SCOTT BURNHAM

BEETHOVEN HERO

PRINCETON UNIVERSITY PRESS

PRINCETON, NEW JERSEY

Copyright © 1995 by Princeton University Press
Published by Princeton University Press, 41 William Street,
Princeton, New Jersey 08540
In the United Kingdom: Princeton University Press, Chichester, West Sussex
All Rights Reserved

Library of Congress Cataloging-in-Publication Data

Burnham, Scott
Beethoven Hero / Scott Burnham.
p.   cm.
Includes bibliographical references and index.
ISBN 0-691-04407-4 (alk. paper)
1. Beethoven, Ludwig van, 1770–1827—Criticism and
interpretation.   2. Beethoven, Ludwig van, 1770–1827—Appreciation.
I. Title.
ML410.B42B84   1995
780'.92—dc20   95-8981

Chapter 1 has been adapted from "On the Programmatic Reception of
Beethoven's *Eroica* Symphony," in *Beethoven Forum*, vol. 1,
by permission of the University of Nebraska Press. Copyright © 1992 by the
University of Nebraska Press

This book has been composed in Palatino
Music typeset by Don Giller

Princeton University Press books are printed
on acid-free paper and meet the guidelines
for permanence and durability of the Committee
on Production Guidelines for Book Longevity
of the Council on Library Resources

Printed in the United States of America
by Princeton Academic Press

10 9 8 7 6 5 4 3 2

For Dawna Lemaire

IT IS NOT EXPECTED of critics as it is of poets that they should help us to make sense of our lives; they are bound only to attempt the lesser feat of making sense of the ways we try to make sense of our lives.

Frank Kermode, *The Sense of an Ending*

CONTENTS

ACKNOWLEDGMENTS

I OWE MUCH to Elizabeth Powers, fine arts editor at Princeton University Press, who has been a guiding spirit in this project from its first glimmers to its completion. Production of the book was enhanced tremendously by the fine work of Lauren Oppenheim.

For making possible liberal amounts of leave time from my teaching duties, I gratefully acknowledge fellowships from the National Endowment for the Humanities and from Princeton University.

For intellectual sustenance, I need especially to applaud and thank Ian Bent, Robert Hatten, and Charles Rosen, whose generous and close readings of the manuscript proved absolutely crucial to the well-being of this book. They collectively saved me from many errors and potential mishaps; those that remain are all my own. In addition, Christopher Reynolds and James Webster made many helpful suggestions for an earlier version of chapter 1, and Richard Kramer offered indispensable advice at a still earlier stage. Two professors from Brandeis University also deserve mention here. The spirit of this book would surely have been diminished without Leonard Muellner, my cicerone in the Homeric world. And my single greatest intellectual debt is payable—as always—to Allan Keiler. It is my pleasure as well to acknowledge my esteemed colleagues in the music department at Princeton, both composers and musicologists, current and emeritus, and to thank department manager Marilyn Ham and her staff; I cannot imagine a more supportive and enriching academic environment.

Any work of this sort undertaken without the occasional accompaniment of interested friends is doomed to whistle tunelessly in the dark. Some of the friendly souls with whom I have had enlightening conversations about Beethoven and related matters include Paul Bertagnolli, Lee Blasius, David Cohen, Taylor Greer, Jeffrey Gross, Kristin Knittel, Igor Korneitchouk, Stan Link, Melanie Lowe, Roger Lustig, Michael Marissen, Brian Mohr, Tina Muxfeldt, Michael Schiano, Jeffrey West, and Lawrence Zbikowski.

Finally, I owe the deepest gratitude to all three of my families—the Burnhams, the Lemaires, and my own—for their abiding support and confidence. In particular, my grandmother Luisa Heyl Foote has been a benevolent star forever bright on the horizon—while the light of Dawna and Emmett shines warm and clear at home.

INTRODUCTION

BEETHOVEN. When asked to name the single most influential composer of the Western world, few would hesitate. And the specific style that has come to define the nature of Beethoven's accomplishment is his heroic style, a style to which only a handful of his works can lay unequivocal claim: two symphonies, two piano sonatas, several overtures, a piano concerto.[1] For nearly two centuries, a single style of a single composer has epitomized musical vitality, becoming the paradigm of Western compositional logic and of all the positive virtues that music can embody for humanity. This conviction has proved so strong that it no longer acts as an overt part of our musical consciousness; it is now simply a condition of the way we tend to engage the musical experience. The values of Beethoven's heroic style have become the values of music. This book asks how this came to be, and why this came to be—in short, why this music matters so.

"With Beethoven, the human element first came to the fore as the primary argument of musical art." The words are Busoni's, the perception an eminently common one. Yet it offers perhaps the most viable explanation for the compelling and perennial appeal of the heroic style. Busoni's declaration is cited by Hans Heinrich Eggebrecht in his 1970 monograph on Beethoven reception, a veritable anthology of apothegms culled from a wide range of the Beethoven literature.[2] Eggebrecht chronicles the persistence of a small but potent group of topoi informing the reception history of Beethoven. Common to many of these topoi, which Eggebrecht calls "reception constants," is the feeling that Beethoven's music somehow encodes real-life experiences. For example, Eggebrecht's topoi include such portmanteau words as *Erlebensmusik* (music-as-experience), *Leidensnotwendigkeit* (the necessity of suffering), and *Überwindung* (overcoming). In Eggebrecht's view, the whole of Beethoven reception can be read as if it were "one book written by one author,"[3] the prevailing theme of which is the importance of the "human element" in Beethoven's music. For Beethoven has arguably been to music what Socrates was to ancient philosophy: humankind becomes his fundamental subject; his music is heard as a direct expression of human values.

In another citation appearing in Eggebrecht's anthology, Friedrich Nietzsche claims that "with Beethoven, music first began to find the speech of pathos, of the impassioned will, of the dramatic vicissitudes in the soul of man [im Inneren des Menschen]."[4] Nietzsche purports to tell *how* Beethoven's music engages the human element—it is heard to reach within us, to the very root of passion. His music thus offers a privileged testimony to the human will and its struggles, both with itself and with a recalcitrant external world. The interiority Nietzsche speaks for implies a deep sense of engagement at the individual level, and yet Beethoven's music has always been felt to wield the broad power of universality. But his is not a faceless universality, not some blunted common denominator; his is a universality that embraces all individualities. As Victor Hugo avers: in Beethoven's music "the dreamer will recognize his dream, the sailor his storm, . . . and the wolf his forests."[5] This is indeed music of universal human experience, but of a very particular type: human experience is here cast as heroic experience. The repeated claims on behalf of this music for universality testify to the profound satisfaction this scenario offers, how it appears to engage each of us at a deeply personal level, and yet engages us all in roughly the same way, such that the fundamental experience of the heroic style is always described similarly.

And what is the nature of the heroic experience represented in this music? The short answer usually invokes the necessity of struggle and eventual triumph as an index of man's greatness, his heroic potential. As a character in one of Milan Kundera's novels puts it, "We believe that the greatness of man stems from the fact that he *bears* his fate as Atlas bore the heavens on his shoulders. Beethoven's hero is a lifter of metaphysical weights."[6] Who, we may ask, is Beethoven's hero? Is he really an Atlas, marked most signally by the presence of strain? And is the heroic style then a celebration of heaviness, a way to confirm fate as weight, making the contemplation of the human condition a branch of the science of load bearing? Such a one-sided caricature of the heroic experience is belied by the accounts of Beethoven's hero that arise in programmatic treatments of his music.

Within the tradition of programmatic interpretations of the *Eroica* Symphony that constitutes the primary strand of that symphony's reception history, there have been a number of candidates for its hero— Napoleon is merely the default choice. In many of these readings, the hero of the first movement shares important features with the heroes in contemporaneous German drama. Just as the great historical dramas of the German *Klassik* turned from the portrayal of mythological figures (as in French classicism) to that of real human beings, Beethoven's heroic concept is heard to be rooted not in some divinity but in man himself, in the rhythms of self. And it has not been heard merely to portray the predicament of a particular hero but to speak to the hero within all of us, to empower that hero. This is put most directly by Wagner, writing in 1851: "If by 'hero' we understand the complete, whole Man, to whom belong all the purely human feelings—of love, pain, and power—in their highest fullness and strength, we then grasp the correct subject that [Beethoven] shares with us in the gripping musical speech of his work."[7]

The course of the entire four-movement work signifies for Wagner the coming together of the whole man, a process we would today be inclined to call self-actualization. This hero rejoices in his mildness as well as his might, his anima as well as his animus. By raising such a view of man as the hero of Beethoven's *Eroica*, Wagner goes beyond Kundera's invocation of the metaphysical weight lifter. Doing so, he touches on the nature of the effect of the heroic style on its many listeners, for one's concept of self is here engaged much more broadly.

But the study of our prepossession by the heroic style urges another step. In addition to arguing for a view of Beethoven's heroic style that helps us understand that its profound appeal is an appeal to a particularly rewarding sense of self, I shall consider the process by which we have come to transform that compelling appeal into the compulsions of institutional thought about music. As an articulation of this crucial shift, we may again turn to Wagner and the *Eroica* Symphony. For Wagner had yet another idea about the hero of the *Eroica*. A character in one of his Parisian short stories ("Ein Glücklicher Abend," written in 1841) discourages his friend from hearing the *Eroica* as a musical portrait of Napoleon or of any other specific hero. He argues instead that the symphony is itself an act of heroism, an emulation of Napoleon: "He [Beethoven], too, must have felt *his* powers aroused to an extraordinary pitch, his valiant courage spurred on to a grand and unheard of deed [unerhörte Tat]! He was no general—he was a musician; and thus in *his* realm he saw before him the territory within which he could accomplish the same thing that Bonaparte had achieved in the fields of Italy."[8]

Even though Wagner's story was to have no effect on the steady stream of heroes who continue to figure in programmatic interpretations of the *Eroica*, his words serve well as an articulation of the prevailing view of Beethoven's stature in music history. For Beethoven himself is acknowledged as the hero of the *Eroica* Symphony. This pronouncement transforms the symphony from the portrayal of a hero to an act of heroism, and Beethoven from the portrayer of heroes to hero himself. His symphony both describes and is an "unerhörte Tat." In a fundamental and emblematic move in the reception of the heroic style, Beethoven, the original teller of a heroic story, has become the protagonist of a similar story. Thus the understood meaning of the *Eroica* and the act of its creation are merged; this establishes a symbolic conjunction of this work and this artist that will prove singularly tenacious. For with the *Eroica* Symphony, Beethoven becomes the hero of Western music, "The Man Who Freed Music." With this one work, Beethoven is said to liberate music from the stays of eighteenth-century convention, singlehandedly bringing music into a new age by giving it a transcendent voice equal to Western man's most cherished values.

Beethoven is thus deemed a force of history, the prime mover of musical necessity. Accordingly, two other constants of Beethoven reception noted by Eggebrecht are *Autorität* (authority) and *Inbegriff* (epitome).[9] These imply that Beethoven's music instantiates something felt to be fundamental to music itself; indeed, Beethoven is treated as the embodiment of music, the indispensable authority on the question of how music ought to go. We have moved from Beethoven's hero to Beethoven Hero; the hero with whom we identify becomes subsumed within the figure of a demigod whom we can only serve.

It goes without saying that several very suggestive aspects of Beethoven's life have lent crucial support to our continued treatment of him as the quintessential artist-hero. In a letter to the Countess Erdödy, written in 1815, the composer made the following declaration: "We mortals with immortal spirits are born only to suffering and joy, and one could almost say that the most distinguished among us obtain joy through suffering."[10] It would be hard to imagine a more direct transcription of the popular view of the meaning of Beethoven's heroic style. And I need hardly invoke the impassioned rhetoric of the Heiligenstadt Testament, another of Beethoven's imposing gifts to posterity. But I shall not be discussing these features of Beethoven's biography, for in the end I am concerned not with how the facts of his life impinge upon his work (there are plenty of scholars better equipped than I to deal with that question) but rather with how his work has impinged upon us. A knowledge of the facts of his life may deeply influence the way we hear his music, of course—and yet if the music did not hold such a fascination for us, the facts of his life would hardly matter. For there are plenty of embattled artists peopling the tapestry of modern human history, but only one of them has written the music of the heroic style. Thus my emphasis will be on the music and how we have been hearing it.

At the outset of my investigation stands the *Eroica* Symphony, as the fulcrum upon which generations of critics have levered the subsequent history of Western music. And not only is the *Eroica* Symphony said to have changed the course of music history but, more astonishing still, it is primarily the first movement of the *Eroica* that carries the force of this historical turn. Epitomizing the type of plot most readily attributed to Beethoven's heroic style, this single movement stands in a uniquely influential position in the history of Western music: if not the progenitor of numberless epigonal openings—the fate of the first movement of the Ninth Symphony—then surely it has provided the template by which the dramatic potential of sonata-form composition would subsequently be gauged. Programmatic critics have repeatedly interpreted this movement as a deeply engaging psychological process not unlike the archetypal process depicted in mythological accounts of the hero's journey, with the result that sonata form takes on an ethical trajectory, one that would sustain the form well into the twentieth century. And this is why it is so important that our own trajectory begin here, with the first movement of the *Eroica* Symphony.

What is it about the heroic style that grants it such an imposing presence, a presence that indeed registers as myth, combining the power, grace, and spontaneity of autochthonic expression? What is it that fosters the reported intensity of listeners' engagement with this music, their often overwhelming sense of identification with its musical process? And how does the heroic style control our discourse about music; how in particular has Beethoven come to embody Music? These questions set the tasks of chapters 2 and 3, where we will first explore the musical values that contribute to one's sense of identification with this music and then the ways in which these values have been inscribed, through the work of some of the most influential Germanic tonal theorists of the last two centuries, as the cardinal values of musical thought in the West.

With this appeal to musical values I do not mean to stake out some sort of neutral level of purely musical significance. But I believe we can still profitably make music the primary, or at least initial, locus of our investigation. We can look to the music of the heroic style and attempt to account for the level of engagement these works inspire by thinking about what things we are responding to in the music and how we tend to characterize those things. This is how such things become musical *values* after all. In other words, we are examining our reactions more than imputing any sort of immanent essence to the music, and it is in this sense that I shall be using the term musical values—as those things that we come to value in the music.

Another way to say all this is that instead of looking for a strictly musical basis of our prepossession by the heroic style I am looking for the phenomenological basis. This involves taking note of our reactions to the music and finding out how the music makes such reactions possible, how it nurtures and sustains them even to the point of making them seem inevitable. These reactions are always expressed metaphorically, and it is on this footing that I shall continue to address them. As we shall discover throughout this book, the musical processes heard in the heroic style tend to elicit a family of related metaphors, no matter what the explicit analytical language of the critic. At bottom, there seems to be no other way to deal with them, no other way to hear them. This is in fact their power (rather than our weakness, or some collective failure of imagination): analytical discourse cannot but ground these processes once again in the same metaphorical scenario. Thus the scenario of an embattled and ultimately prevailing subject seems to be the only commensurate response to this music. Of course this scenario is tremendously compelling in its own right, with the result that its conjunction with Beethoven's music proves irresistible.

With its projection of a self struggling to create and fulfill its own destiny, the music of Beethoven's heroic style is strongly rooted in the cultural and intellectual impulses of its own age. In chapter 4, I shall characterize that age as a watershed era in the formation of our modern concept of self, an end to which many of the diverse currents of romanticism, classicism, and idealism prove to be kindred streams. Although I shall for convenience refer to this age as the *Goethezeit* (Age of Goethe), I ultimately argue that it is Beethoven who sounds its deepest and yet most vivid keynote, joining, in the *élan terrible* of his heroic style, the Goethean dynamic of contemplation and deed with the Hegelian dialectical trajectory of the self and its consciousness.[11] Our allegiance to the heroic style will thus be understood to be distinctly ethical, bound inextricably with the values of self that flourished in the early nineteenth century and are still maintained, albeit covertly, in much of our current musical discourse. As part of its critique of the Beethoven paradigm, chapter 5 will address the unhappy results of our collective repression of this ethical dimension.

The conviction that our mainstream musical discourse has come to be fundamentally constructed by a single compelling musical style begs the question of the possibility of getting beyond this paradigm. My final move in this book will thus be to suggest a model of musical experience based on what I shall call "presence." I invoke this model as a strategy bent on attenuating the prevailing Beethovenian view of music as exclusively process-oriented. My proposed model must unfortunately remain clothed in the loose lineaments of suggestion; a more finished argument would transcend the reach of this study and may not even be possible within the field of its terms.

Finally, I would like to acknowledge right at the outset what may seem to be curious omissions, odd swerves from the accepted track of musicological scholarship on Beethoven. First, I shall not address the heroic style in terms of its development or its musical precedents.[12] Second, there will be no discussion of the music of the French Revolution, no speculation about Beethoven and Napoleon, nothing at all, in fact, about the biographical issues surrounding the Beethoven myth.[13] Third, I am not interested in presenting a highly detailed reception history, abundantly adorned with documents, debates, and other "debris" (to borrow Dahlhaus's trenchant term for the materials of reception histories).[14] Again, there are many vastly capable scholars who have worked, or are currently working, in all these quarters.

Instead, I wish to deal with what is most overt about the heroic style, its best-known footprint. My goal is to engage as directly as I can the fundamental importance of this music. It is admittedly difficult to say anything new about Beethoven's music when facing it head-on in this way. But this very difficulty is a crucial part of my story, for it raises the suspicion that it may in fact be impossible to say anything genuinely new about this music (or any music) when all that we say about music in general is conditioned by this very music. The attempt to talk about how we hear this music is really an attempt to deal with the question of what we value in music—what we want from music and what music does for us. These broad concerns form the backdrop of this study. Yet my motivation here is not to critique and then dismantle the status quo, to condemn out of hand our unconscious acceptance of what may now register as unconscionable values. Rather, I hope that these pages will reveal a fundamentally ethical crux; I hope they will capture some trace of the poignancy that obtains when the attempt to understand what we have come to love in the heroic style becomes the attempt to understand what that love has brought us to. For I want to believe that the tradition that has accumulated in the wake of Beethoven's music is not simply the unwitting dupe of ideological prejudice; I want to believe that the values of the heroic style are truly of value. And yet, the time has come—not to disown these values, surely—but to discern the ways in which we have become invested in defending them, to discover the cost of such defense mechanisms to the well-being of our musical ecology. We may even find that Beethoven no longer needs to be defended.

A NOTE TO THE READER

Because of the general availability of scores of Beethoven's symphonies, discussions that include these works are not accompanied here by music examples. Examples are provided for most of the other works discussed in the text.

BEETHOVEN HERO

Chapter One

BEETHOVEN'S HERO

WE BEGIN BY retelling a story that has been told for almost two hundred years: the story many generations of listeners have heard in the first movement of the *Eroica* Symphony. Like a great myth, this story is told in numberless ways, fashioned anew by each generation. Different agents move through its course to similarly appointed ends: we hear of the destiny and self-realization of real heroes, mythical heroes, or even humankind itself. These sorts of programs are still generated today, though much less frequently, and even at the height of the formalist disdain of such interpretations, earlier this century, the old story is preserved—if only in a translated version with new metaphors, telling of the animadversions of a process or a structure, or the development of a theme and its motives. For the trajectory of these stories is always the same, or nearly so: something (someone) not fully formed but full of potential ventures out into complexity and ramification (adversity), reaches a ne plus ultra (a crisis), and then returns renewed and completed (triumphant). The use (whether overt or covert) of such an anthropomorphic scenario is a sign that the stakes are high, the game played close to home.

To expedite the telling of this story, I shall concentrate on those passages that have attracted the most commentary and that are heard as crux points, hinges, turning points, ends, and beginnings. These include the first forty-five bars, the new theme in the development and its climactic exordium, the horn call, and the coda. The interpretive readings of several different generations of critics and analysts—ranging from A. B. Marx and Aléxandre Oulibicheff through Heinrich Schenker and Arnold Schering to Peter Schleuning and Philip G. Downs—will combine to form a composite narrative.[1] Emphasis throughout will be on the similar ways in which all these commentators react to the musical events of the movement, however dissimilar their language and explicit agenda.

I am purposefully limiting the discussion to the first movement. Wilhelm von Lenz once observed that this movement is closed within itself, "like an overture raised to the power of a symphony."[2] Many of the other writers I have looked at implicitly subscribe to the same view, for most of their interpretive energy is pledged to the first movement, with the remaining movements receiving progressively less and less coverage. Critics attempting to develop a programmatic interpretation that satisfactorily links all four movements of the *Eroica* face a number of stiff challenges, not the least of which is the presence of two movements after the hero's funeral. If Berlioz hit upon the happy expedient of hearing the Scherzo as a musical transcription of ancient Greek funeral games, there still remained no comfortable way to incorporate the finale. Most critics allow the finale to pick up a very different narrative strand from that projected by the first three movements—here, Beethoven's use of the theme from his ballet *The Creatures of Prometheus* provides a convenient and irresistible extramusical clue. The recent Prometheus-based interpretation of the *Eroica* by Peter Schleuning attempts to make a virtue of this situation, by claiming that the finale is the programmatic goal of the entire symphony, which allegedly follows the Prometheus story of Beethoven's earlier ballet through all four movements. Wagner, as we saw in the introduction, preceded Schleuning in the view that the finale crowns one long process; for him, the finale works to unite the facets of Mankind projected by the earlier movements into a heroically complete man. I would argue that the urge to create an embracing narrative for the entire symphony arises at least partially from the ease with which such programs are generated for works like the Fifth and Ninth Symphonies, and from the perception that such "through-composed" multimovement designs represent a higher form of the symphony.[3]

But it is not merely to avoid the interpretive challenges of the subsequent movements that I propose to limit this discussion to the first movement. As I stated in the introduction, it is primarily this movement that has been responsible for the stature of the *Eroica*, for its role as a turning point of music history. The unexampled drama of this movement singlehandedly altered the fate of sonata form, the defining form of the classical style, not to mention that of the symphony. And the homogeneity of its reception, the nearly universal feeling that it is most meaningfully heard as a powerfully stirring version of that premier story of Western mythology, the hero's journey, fairly demands that it be placed at the outset of our own journey.

I

The first forty-five bars of the *Eroica* Symphony comprise one of the most raked-over pieces of musical property in the Western hemisphere. No one denies the overtly heroic effect of the two opening blasts, and it is almost comic to see how programmatic interpreters inevitably rush off with the impetus of these two chords only to stumble a few bars later when they realize that something distressingly less than expeditious heroism is implied by the much-discussed C♯ in bar 7. The tendency for critical discourse to slow down when passing this spot mirrors the inability of the piece itself to get started in a convincing fashion. What kind of a hero would pause so portentously at the very outset of his heroic exploits?

A. B. Marx and Aléxandre Oulibicheff offer a neat solution to this dilemma in their Napoleon-oriented programs, both dating from the 1850s: elements that impede the forward progress of the music or undermine its tonality are seen as external to the hero Napoleon and do not signify any weakness or vacillation on the part of the great general.[4] Napoleon himself is stuck in forward gear, and the concept of the heroic implied in these interpretations is that of a singularly obsessed hero fighting against a recalcitrant external world.[5] For both Marx and Oulibicheff, the music of the first forty-five bars represents morning on the battlefield, thereby establishing a setting for the ensuing battle. Marx, for example, notes that the theme (which he explicitly associates with Napoleon) first sounds in a lower voice and is raised in three successive stages to a full orchestral tutti statement. His program acknowledges this musical process by casting the entire section as a conflation of the rising of the sun on the battlefield with the rising of Napoleon onto his battle steed. Moments of tonal vacillation, such as the C♯ at bar 7 or, in the next statement, the sequential move to F minor, are associated with shadows and mists—things that hide the light of the sun (and of the rising hero).[6] These moments are always followed by an even more decisive statement of the theme, and a pattern of statement–liquidation–stronger statement is established. Not only does the hero persist; he grows stronger.

This pattern, which is noted in programmatic terms by both Marx and Oulibicheff, can help us identify what is surely one of the most striking features of this opening section: it functions simultaneously as an introduction (setting) and as an exposition of the first theme. That is why the theme cannot appear in full tutti splendor (Napoleon cannot appear in the saddle) until after the big dominant arrival and prolongation in bars 23–36. The dual image of sunrise on the battlefield and the hero preparing to present himself to his troops captures an important aspect of the musical process.

But that is not all. There is also a sense of musical development in these first bars. Both Marx and Oulibicheff note that the ambiguity provided by the C♯ in the bass and the subsequent syncopated G's in the first violins works to extend a simple four-bar phrase into a thirteen-bar *Satz*.[7] The fact that the theme always veers away from E♭ through the introduction of chromaticism is a mark of developmental instability as well as developmental extrapolation. In Marx's reading, this kind of vacillation contributes to a pattern of action and reaction that extends throughout the entire movement.[8] The identification of the main theme of the movement with the protagonist Napoleon, who must exhort his troops to victory, conforms to the tendency of this theme to act more as a developmental force than as a melodic entity, even during the course of its own exposition.

Several critics of the twentieth century give the developmental and transitional features of this opening section a psychological reading. Alfred Heuss elaborates a view of the hero as a willful and wily leader, whose strategic mainspring is his quicksilver unpredictability, heard in the "demonic uncertainty" of the famous C♯.[9] The opening forty-five bars represent for Heuss a process in which the hero becomes conscious of his inner nature (expressed by the cello line at the outset) and transforms it into his public exterior (the transference of the theme to the upper register); when the theme is heard in both bass and soprano (bars 37ff.), Heuss exclaims: "And now . . . the hero looms before us as a giant, fully in tune with himself, both inwardly and outwardly a heroic character of hugest proportion."[10] In this rather more psychologically complex reading than Marx's black and white opposition of hero and external world, Heuss places the vicissitudes of the opening bars within the mind and character of the hero. This type of interpretive strategy, which in its shift of perspective makes the music out to be more a drama of the self in the first person than a depiction of some other self, is echoed in three other roughly contemporaneous interpretations.

Paul Bekker, Arnold Schering, and Romain Rolland all center their interpretations on the dual nature of these opening bars, hearing the passage in the same way as Marx and Oulibicheff but construing it differently. For Bekker, the hero vacillates in his own mind between "vorwärtsdrängende Tatkraft" (forward-driving energy) and "klagend resignierendes Besinnen" (plaintively resigning deliberation). He claims that these two facets of the hero's inner conflict can be followed throughout the entire movement (thereby matching the extent of Marx's narrative structure of actions and reactions).[11] Thus Bekker has transferred the scene of the action from an actual battlefield to a psychological process. At first blush, Arnold Schering's controversial interpretation seems to place the conflict right back on the battlefield, and not even a battlefield from modern European history but the plains of ancient Troy. Hector is said to be the hero of the first movement, the symphony as a whole to consist of selected scenes from the *Iliad*.[12] Yet the starting point for Schering's reading is that of Bekker's: an aggressive/passive duality. Instead of hearing this duality as a conflict within the psyche of the hero himself, Schering personifies the hesitating side of the hero by giving the role to Andromache, wife of Hector.[13] Psychology gives way to mythic archetype. The first section of the exposition thus illustrates, for Schering, the famous scene of Hector's farewell from Andromache in book 6 of the *Iliad*. Finally, Romain Rolland hears the opening section as a battle joined between two souls, figured roughly as the will and the heart (or, as he later puts it, between the "ego of love" and the "ego of will").[14]

All these critics feel the effect of duality and describe it in terms of action and reaction, whether the action is the rising of the sun, the deed-oriented drive of the hero, the urge of Hector to defend his city, or simply the will, and whether the reaction is morning mists and shadows, the passive contemplation of the hero, the wifely remonstrances of Andromache, or simply the heart. Among those latter-day analysts who seek to eschew programmatic interpretation, David Epstein sees this duality in terms of downbeat orientation versus upbeat orientation.[15] In my view, this is yet another translation of what is felt by those who account metaphorically for the musical process at work here. Moments of retarded action, which act as extended upbeats and build to a big dominant, enable a higher level of energy to be attained from which a new downbeat-oriented section can follow. Thus a kind of systole-diastole rhythm permeates this opening section and can be said to continue throughout the movement at several different rhythmic levels. At a local level, for example, the syncopated, upbeat rhythm of the first violins in bar 7 initiates a long intake of breath before the downbeat of bar 15; more globally, the so-called second theme as well as the so-called new theme provide large-scale reactive upbeats to ensuing downbeat sections.

Pausing to take stock of the various readings of the first forty-five bars, we notice that all our critics have identified in one way or another those aspects of Beethoven's style which are particularly characteristic of his middle period. These include the alternation of active downbeat-oriented sections with reactive upbeat-oriented sections, the liberation of thematic development to the extent that it may even take place during the initial exposition of the theme, and the polysemic formal significance of the opening section, understood as combining the features of introduction, exposition, and development. All the programmatic interpretations mentioned so far have equated these innovations with the will of a heroic protagonist, a hero preparing—either mentally or physically—for heroic action. Just as the protagonist himself has not yet gone through the fateful trials that will define his character as a hero, so too has Beethoven's theme remained, in a sense, unconsummated: its urge to slide immediately away from E♭ through chromatic alteration, even in its tutti presentation, never allows it to behave as a truly melodic theme with a stable harmonic underpinning and normative phrase structure—in fact it will have to wait until the coda before it is granted that sort of themehood. Thus there is a strong sense in the opening section that this theme has not yet submitted to its destiny, has not yet exercised its full power or received its full due. The same might be said of any theme heard within the context of sonata form. But the fact that this theme must so submit in order to become more like a theme is unprecedented in musical discourse. This process establishes a new way in which music can be about a theme.

At this point I would like to suggest that the programmatic equation of theme and dramatic protagonist makes explicit a certain attitude about the nature of Beethoven's use of thematic development in his middle-period style. It was this dimension of Beethoven's style that was felt to be revolutionary and deeply engaging by his first critics; programmatic interpretation allowed them to address this specific aspect while downplaying the more generic and easily describable categories of musical form and harmonic syntax. There was no analytical metalanguage that could account for overall thematic process comparable to that which could describe periodic structures and other features that the *Eroica* shares with stylistic practice that had already been codified. Most of these critics were perfectly capable of describing the music in terms of form, thematic structure, and harmony.[16] They simply chose not to, for those things were not what was most meaningful to them about this music.

Yet it would be limiting to imply that the nineteenth-century prevalence of programs was solely a matter of exigence, of the need to find an analytical metalanguage that could map onto the elusive logic of thematic process. To take a broader view, such programs may simply be indicative of the need to approach works of imagination with imagination. Anthropomorphic metaphor was not the only available language for romantic critics, but it may well have been the only commensurate language for what they felt was the deep imaginative potential of this music. Metaphors involving human actions engage the imagination more directly, overtly, and powerfully than those detailing faceless processes that are merely organic. And the concept of theme as protagonist reflects the dynamic nature of the thematic process in Beethoven's heroic style while offering an available and easily identifiable model for the engaging drama of this music.

This is a more portentous critical turn than one might think, for in musical thought since Beethoven, themes and motives have often been conceptualized as dramatic protagonists.[17] This interpretive reflex provides a mode of identity with the theme, a way to be present in the musical experience. And it has since come to characterize our general perspective on Western tonal music: in such music we like to hear a temporal dramatic process featuring a theme or motive. Because first movements of symphonies most readily exemplify this model, they have received the most attention in critical and analytical writings. The imputation of dramatic agency to music finds in Beethoven's heroic style something of a *locus colossicus*; for here, in Wagner's terse formulation, all is melody, and the entire symphonic texture is heard as somehow moving into dramatic action as a theme might.[18]

II

For many writers, the most explicitly novel feature of the first movement of the *Eroica* Symphony is the theme in E minor that enters in the development section after a climax of shattering force.[19] The newness of this "new" theme has been challenged by analysts who have unearthed more or less hidden connections to previous thematic material.[20] Such analytical observations often put on a self-congratulatory air of discovery, as if the fact that this theme bears latent resemblances to other aspects of the thematic, rhythmic and harmonic arguments of the movement would somehow negate the overwhelming reality that it is, in fact, a *new theme*.[21] Moreover, it is arguably the only theme yet heard in the movement—none of the thematic utterances within the exposition can claim the melodic and harmonic character of a theme to the same degree. And it is clearly meant to be heard as a major statement, for Beethoven marks its entrance with incomparable drama. This is no place, then, for clever compositional subtleties; rather, the new theme somehow bears the brunt of the entire conception of the movement. How have our critics dealt with it?

In characteristic form, A. B. Marx dissociates the new theme from his hero. Marx leaves the question of the theme's precise meaning open; he offers a number of possible interpretations, all of which represent the utterance of an outside agency reflecting on the sad business of human carnage.[22] As such, the theme stands in Marx's reading as the culminating reaction in a series of action-reaction configurations. In the exposition and earlier part of the development these involved the interaction between Napoleon and his troops; here the reaction is expressed by some greater entity that stands beyond the field of action. Peter Schleuning, in his recent interpretation of the *Eroica* as a symphony about Prometheus, recognizes the new theme as a turning point in the musical process, one that signifies an "internally heard higher voice" warning Prometheus not to destroy his own work (an act that he had almost managed in the preceding bars).[23] The similarity to Marx's reading is striking.

For Wilhelm von Lenz, the new theme records the moment immediately after the hero is slain. Lenz provides the following stanza as a poetic equivalent to the theme:

> I feel I have lived for all the ages
> And hitched my fame to the stars.
> The world shall know that the lion now dies,
> And *Vienna* shall light his funeral torch.[24]

The hero, and the music, have clearly crossed the line into the afterlife; the otherness of this realm is expressed in the otherness of the new theme. Lenz's interpretive stanza also resonates with the Homeric notion of *kléos* (glory), a concept to which I shall return presently.

Oulibicheff's reading calls for a change of scene: hearing an oriental note in the new theme, he speculates that Napoleon, staggered by the force of the preceding music (is it forecasting his disastrous Russian campaign?), turns his thoughts back to his campaigns in Egypt and the Indies. As in Marx's program, the new theme thus represents a turning away from the action at hand. Like Oulibicheff, several critics of our own century also prefer to hear the new theme as indicative of an internal process taking place within the mind of the hero. For Paul Bekker, the new theme represents a catastrophic impasse reached by the conflicting sides of the heroic personality, a paralyzing disjunction that results in brooding and languishing exhaustion.[25] In the Homeric scene envisioned by Schering, the new theme illustrates Hector's Christian reluctance to kill Patroklos after a protracted standoff. This moment of anachronistic morality is Beethoven's addition to the Homeric tradition, claims Schering.[26] Schering's version thus shares with those of Marx and Schleuning the aspect of an outside agency (Christian humanity) that intrudes at the crucial moment upon the action (Hector's urge to kill Patroklos).

All these views emphasize the otherness of the new theme, the effect of supreme disjunction that it brings to the musical discourse. Yet this very disjunction is somehow seen as a necessary stage in the psychological and dramatic process of the movement. Marx, the premier nineteenth-century theorist of form, acknowledges the disruptive effect of this theme on his notion of sonata form and seeks to assuage his discomfort by appealing to Beethoven's ability to create dramatically compelling *Sätze*: each *Satz* leads to the next in such a way that the listener is prepared to "take it up."[27] The new theme is thus made to sound inevitable or at the least, credible, and that which is unjustifiable in terms of formal analysis is justified in terms of dramatic process. In the interpretations of Bekker and Schering, the new theme is felt to be a necessary, if extreme, component of the hero's psychology.

Heinrich Schenker fleshed out Marx's intuition about our willingness to accept this "unerhörte Tat" by showing how the motivic preparation for the theme starts some forty bars before its appearance.[28] Furthermore, Schenker understands the remote tonality of the new theme as made necessary by a chromatic upper neighbor to B♭ in the bass, indicative of the *Aufwärtsdrang*, or "urge to ascend," an emblematic—and distinctly heroic—trait of the musical process, which he tracks throughout the entire movement (see example 1.1).[29]

Example 1.1. Beethoven, Symphony no. 3, first movement, development section: voice-leading graph. From Schenker, *Das Meisterwerk in der Musik*, vol. 3, supplement, figure 3.

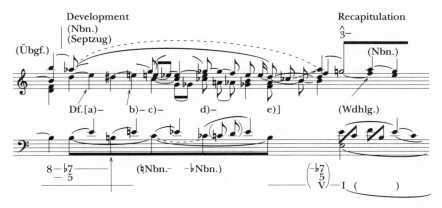

In terms of harmonic progression, there is a long-ranging string of rising fifths that starts in the fugato and leads, with some prolongational episodes, to E minor (F minor, bar 236; C minor, bar 239; G minor, bar 242; D minor, bar 245; A minor, bar 254; E minor, bar 284). The positioning of the A-minor sonority, as a iv^6 about to land on V^7 in E minor, undermines its identity as an independent tonicization. Instead it marks the beginning of a thirty-bar approach to and elaboration of the dominant of E minor, culminating in the clash between E and F at the top of the orchestral texture, a clash that makes explicit the implied dissonance respective to the tonic of the ♭II sonority. The energy of this clash is shunted off gradually in the following bars by the repeated pulses of the dominant with minor ninth—a toned-down, more normative presentation of half-step dissonance—followed by the dominant seventh. Analysis of this long-range underlying tonal preparation of E minor, whose path leads locally through some disorienting diminished seventh chords (bars 266–71 and 272–73) as well as the harrowing impasse of bars 276–79, supports the insights of a Marx concerning our willingness to accept the seemingly unacceptable. For if we do find ourselves in what may retrospectively be adjudged an impossibly remote harmonic realm, we are made to feel the ineluctable continuity of the process through which we arrived there.[30] This continuity, both long-range and short-range, is compelling enough to make us believe in anything.[31]

While analysis such as Schenker's gives the impression of careful and strategic preparation of an end determined by the deep structure of the movement, most programmatic reactions to this section of the development indicate a process carried dangerously afield by its own destiny-driven engine. The effect of the continuity in this scene is rather like a movie camera tracking in one shot the progress of two combatants, whose heated struggle takes them far away from where they started. Their struggle has its own coherence in the long-range harmonic progression detailed above; no single step of this progression is unorthodox, and there are no magic doors, no remote modulations. Yet this progression moves far beyond the precincts of E♭: the shock of this distance is accentuated by the grinding halt on an "evil chord" standing on the brink of E minor.[32] This moment of dissonant climax has been described by all programmatic commentators as a catastrophic impasse, either a standoff between two fighters or two armies (or two states of mind), resulting in death (or mental paralysis), or an extreme state of Promethean frustration and enraged despair.[33] In either case, the agency we have been tracking through this movement has forgotten itself and risked everything in its fatal progress, has moved to an ultimate point beyond which lies nothing and from which there can be no turning back.

The movement has thus reached an antipode.[34] This important arrival has occurred in the development section, a section normatively reserved for working on thematic material and building up to the recapitulation. Again we see that one of the central critical intuitions about this movement, that its opening theme is somehow less a musical object than a potential to act, less *ergon* than *energeia*, is borne out by the progress of the musical discourse. The point here is not to showcase a given theme by first exposing it, then moving away from it, and finally returning to it in triumph. Rather the theme embodies from its outset a process of action and reaction that culminates at the arrival of the new theme, a kind of photographic negative of the initial theme itself (which may be a more fruitful way of assessing the hidden features the new theme shares with the main theme). This arrival is just as important to the psychology of the movement as the moment of syntactical climax, the recapitulation.[35] For here the first theme has engendered its complement, a true alter ego.[36] The ensuing dramatic juxtaposition of this complement with the first theme itself further profiles their charged relationship. After bursting onto the scene in a militant C major (bar 299), the first theme's arpeggiated thrust darkens to C minor, muscles its way up to E♭ major, and then darkens again, now to E♭ minor. That the new theme then takes up this key—the tonic minor—indicates a psychologically complex irony: for if it here seems that the new theme has in fact succeeded in usurping the place of the first theme, its role in the larger harmonic design is that of a minor-mode inflection of tonic that will eventually settle onto the protracted dominant pedal leading to the major-mode recapitulation and the renewal of the first theme.[37]

Analytic methodologies that attempt to demonstrate the presence of a web of thematic relationships emanating from some initial thematic utterance will perforce neglect the otherness of the new theme in an aesthetically motivated zeal to assimilate it into a larger organic whole.[38] Programmatic criticism, on the other hand, does not seek to *explain* the new theme by showing secret organic connections to the first theme but rather attempts to understand the effect of this important disjunction and how it arises, by describing the entire process metaphorically. By interpreting the new theme as an important turning point in a psychological or dramatic process, metaphorical programs suggest a significance at once deeper and more immediate than one based solely on hidden motivic relationships.[39]

III

If the old story is true, the next musical crux in the movement moved even Beethoven to violence at its misapprehension. The impact of poor Ries's boxed ear has resounded on through the years of this symphony's critical reception. In view of that reception, Beethoven's imputed action takes on a symbolic cast, for most of the programmatic critics interpret the famous horn call as a bold reminder, a recalling to duty, an *Ohrfeige* for the exhausted hero. For Schering, the horn call brings Hector back to his senses as if calling him by name.[40] In the words of Bekker, "Then, like a spectral exhortation full of promise, the horn motive sounds, leading [the hero] away from his dusky brooding back into the living world of the deed."[41] Commenting on the horn call's apparent temporal displacement, Marx characterizes the passage as "drifting entirely out of a lost distance, strange, a summons not at all belonging to the present moment but which augurs and heralds those to follow—namely, the return of the heroic theme after the struggle seemed extinct."[42] With the word "strange" (*fremd*), Marx implies that in the world of the second theme and its aftermath, the first theme itself has become alien, heard from a "lost distance." Here in the midst of doom the horn call sounds both as a monitory utterance from the beginnings we have so utterly left behind and as a premonition of the redeeming glory to come. A reminder from destiny, linking past and future?[43]

Critics like Oulibicheff and Lenz treat the striking harmonic juxtaposition of dominant and tonic during the horn call as one of the moments in this grand conception where the idea of the piece overrides musical considerations. As Lenz puts it, "It is not the ear but the *idea* which acts as judge, when *storm cloud* and *lightning* appear all at once in this manner. . . . Tragedy need not flatter the senses but ought to uplift the soul, and the *Eroica* is a *tragedy* [expressed through] *instrumental music*."[44] Schenker, ever the man to deflate such speculation, justifies the moment harmonically by showing that it is based on a rather common mode of dominant prolongation (see example 1.2).[45]

Example 1.2. Beethoven, Symphony no. 3. From Schenker, *Harmony*, 162–63.

Other critics point to similar juxtapositions in works like the *Les Adieux* Sonata and the "Pastoral" Symphony, presumably to identify this type of harmonic conflation as a style trait rather than as something that needs interpretation in this specific context.

We would do well to examine this context to understand how the syntax of this passage has brought on the unanimous programmatic response that something both momentous and mysterious is afoot.[46] Starting as far back as bar 338, the retransition section that eventually includes the horn call is regularly articulated in four-bar groups, generally consisting of one harmony per group. After working slowly up from the B♭ of bar 338 to an E♭ in bar 358, the bass drops suddenly to

C♭ at 362, an arrival given climactic status by the prolonged fortissimo and tutti projection of the C♭-major sonority.[47] The energy of this fanfare is slowly dissipated in the exchanges between winds and strings that follow; at bar 378 the bass returns to B♭, and by bar 381 the upper voice has been coaxed down from G♭ to D. The C♭ in the bass of bar 362 has thus taken sixteen bars to complete a long-range resolution to B♭.

Now the winds drop out for two bars and the tremolos begin. The C♭ appears once more, this time as a minor ninth now taking four bars to resolve to the B♭ in bar 386. At bar 390 the resolution of C♭ to B♭ is further compressed to just two bars. The drama of this progressive compression is matched by the sustained suspense of the violin tremolo, now uninterrupted by the winds or by any bass articulations. Beethoven carefully prepares the disappearance of the bass by staging its gradual reduction from quarter-note arpeggios (bars 369 and 373) to eighth-note arpeggios (bars 374–77) to single-note pizzicati in each bar of the four-bar group (bars 378–81) and, finally, to pizzicati in bars 3 and 4 only (bars 384–85 and 388–89).

Everything has died out save the pianissimo violins, and yet there is an eerie sense of energy in the air; the quietly humming presence of dissonance voices a suddenly brimming sense that an issue is imminent. Progressive textural reductions have reinforced the four-bar regularity of this section (initiated back in bar 338) while building dramatic tension in conjunction with the compressed resolutions of C♭ to B♭; further reduction or further compression is unthinkable. We are being set up: the predominant pattern of chord change every four bars leads us to expect yet another chord change at 394, and the local dramatic conditions demand it. Syntactically, this is a good place to arrive at E♭—but are we really prepared for the thematic recapitulation? Can Beethoven simply die away into his heroic return? That would surely be a *resurrectio ex abrupto*, for we have been told all along in no uncertain terms that the arrivals of important statements of the first theme need a strong upbeat to send them off.[48]

Beethoven has it both ways. He brings E♭ back at the right spot *and* provides the needed upbeat. The reference to E♭ major supplied by the horn call becomes in fact the necessary condition for initiating the critical upbeat. For the effect of the horn call overlaid on the continuing, albeit pianississimo, tremolo of B♭ and A♭ is to challenge this remnant of V^7, releasing the latent energy of its quiet persistence and instantaneously transforming a glowing ember into an explosive force. The tremolo had reduced the V^7 to its barest dissonant combination, the major second, an interval that could preserve the energy for a big move to tonic but could not resolve there directly. The A♭ needs to attain a higher register—it cannot remain as a bass line. After the explosion in bars 396–97 scatters the voices of the V^7 sonority into a resolution-worthy configuration, the recapitulation may proceed.

Just as striking as the harmonic juxtaposition, with which critics have been exclusively concerned all these years, is the rhythmic juxtaposition of downbeat (reference to first theme) and upbeat (the move to the recapitulated theme). We have explored the rhythmic pattern of the presentation of the first theme in the opening forty-five bars as an increasingly intense succession of large-scale downbeat and large-scale upbeat sections, usually coordinated with tonic and dominant areas respectively. The horn call combines in one mysterious utterance the essence of the theme (a triadic call) and the essential crux of its presentation (the downbeat-oriented tonic configuration that becomes upbeat- and dominant-oriented). The two poles of this basic rhythmic/harmonic pattern of respiration occur at the same moment, an observation that deepens the preceding interpretive characterization of the horn call as both a warning from the past (downbeat) and a premonition of the future (upbeat). Remarkably, the horn call performs this feat by matching an utterly simplified V^7 with the simplest triadic statement of tonic, as if answering the elemental with the elemental—whispering, as it were, the magic word.

And there is yet another dimension to the magic of this word. We must remember that in terms of the thematic material of this movement, the horn call is nothing other than a baldly stated two-bar citation of the first theme in its original mode and register. The appearance of the first theme as a military horn call takes on a communicative function hovering suggestively between the referential and the phatic. In other words, the horn call both represents the hero and summons him by name. As a representation of the hero/theme, this terse reduction refers both to the musical essence of the first theme, by revealing that component of the theme which remains invariable throughout its many appearances, and to the poetic essence of the hero, by metonymically symbolizing the hero as a military horn call. But the abstracted essence of the first theme here heralds rather than enacts the important thematic return; or, semantically speaking, this use of the theme stands not for the hero himself but for his name. Thus the poetic essence of the character of the hero (a military horn call) is used to name the hero. This is precisely the sense in which the heroes of Greek mythology are often named. Hector, for example, takes his name from the verb *ékho*, in the sense of "protect": Hector is named as he who protects the city of Troy.[49]

The programmatic interpretations of Marx and Schering recognize the function of naming enacted by the horn call and the powerful effect it has on the musical process—an effect of recalling, in a trice, a development that has hurled itself into territory representing the extreme implications of the opening argument (the new theme and its aftermath) back to the return of that argument itself. Perhaps the most overt aspect of this effect of the horn call is quite simply its reminder of E♭ major at the end of a long retransition exclusively concerned with E♭ minor: the same utterance that names the hero/theme thus names the home key in its appropriate mode while forecasting the important formal event of that key's return.

Those critics who, like Oulibicheff and Lenz, interpret the horn call as one of many moments in Beethoven's symphonic works where the *Idee* overrides musical considerations are also on to something important about this moment. It is a classic case of the "stroke of genius": the horn call solves a syntactic problem (the arrival of tonic, which cannot yet be the arrival of the recapitulation) while at the same time naming the hero (reminding the music of its original mode as well as its initial thematic and rhythmic premise), releasing the explosive potential of the major second tremolo, and merging the two poles of the movement's thematic complex—tonic/downbeat over and against dominant/upbeat—into one synoptic moment. Our *Idee*-minded critics are reacting to a representation of something "unerhört," something that defies convention and defines genius, as conceived in the early nineteenth century.[50] When they invoke the notion of a poetic *Idee* to account for this type of passage they are not simply at their wit's end but realize that more is at stake than a daring harmonic anomaly: there is a higher significance that goes beyond the local effect. We detect a wonderful symbiosis, for the *Idee* serves the form (articulates its major juncture), and the form serves the *Idee* (provides for a return to the hero's identity after the exploration of some "other" state).

The case of the horn call illustrates the point that programmatic critics are responding metaphorically to something of great moment in the musical process, something that we would today be inclined to describe syntactically or stylistically. From this we should conclude not that we are only now able to understand these aspects of the music but rather that we are making these same aspects explicit with a different type of analytical language. Neither would I wish merely to reduce earlier metaphorical accounts of the *Eroica* to a series of analytical statements closer to our own customary discourse about tonal musical processes. To do so would be to treat such metaphorical language as protoanalytical, to patronize this mode of musical understanding by imputing to it the inchoate glimmers of our own analytical discoveries. Much more germane, I believe, is the observation that practitioners operating from a wide range of critical and analytical standpoints notice similar things in this music and express these things in the different languages available to them. Yet the persistence of programmatic criticism throughout the reception history of the *Eroica* signals a need to characterize the process of this movement in terms more universal and fundamentally meaningful than those of musical syntax or morphology.

IV

We left the heroic presence in our composite story poised at the return of the opening music after facing the danger of the climactic standoff and experiencing the mysterious voice of the new theme. In the midst of a dramatic standstill the horn call summons the hero into action once again, and the expansive surge of bars 430ff. tempered by the warming influence of the preceding sections in F and D♭ suggests that the hero has grown as well as triumphed.[51] As this scenario already indicates a process of journey and return, of loss and greater gain, and of quest and discovery, we might imagine that the story is in essence over. Everything that happens now would then be the mere playing out of a musical form, a kind of travel expense owed to the vehicle of this journey, symphonic sonata form. Yet the coda adds perhaps the most important stage to the story, in that it provides a consummate ending, one that is both goal and closure, telos and epilogue.

It would be hard to find music more exemplary of one's general notion of the heroic style than the music of this coda. This perception, coupled with the embarrassment of trying to fit a large-scale repetition into a dramatic narrative, makes it no surprise that not all our critics bother to account programmatically for the repeated music of the recapitulation, moving instead from the onset of the recapitulation right to the coda.[52] Marx, for example, leaps to the very end of the coda in his program—he relegates the entire body of the recapitulation to the general category of victoriousness and hears the fourfold return of the first theme in the last section of the coda (from bar 631 on) as the absolute culmination of victory.[53] Wilhelm von Lenz suggests that the recapitulation expresses the hero's posthumous fame, in a manner perhaps not unlike the epic retelling of heroic exploits.[54] This reading, in conjunction with Marx's comments on the thematic return at the end of the coda, could supply us with the final programmatic stage of our hero's journey: after the hero's life and death, his eternal glory resounds to the heavens.

In the culminating passage of the coda, from bar 631 to the end, the first theme is provided with a regular harmonic underpinning of tonic and dominant and regular four-plus-four phrasing. The power of this square treatment of the theme is precisely in its presentation: the theme becomes more like a real theme, for it is now an actual melody. That is to say, in its previous manifestations the first theme acted more as a bass line in motivating harmonic development; now it is freed from its compulsion to act as an unstable, driving force and is able to enjoy a truly melodic character.[55] In the context of this movement, such stability could inform only the final manifestation of the theme, where it marks the tonality of E♭ major in such a way that we need never again fear its imminent dissolution.

Yet the melodic repetitions at the end of the coda do not constitute a theme in the usual sense, for they do not represent a closed melodic structure.[56] Rather, they are left open—harmonically, by the symmetrically balanced exchange of tonic and dominant, and melodically, by the insistence on the fifth scale degree, keeping alive the unresolved feeling of a dominant-heavy melody.[57] This openness suggests the possibility of endless repetitions, endless affirmation. It takes another, and stirringly powerful, manifestation of Schenker's *Aufwärtsdrang* to close the cycle, a chromatic swell in the first violins (bars 663–68) that reaches a high A♭ and resolves it to G (a final culmination of the first violins' opening move from G to A♭ in bars 7–10). This is followed by the completion of a cadential gesture that had been kept open in all its previous appearances.[58]

Thus the final melodic utterance of the opening theme has thematic stability but not thematic closure—again, what an appropriate way to signal an apotheosis: the unstable and volatile theme of the opening bars is now heard as a stable, indeed, potentially unending iteration. Another aspect to this apotheosis is the almost childishly simple nature of this final version of the theme. Imagine how impossibly banal such an utterance would be if heard at the outset of the movement. Yet this stripped-down version plays well as a monumentalization of the theme—here it can truly transcend any notion of a worldly theme; it has no need for a closed structure as it hymns eternally on tonic and dominant. Although this version of the theme is thus kept open harmonically, it indeed assumes a cumulative progress in the way its iterations are treated orchestrally and dynamically: the slow rise to the height of orchestral sound and the top of the orchestral register triggers the closural sweep of the *Aufwärtsdrang* and final cadences.

Regarded metaphorically, the thematic process of the entire movement seems to realize Heraclitus's famous apothegm, "character is destiny": we are made to hear that the hero's fully revealed character entails the process of his destiny. In Marx's interpretation, Napoleon can become Napoleon only through successful interaction with his troops. For Lenz, the hero must die in order to obtain eternal glory. This was the fatal transaction made explicit by Achilles in the *Iliad*; as he says in book 9, lines 410–16: "I carry two sorts of destiny toward the day of my death. Either, if I stay here and fight beside the city of the Trojans, my return home is gone, but my glory [*kléos*] shall be everlasting; but if I return home to the beloved land of my fathers, the excellence of glory [*kléos*] is gone, but there will be a long life left for me, and my end in death will not come to me quickly."[59]

Marx's description of the final moments of the movement as a culmination of the hero's glory works well with the notion of *kléos* that Lenz invokes. The standard Homeric formula for *kléos* is that *kléos* reaches the heavens (*kléos ouranòn hĩkei*). Such an image aptly captures the impression made by the soaring conclusion of the movement: the theme (the hero) flies to the heavens, liberated from the battles of mortality. His final form is that of a true melody; this was a form forbidden to him until he lived through to the uttermost consequences of his heroic character. As a melody, he can now be sung by posterity. Thus the heroic journey here envisaged ranges from life to death (or some related experience symbolizing death) to the eternal glory of epic song.

In order to increase our understanding of the coherent musical process that informs this kind of reading we must consider one final musical crux: the famous passage at the outset of the coda, where the music plunges directly through D♭ major to C major (bars 551ff.). In his eagerness to get at the movement's final peroration, Marx omits any account of this striking passage from his program, although he comments on it elsewhere when addressing Oulibicheff's criticism of the same bars. Both critics see the passage as expressive of the tenacity of the hero's will. In the words of Oulibicheff: "It is the voice of the hero, the summons of glory. . . . In whatever land or whatever circumstances this summons is heard, . . . the hero always wants the same thing, and he is always sure of being obeyed."[60] Marx, somewhat more in the Prussian manner: "The [hero's] word shall prevail! And it has triumphed! And it shall triumph and rule!"[61] Do these critics hear the passage in this way simply because its harmonic syntax seems so willfully arbitrary, or is there something in the process of the coda that makes such a compact expression of the willful nature of the first theme indispensable at this very spot?

The work of Joseph Kerman and Charles Rosen has shown that one of the primary roles of the Beethovenian coda is that of finishing any business that cannot be transacted within the recapitulation proper.[62] In the case of this movement, several pieces of thematically related business remain: the new theme, as the essential second theme of the movement, needs its own recapitulation, and the first theme needs to attain its final form. There is also a tonal agenda that arguably needs to be completed. In order to understand the nature of this agenda we must invoke the very beginning of the recapitulation.

The recapitulation in classical-style sonata form more often than not emphasizes the subdominant area before proceeding to the second theme group. As Charles Rosen points out, this requirement is met in a most unusual way in the opening moments of this particular recapitulation. At first it seems as if the music will move toward the subdominant, as the C♯ from bar 7 now drops down to C♮—but the key that shows up is not F minor, which would stand for the subdominant A♭ major, but F major, which is in fact the dominant of the dominant. Beethoven's particular approach to this F major neutralizes its function as an applied dominant, however; there is no aural sense that this key will move to B♭. The following passage in D♭ plunges deeply into the flat side of E♭, as if to compensate for the ambiguous use of F major, thereby suggesting a subdominant orientation for the entire section.[63]

One might expect that another, less equivocal move to the subdominant area would be attempted in the coda, if it is indeed the locus for unfinished business. And this is in fact the case. Beethoven establishes the subdominant area with the key of F minor, heard as the functional representative for the subdominant key of A♭ major. This is the F minor we missed at the outset of the recapitulation but that is much more at home here as the tonality of the new theme. The passage at the outset of the coda sets up F minor by passing in short order from E♭ to C major and then fashioning the latter as a dominant. But can we hear this passage merely as a grandiose yet awkward preparation of F minor? The notorious chord progression, with its bald parallels, frustrates the search for local harmonic logic and seems to point to some larger requirement.

The D♭ that makes a momentous appearance at the beginning of the coda (in bar 557) is the ultimate manifestation of the C♯s at bars 7 and 402, as many have pointed out; now it sounds as the root of its own triad, and the passing motion of E♭ to D♭ to C is hypostatized with triads built on each of these tones. Perhaps it is not too farfetched to argue that the unusual manner of touching on the subdominant that Rosen notices at the head of the recapitulation has left the C♯/D♭ with some latent energy still unspent. Or, if we would rather talk in terms of a pitch story, the transformation of the C♯ of bar 7 to D♭ is not yet complete in bar 402; D♭'s greatest role is played in the coda. This is to read the D♭ as signal of the impulse to move to the subdominant. In its early guise as C♯ (bar 7) it has a "noch nicht" effect; moving here to the subdominant would be premature and disastrously enervating. But we can read that C♯ as a latent aspect of the theme to move toward the subdominant or other flat-side tonalities.

As was the case with the horn call, the "unerhört" quality of the passage at the outset of the coda can be linked to the simultaneous fulfillment of several requirements of the musical process of the movement. The need to recapitulate the new theme is merged with the story of the transformation of C♯ to D♭ and the previously suppressed harmonic necessity of a move to the subdominant area. Thus the business of the underlying form is again combined with an ongoing, end-oriented musical process: the formally necessary coda is articulated by the clarification of an enigmatic and latent aspect of the first theme.

The related appearances of the D♭, the subdominant function, and the new theme can be translated into the metaphorical myth of the hero if we consider that the recapitulation, if it is to represent the epic retelling of the hero's exploits, must indeed recount the hero's chthonic experiences. These experiences form a vitally important part of the heroic journey, and they take the form of some sort of symbolic death, generally entailing a visit to the underworld. Beethoven's coda uses the D♭ as a direct lever into the relevant tonality for the recapitulated new theme, the theme that represents the hero's brush with death in the development. And it makes sense that the epic retelling of the chthonic episode implied by the new theme should be assimilated into a "safer" harmonic area than was the case when the theme was heard in the "present tense" in the development.

Looking back across the entire movement, very much now in the spirit of our programmatic critics, may we not speculate that the C♯ of bar 7 represents something like the latent trend toward death inherent in any mythic hero of epic stature?[64] We should remember that a C♯ initiates the thematic argument in the development that ultimately leads to the new theme. I am referring to the passage at bars 178–86, where a 5–6–5–6 voice-leading progression leads from C minor through C♯ minor to D minor. It is clear that this arrival of D minor marks the commencement of an extended section that culminates at the climactic bars before the new theme. Marx, for example, identifies this scene as the actual battle, which grows to a standoff immediately before the puzzling reaction of the new theme.[65] The passage from C through C♯ to D represents another example of Schenker's heroic *Aufwärtsdrang*, whose presence is felt again at bars 219–20 and, climactically, at the move from E to F in bars 274–76. The motion from C♯ to D in the bass of bars 7–9 can be seen as the first glimmer of this powerfully consequential realization. Only in the recapitulation, the epic retelling, can the C♯ be transformed into a D♭. No longer will it initiate the action-oriented *Aufwärtsdrang*. It will henceforth resolve down, as a D♭, and will signal the imminent presence of the subdominant area, the area wherein it is safe to talk of death, symbolic or otherwise.

The coda brings together the main elements of the archetypal process suggested metaphorically by narrative interpretations of the movement: the plunge from E♭ through D♭ to C is heard as the hero's will, the fatal consequences of which are symbolized by the recapitulated new theme, which in turn leads to the final affirmation of eternal glory. Thus the process played out by the entire movement is recapitulated and confirmed in the coda. The momentous events at the beginning of the coda serve as a local preparation for the culminating repetitions of the first theme at the end of the coda,[66] a preparation just as necessary as was the horn call for the climactic return of the recapitulation proper. Both passages represent downbeats that act simultaneously as upbeats to the successive stages of climactic affirmation that are needed to balance the climactic—and psychologically portentous—disjunction in the development section. Beethoven's first movement is thus expressive of an almost universally accessible psychological process: a dangerous yet necessary exploration of some unconscious aspect of the psyche is followed by a tremendous sense of reintegration and affirmation. And this process is no secret, told only to initiates—for every listener who accepts Schenker's view that the final section of the coda has no structural function save that of bringing the upper voice back to the obligatory register, untold legions will understand the waves of affirmation signaling the triumphant closure of a meaningful process.

Hearing the coda as recapitulating the entire process of the movement brings into play a reflexive dimension that goes beyond the enactment of a narrative. For here not only does the music appear to enact epic events, it can be said to effect the distancing narration of the genre of the epic: the coda sings the events of the movement in something like stylized epic form.[67] Of course the whole process is much more complex, for in the coda the idea of retelling the movement is merged with the culminating release, or telos, of the movement—the distancing implied by readings of the coda as a narrating summation of the entire movement is paradoxically at the same time a moment of complete identification. The acts of telling and enacting are merged; distance from and identification with are made inseparable. We shall explore this aspect of Beethoven's music further in chapter 4; for now I shall pause only to say that this paradox of distance and identification is a secret of human consciousness for which Hegel could find expression only in the mirrors and mazes of a densely forbidding pro-lixity—and yet it is no secret at all, for it is our oldest companion, the basic condition of our self-consciousness.

It is here that we start to understand the power of Beethoven's heroic style as an expression of the conditions of selfhood. Of pri-mary importance in this music's projection of the experience of self-consciousness is its ability to enlist our identification, to make us expe-rience its surging course as if it were our own. Especially astonishing in the first movement of the *Eroica* is the power of the banal thematic statement in the coda, which has been heard to express the epitome of victory. For "victory" itself is banal: it is not a complex experience. What Beethoven's coda succeeds in doing, to judge by its reception, is to express victory not just as Victory but as the listener's own victory (how tiresome to watch or listen to someone else's celebration)—and yet also as Victory. (This may be what separates Beethoven's heroic music from the French revolutionary music it is at times claimed to be modeled on.) Thus it is not just the monumental tread of the story, or the paradoxical merger of telling and enacting, it is also simply and at bottom the way in which we are drawn in to identify with the music that helps explain the power of Beethoven's heroic style. We shall take up the task of understanding the nature of this identification in chap-ter 2. Among other things, we will find that we ourselves appear to become mythologized in the process of identifying with this music. Without this fundamental sense of identification, the heroic style—if even possible—would perhaps still constitute a brave and intriguing chapter in musical history. With it, this music creates such a history.

V

In retelling once again the tale the *Eroica* Symphony has been heard to tell I have conflated many different versions into a master trope that I believe sounds the deepest common denominator of all the others. This trope shares significant features with the quest plot, or hero's journey, and as such carries significant mythic and ethical force. By now it should be obvious that I have taken my cue from the long tradi-tion of programmatic interpretations of this symphony and that I have attempted to justify this maligned mode of criticism by contrasting it favorably with more recent analytical methods. Yet my defense of the value of programmatic criticism should not be allowed to harden into prescription. I do not wish to suggest that it is necessary to read or practice programmatic criticism in order to understand works like the *Eroica* Symphony. To make such a suggestion would be to confuse the relationship between the narrative programs and the symphony. We must not for a moment think that the symphony is about these narratives, for it is precisely the other way around: the narratives are about the symphony. Failure to heed this seemingly obvious caveat drastically foreshortens the work's interpretive horizon and unites critics as outwardly antithetical as Arnold Schering and Heinrich Schenker in the same mistaken assumption—for both claim that they are revealing the true content of the work, in the form of either a literary key or a reductive graph.

Schering's assumption of a programmatic key misses the spirit of the nineteenth-century critic's encounter with the work.[68] The *Eroica* served its earlier critics well as an example of music rising to the level of an *Idee*, but not to an exclusive *Idee* from a specifiable source (such causal argumentation could infiltrate the hermeneutic enterprise only in a more positivist age) or to an abstract and disinterested Platonic construction: the type of *Idee* that A. B. Marx had in mind rose above any one exemplar—his *Eroica* first movement is the picture not of any given battle but of the "ideal battle"—yet was fundamentally interested in the human condition.[69] It would be easy to be lured at this point into the storied convolutions of Hegelian metaphysics, specifically those concerning the concretion of the *Idee*. Almost more important, however, is the *type* of *Idee* that Marx and others ascribe to Beethoven's music, for it invokes nothing less than the highest values of their age, those of freedom and self-determination, as well as the decidedly human (as opposed to godlike or demigodlike) nature of the heroic type. The trajectory of a work like the first movement of the *Eroica* is typically characterized as a spiral process in which a human hero goes forth (outwardly or inwardly), suffers a crisis of consciousness, and returns enriched and renewed. In Idealist metaphysics, the *Weltseele* is similarly brought to a state of self-conscious freedom, thus constituting the largest loop of the same spiral—but it is the tighter circle of the humanly heroic, the realm in which the *Deutsche Klassik* staged its most successful dramas, which forms the ethical backdrop for early interpretations of the heroic style. While Idealist thought lends critics like Marx philosophical legitimacy for their view of the momentous impact of Beethoven's music, it is the general moral tenor of the *Goethezeit* that ultimately sustains them.

Although I would seek to detach the narrative program from the role of an explanatory code key (thus refusing to consider this most outspoken of works as encoded and secretive), it is clear that programmatic criticism is metaphorically suggestive of underlying and archetypal processes. These more or less universal paradigms are evoked in response to the intense engagement many listeners feel when confronted with the music of Beethoven; the narrative programs that evince these patterns serve as a way of communicating the spirit of such an engagement. They imply by analogy that this music functions like myth, as a metaphorical translation of something fundamentally meaningful in human experience.

This is important, for it may help explain, better than any formulation of Beethoven's musicotechnical prowess or organic-artistic instincts, the tenacious hold the heroic style has exercised on the very foundations of post-Beethovenian musical thought. As I shall argue later, our celebration of the musical virtues we prize in Beethoven and prise out of all the other pieces we admire is grounded in a sense of self that is aided and abetted by the mythmaking power of this music and its composer, and that runs deeper than the merely aesthetic, even though this deeper sense is often translated into a celebration of just that aesthetic consciousness. Philip G. Downs concludes that the *Eroica* acts as an analogue of the listener's own "potentiality for perfection":[70] such an assessment clearly places the reception of this movement beyond aesthetic contemplation and confers upon the music a morally exalted agenda. The programmatic reception of this symphony addresses its perceived ethical dimension directly and overtly; there is a sense in which these authors, whatever else their motivation, are closer to telling us how this work engages them, how it makes them feel, than are their formalist counterparts.[71]

Yet the question arises whether the music actually projects such a trajectory for these critics or if the extramusical associations brought on by the designation "Eroica" may not in fact form the basis of an intertextual tradition of *Eroica* interpretation. In other words, are the programmatic readings largely reacting to one another?[72] We may accept that the tradition of *Eroica* interpretation is homogeneous at least partially because of an intertextual urge (a tendency to react laterally to other interpretations, as well as frontally to the symphony), for intertextual skirmishes stay on the same field: they all assume the underlying heroic trajectory and stake their claim to individuality in the designation of specific protagonists. Hence the force of Wagner's 1851 claim that the real hero of the *Eroica* is humanity itself—Wagner's reading thus seems to transcend the narrow compass of a hero who is a specific and time-bound historical figure.[73] Likewise, Arnold Schering's pride in claiming to have found the key to the symphony rests on his positivist faith in the type of specific connections that characterize the logic of causality. Wagner rejoices in locating the highest common denominator, the transcendent index of the work; Schering is pleased to uncover the work's secret source. Both leave unquestioned the basic trajectory of the work and its heroic implications. But is such unquestioned acceptance of the underlying paradigm a function of the power and direction of the music, or of the power and direction of the designation "Eroica" and its famous associations with the real-life hero Napoleon? Such a question is impossible to answer and is ultimately misleading. For it is precisely the conjunction of just this music with just these extramusical implications that has become so firmly planted in our collective musical consciousness.

The power of this conjunction of Beethoven's music with the ethical and mythical implications of the hero and his journey holds the entire reception history of this symphony in its sway, for there has never been a reaction against the basic heroic trope, no deconstructive readings of the *Eroica* as antihero or antiwar or antiself. Perhaps the most immediate sign of this power is the curious persistence of the urge to produce programmatic readings of this work, even in periods marked by a general reaction against such extramusical interpretations, such as the antiromantic reaction to Beethoven in German scholarship around the time of the centenary of the composer's death,[74] or the structuralist analytical bias of the last thirty years.[75] Such persistence argues for an intriguing resistance to the mainstream formalism that has characterized analysis and criticism in this century. On the other hand, the work of Lorenz and Schenker specifically positions itself against a programmatic approach and gains thrust and influence from this opposition— but as I suggested earlier, their analyses share some features with the readings from which they claim to have distanced themselves and can be read as newer translations of the same story. The irony arises that Beethoven is used both as an example of the power of formalism and as an example of the continued viability of programmatic interpretation. The formalist challenge is to show how this highly characteristic music could in fact be accounted for in terms of latent unity and often subsurface coherence, how its idiosyncratic surface is actually but the face of a richly wrought and integral aesthetic structure. The hermeneutic challenge is to understand the message of the music by creating a metaphorical gloss, often taking the surface at "face value." Formalist analysis seeks to explain surface phenomena in terms of a theory of underlying coherence; hermeneutic analysis seeks to understand the face of the music in relation to other meaningful human experiences.

What is interesting is that for all the power of its twin metaphors of depth and origin, the formalist model did not succeed in supplanting the programmatic impulse. This is most likely because they are not really rival paradigms at all in the way they relate to Beethoven's music: their language may seem incommensurable, but their fundamental view of the musical process is constrained in the same ways. The overmastering coherence heard in works like the *Eroica* Symphony has both inspired the use of heroic metaphor and encouraged the coronation of such coherence as the ruling musical value of the formalist agenda. That is why I would argue not only that we have never fundamentally changed our view of this work but that because of the position and influence of Beethoven's heroic style in subsequent musical history, we have never since fundamentally changed our view of music.

Chapter Two

MUSICAL VALUES

PRESENCE AND ENGAGEMENT IN THE HEROIC STYLE

LISTENING TO music is a two-way street, regardless of the efforts of various factions of musical academia to legislate one-way traffic, either from an absolute and self-sufficient musical work to the listener or from the relative situatedness of the listener to a decentralized musical work. In the latter view, strictly musical values become suspect, as do all other apparent claims to music's immanence. Yet if we define musical values as those things that we as listeners have come to value in the music, we keep the idea of a two-way interaction open while allowing ourselves to address musical issues. In looking for the phenomenological basis of our engagement with Beethoven's heroic style I shall thus be looking for the things we hear in this music, how we tend to characterize them, and why they are important to us.

Beethoven's heroic-style music is engaging in the sense of being compellingly involving. It is not difficult to cite and demonstrate the overwhelmingly dramatic rhetoric of Beethoven's heroic style—the heart-stopping pauses, crashes, register shifts, and startling harmonies—when searching for reasons for this engagement. But these things alone could hardly engage us in a dramatic process commensurate with a representation of human destiny, or even with that of any narrative plot. Indeed, an emphasis on these sorts of surprises would make the Beethoven experience seem more like a ride in an amusement park. The phenomenon of listener engagement entails as well a marked sense of identification with the music. Conspicuously dramatic features in the music must be heard to issue from the past and to be decisive for the future; they must inspire an intense degree of involvement in a recognizable yet experientially individual temporal process. This is why Beethoven's internalization of classical syntax and phraseology may be seen as paramount: he is thus provided with a style stable enough in its sense of both local and global balance to assimilate and project a highly dramatic sense of temporality.[1] (We shall return to this point presently.)

To consider Beethoven's music as a projection of experiential temporality presupposes some sort of temporal actant. That we understand the music in these terms is manifest in the ready identification of thematic process with dramatic protagonist assumed in most interpretations and analyses of this music. Such identification goes further than the general attribution of human agency (be it voice or persona) to musical processes, for here the particular emphasis is on the concept of protagonist. Just as the word itself derives from terms related to combat and contest, so the agency in interpretations of Beethoven's heroic style is styled first and foremost as a struggling, contending "agonist." We take this type of scenario for granted to such a degree that it is difficult even to ask why it should have come about. Surely the extramusical connotations of many of Beethoven's dramatic works (*Egmont*, *Leonore*, *Coriolanus*) suggest and condone such a scenario. The musical portrait of a dramatic hero is bound to include music representative of conflict and strength. But such connotations alone cannot guarantee the consistency of the heroic paradigm as applied by critics and analysts both explicitly and implicitly for the last two hundred years. In other words, even if the extramusical preconditions of some of these works let specific heroes into the critical arena, something else operative in the music helped transform these pieces from works about specific heroes to works about Heroism.

Even in interpretations insisting on a specific hero, the emphasis is often on an ideal portrait of such a hero. For example, Marx, in his account of the *Eroica* first movement as Napoleon in battle, warns the reader that he has no specific battle in mind but rather an "ideal battle." For Wagner in 1851 the hero of the *Eroica* is Man; Philip Downs interprets the first movement of that symphony as a record of heroic self-overcoming.[2] All these interpretations are offered in the spirit of a corrective, freeing the music from any all-too-narrow association with one hero and from the less exalted company of program music. The transformation from program music to ideal music (in Marx's sense) hinges on a heightened sense of identification with music heard not simply as mimetic representation but as dramatic enactment itself.

In his essay on the *Leonore* Overtures, Tovey remarks that classical-style instrumental music is much more dramatic than would be suitable for theater music.[3] With the support of an immediately visible and viable dramatic situation, theater music has no use for the overpowering intensity of a piece like the Third *Leonore* Overture (that the performance tradition of *Fidelio* cannot resist including this overture within the body of the opera itself is more a tribute to its power than an acknowledgment of its operatic suitability). Here, then, is a possible clue to the effect of engagement that Beethoven's heroic style engenders: in the absence of a clearly defined dramatic subject the music's overabundant drama seems to address and enlist the nearest available subject—the listener.[4]

For Tovey, such music cannot map onto the concrete events of a staged drama (whether real or imaginary); its dramatic power is too overwhelming, too concentrated. Yet this apparent underdetermination may in fact compel the music to attract and map onto something commensurable in the listener. In other words, the music is not so much *about* anything in a directly referential sense but acts as a disembodied yet compelling force that attracts whatever is at hand as long as it is remotely commensurable.[5] Freed of the consideration of some specific dramatic process, the listener may confront the music, and be confronted by the music, more directly. This results in a sense of identification as well as a feeling of universality. For if this music engages us so distinctly and directly, and yet is so referentially disembodied, so bereft of explicit attachment, are we not made to feel that our individuality is enlisted in some collective universal? Thus the music is ultimately about us, but not in the banal sense of a portrayal: rather, it is about our susceptibility to, and understanding of, processes that model the merger of individual and universal. Before we can explore the mechanism of this merger more closely, we must first take up the music's almost coercive immediacy, its apparent ability to generate and sustain a feeling of presence.

I

"For in Beethoven's music the factor of so great moment for the history of Art is this: each miscellaneous technical convention employed by the artist for the sake of making himself intelligible to the outside world is itself raised to the supreme importance of a direct outpouring of his spirit. . . . Everything becomes melody, every voice in the accompaniment, every rhythm, even the pauses."[6]

With these words, written on the occasion of the Beethoven centenary in 1870, Richard Wagner specifically locates Beethoven's historical importance in a radical vitalization of musical language, in which every peripheral detail becomes galvanized with significance, as part of a unitary and unmediated effusion. When he exclaims that "everything becomes melody," that the entire musical texture assumes the forward flow of a melodic line, Wagner employs the concept of melody figuratively in order to characterize the feeling of engagement elicited by Beethoven's music. He thus provides the reception of the heroic style with a guiding metaphor: the concept of line, of a never-flagging sense of presence. But if it is in fact generally acknowledged that we hear the works of the heroic style in this way, to what do we owe the impression not only of an ever-present effusion but of an engaging and irresistible surge that actually seems to carry us along instead of flowing past us?

To feel the force of this claim, one need only make a quick comparison with a typical reaction to Mozart. For if it sometimes feels as if one is compelled to move along with the music of Beethoven, the music of Mozart remains, always, at a remove. It is common to refer to Mozart's music in this way, as a form of perfection, the likes of which can be apprehended only from an all-too-human distance. Descriptions of Beethoven's music, on the other hand, sound like experiences in a flight simulator.[7] There is a visceral element immediately perceptible in this music, a disturbing, invasive, and ultimately compelling interaction with the listener.

Let us begin with the best-known example: the first movement of the Fifth Symphony. The famous opening itself already compels the type of listener engagement characteristic of this style. We can understand this opening as an extreme case of a more or less common rhetorical exhortation, examples of which are not lacking in classical-style music—one thinks of the opening of Mozart's "Prague" Symphony, or Haydn's "London" Symphony, or even the *Eroica*. But whereas such exhortations generally form terse rhythmic totalities (usually with dotted rhythms) that often assert both a meter and a tonality, Beethoven's does neither. (E.T.A. Hoffmann's observation that the opening implies $E\flat$ major more than C minor is the type of thing an intelligent musician would notice who had no precedent for such an opening.[8]) Instead, the listener is immediately put on his or her mettle, thrown into an unknown situation—and not by a mysterious and enticing piece of ambiguity but by that most unsettling of all utterances, the imperious command to do one knows not what. (Imagine an authoritarian supervisor crashing into an employee's office, shouting an urgent yet incomprehensible command, and immediately rushing out. All the poor functionary can do is to rush out after him—one would hardly just sit there thinking, "Now, I wonder what he meant . . .") In this way the listener is irrevocably drawn into Beethoven's drama with this opening that is more a direct command than an exhortation. This is to construe the opening not only as an expression of self but as a challenge to self, a combination that of course constitutes the characteristic force of a command: the invasive expression of a will.

Ambiguity alone is not imperious, nor is it invasive. A good part of the effect, the presence, of the opening utterance may be expressible in terms of metric or tonal ambiguity, but its force is bound up in its scoring, dynamics, rhythm, and contour. Loud, heavy octaves (three separate lines in a two-octave space) articulated with quickly repeated notes are heard to express a willfully instantaneous power, a naked outburst combining force and speed while eschewing preamble.[9] The choice of a middle to low register is crucial here as well—too low becomes too ponderous, too high becomes too shrill. Instead of these extremes, Beethoven's register speaks not so much from the throat but from the diaphragm. To the strings, heard as the natural voice of the orchestra, Beethoven adds clarinets (à 2) in a particularly reedy range, creating more pungent (twelfth-heavy) overtones and the effect of breath: a touch of the ancient aulos and its terrors.[10]

Equally fundamental here is the effect of two descending and interlocking thrusts of a third that combine to descend a minor second—again, the rhetoric is not solely one of questioning or of increasing tension (which would be better expressed with upward inflections), nor is it simply a flat assertion (which would call for some kind of closure). Instead we hear the more complex instance of nonclosural falling motion, only doubly and cumulatively so: G falls to E♭, then F to D, with the result that the sustained E♭ sinks to the sustained D.[11] An opening declamation thus made up of assertively voiced yet descending intervals performs enigmatic and ominous work: the force of assertion does not lift anything up, does not push open a space to be explored, in short, does no such day work, but instead thrusts downward, pushes below, falls like night. Crucial as well is the very compactness of this fall; it does not involve the sublime, awe-inspiring drops of larger intervals, but works within a more humanly gripping space.

Nor may we ignore the portentously dramatic fermatas, two at the outset and two after the first extended phrase, for they affect the listener at perhaps the deepest level. When well performed, these charged pauses allow enough time to mark the listener's consciousness with the intensity of what just happened—thereby increasing that intensity—and yet not enough to dissipate it. The present moment is thus alive with both an assessment of the immediate past and an expectancy of the immediate future. The redoubled force (through the flooding in of consciousness) of what just transpired, coupled with uneasy premonitions of what is to come—this is a classic technique for building suspense, and may even, in an extreme sense, be considered analogous to forms of mental torture employed to break someone's will. If I rush to this melodramatic extreme, it is only to emphasize the power of Beethoven's musical language, its ability to alter our conception of what music is and ought to be.

As Joseph Kerman notes, we must not forget that E.T.A. Hoffmann's reaction to this symphony was one of "Geisterfurcht."[12] Hoffmann's intimation that a supernatural voice finds expression in the Fifth Symphony has been seconded by anyone taking to heart Schindler's story about Fate knocking at the door. For this story perfectly sums up the terror of the opening: a supernatural presence has appeared here below, is at one's very door, and demands entry into that most personal manifestation of the human sphere, the home.[13] The supernatural and the human are face to face, but unlike the famous scene in Goethe's *Faust*, where Faust boldly conjures up the Earth Spirit and then quails in its presence, this spirit arrives without invitation, without warning, and its message is baleful. Thus the sense of presence we detect in this music not only involves the enhancement of the present moment but is intensified to such a degree that that temporal sense of presence becomes an uncanny sense of the presence of another order of being. This is no mere play of words, for here we skirt perilously along the abyssal gape of human consciousness: those moments when we feel most situated in the present moment are also those wherein we feel the presence of a transcendent universal, often characterized as the eternal present.

The power of this opening utterance quite understandably leads to the commonplace assertion that this movement—if not the entire symphony—is built entirely from the initial figure of four notes. Something of such force simply must be essential. Note the switch here from emotional response to aesthetic logic: the assumption that every note derives from the brief initial motive allows the subsequent music—and the analyst as well—to contain and harness the dangerous emotional power of the opening bars, to make it serve an aesthetic conceit. And by making this movement the *locus classicus* of what would henceforth be considered a mark of technical and aesthetic magnitude (hermetic motivic unity), such analysts allow the opening of this symphony to command them in an ultimately broader and historically influential way.

Yet not everyone is willing to argue for the germinal power of the first four notes. Tovey complains that such a view ignores what is truly original in this movement: for him it is not the idea of building up from a brief motive that is remarkable here but the unprecedented length of Beethoven's sentences.[14] He cites the music from the opening to the fermata in bar 21 as the first part of such an extended sentence. In describing it as such, Tovey demonstrates his sensitivity to classical syntax. This first section combines the half-cadence close of a periodic antecedent phrase with a remarkably concentrated use of the augmented-sixth arrival on the dominant, sounding more like the typically high drama of arriving on the dominant of the dominant at the outset of the second theme group.[15] Such emphasis indicates that something of great moment has drawn its first breath, as it were. This conflation of two different levels of formal articulation (periodic antecedent and end-of-transition cadence) dramatizes a normative half-cadence arrival by making it sound like a hard-earned release of tension. Beethoven thus affirms classical-style syntax in a most emphatic way while setting up pressures that more normative periodic structures simply could not contain.

For the arrival in bar 21 is not merely a piece of formal articulation; rather, it culminates the processive intensity of the preceding bars. This intensity is expressed by the cumulative repetitions of the $\hat{5}$–$\hat{5}$ $\hat{4}$–$\hat{3}$ figure in bars 14ff. As seen in example 2.1, the hyperryhthm of these repetitions yields the four-note rhythm of the opening motive at the level of every second bar: $\hat{3}$–$\hat{2}$; $\hat{3}$–$\hat{2}$; $\hat{3}$–$\hat{1}$–$\hat{5}$ (melodically, this reduction answers, by complement, the opening motive's $\hat{5}$–$\hat{5}$–$\hat{5}$–$\hat{3}$).

Example 2.1. Beethoven, Symphony no. 5, first movement: measures 14–21 (first violin).

Thus this rhythmic motive is heard to saturate the first phrase in a way reminiscent of the opening of Mozart's late G-minor symphony, where the anapest rhythm of the opening sounds at the different levels of motive and phrase (see example 2.2).[16]

Example 2.2. Mozart, Symphony no. 40 in G minor, K. 550, first movement: measures 1–3 (first violin).

In this short space of time the music has already played out a drama; the fermata pause allows us to become aware of this before we are drawn back into the storm, while the sustained G, like a cable taut with high voltage, carries the tension over into the next phrase. Imagine the effect of following Beethoven's antecedent phrase with a normative consequent, neatly cadencing on the tonic at the appropriate time. In terms of classical-style equilibrium, the tonic cadence that could balance this half cadence would be too final for any place in the movement except its very close.

The answering phrase results not in a balancing cadence in the tonic minor but in the headfirst arrival at the second theme, a peremptory resolution into the relative major through the use of an enharmonically ambiguous diminished seventh chord (which, if spelled with an F♯, would resolve to V of tonic minor—as it does in the recapitulation—rather than V of the relative major). At the point where such a balancing cadence might have taken place (at bars 38–40: I can imagine it as rhythmically analogous to bars 19–21 and harmonized with something like ii^6_5–V^7–i), the music begins an intensification of all parameters: increased rhythmic activity, addition of winds on the downbeats, rising sequence, accelerated harmonic rhythm, and dissonance over a pedal tone. The arrival on tonic minor in bar 44 is certainly the result of this intensification, and its status as an arrival is justified harmonically by the most involved harmonic progression yet: (from bar 37) i–vii^7–V^7/iv–iv–V^7/iv–iv–vii^7–i. But this arrival does not answer the cadence in bar 21. It is undercut by the tonic pedal tone that precedes it, implying that the entire passage from 33 to 44 is a tonic prolongation (articulated by a Schenkerian octave span). (See example 2.3.)

This would put the harmonic arrival on tonic minor back at bar 33, a rather weak intermediate cadence that cannot even begin to balance the cadence in 21. And the passage starting in bar 44 functions as a climax of the entire first section but not as its closure.

Bars 44 to 51 present something like a summary argument of the harmonic premise of the opening section: the top-heavy tonic that must resolve to, must be followed by, a dominant. It also reverses again what the answering phrase had reversed of the first phrase—the V–i iterations of bars 25–33 had reversed the i–V orientation of the first phrase (which gives the two phrases a clear antecedent-consequent feel, at least in this one parameter). Now at the climax of the section, tonic is again set up as something that must be moved from, rather than toward. The dominant seventh chord onto which this climactic tonic collapses then moves to the surprise diminished seventh chord that finally resolves to the V^6 of E♭ major.

The dramatic sense of presence does not let up until we are thus pitched into the second theme area. This is due in part to Beethoven's use of a modified periodic structure consisting of statement and counterstatement, where the former cadences on V and the latter moves to the new key. Such a procedure is common enough in the classical style; yet it is never employed with such breathless drama.[17] More regularly periodic structures grant us the ability to see some ways into the future. The meter and the phrase structure are predictable enough that we can relax our concern with where we are heading and shift our focus to the local play of detail—a sense of leisure is imparted. Four bars ending with a half cadence means at least four more bars ending

Example 2.3. Beethoven, Symphony no. 5, first movement: measures 34–44.

Example 2.3, continued

with a tonic cadence—without such lulling regularity the "surprise" in Haydn's symphony of the same name would never work. In Beethoven's Fifth Symphony such leisure is revoked: there is no safe projection of the future; no longer can we see a long stretch of the road ahead. Instead we are forced, as it were, to drive at high speed with only the space immediately before us visible—this is indeed one form of living in the moment, and not a very comfortable one. Yet the drama in Beethoven's music is never merely a matter of unpredictability, of the sudden swerve. Working with the manipulation of the temporal experience of periodic phrasing to sustain a feeling of presence is Beethoven's monumentalization of harmony: there is an accretion of mass in the momentum, and what might be merely impetuous becomes inexorable.

For Beethoven creates, among other things, a drama of tonic and dominant. The syntactic business of articulating periodic structures with these polar harmonies is made into something of epic intensity and weight. Like James Joyce's famous sibling rivals, Shem and Shaun, tonic and dominant are inextricably involved in a psychodrama of polar complements. In the first phrase, tonic is a charged downbeat that must discharge into a strong arrival on V. The second phrase reverses polarity, and V discharges into tonic, which, instead of closing the circuit, builds up a higher charge that is discharged into the succeeding dominant seventh and beyond into the second theme. In this scenario, bars 44 and following form a parallel harmonic construction to bars 1–21. Both sections contain tonics that act as points of departure rather than points of arrival and closure. This serves to stamp the whole section from 1 to 58 as an opening, and it is made clear that the balancing resolution to tonic will take most of the movement rather than the more normative eight bars. Many sonata-form expositions can be said to deny closure in such a way that the first theme group has an open-ended character. But the emphatic character of this aspect in Beethoven's heroic style is surely unprecedented, and it has led to the view that the progress of theme is equivalent to the progress of form.[18]

Beethoven's use of tonic and dominant has often been linked to his allegedly elemental simplicity, as if he thus succeeds in penetrating to the naked heart of musical expression and yet somehow avoids sounding childishly abecedarian. In a striking example, Charles Rosen characteristically captures something that, when once pointed out, seems perfectly obvious about this aspect of Beethoven's art. Speaking of the role of the tonic triad in Beethoven, Rosen comments that "it is, in fact, with this fundamental triad that Beethoven attains his most remarkable and characteristic effects. At one point in the G major Piano Concerto, he achieves the seemingly impossible with it and turns this most consonant of chords . . . itself into a dissonance" (see example 2.4).[19]

Because of all the previous alternations with the dominant, the rhythmic acceleration, and the paradigmatic $\hat{3}$–$\hat{2}$ upper voice of the

Example 2.4. Beethoven, Piano Concerto no. 4, Op. 58: measures 23–28, piano reduction.

standard half cadence, the sustained root-position tonic chord of bar 27 clearly requires resolution into the dominant. Rosen goes on to remark that to persist on the tonic in this bar demands an act of sheer will. His example is an extraordinary one, yet this same act of will is surely perceptible in Beethoven's general use of harmonic rhythm in the heroic style. Because Beethoven treats harmonies like monoliths instead of playing cards, harmonic change assumes epic importance, and an act of will is projected.

A large part of the engagement felt when listening to this music is thus compounded of the monumentalization and dramatization of classical-style morphology and syntax. But as we saw in chapter 1, Beethoven's openings may also conflate the formal functions of exposition and development in a way that undermines stability and engenders an imbalance whose immediate consequence is forward momentum. This process can be emblematically styled as *bass composition*, a developmental procedure in which the bass leads, and the music takes on transitional fluidity and impetus.[20] (Conversely, soprano composition would indicate those passages in which an upper voice leads— that is, where a melody is heard over a stable bass line that is most likely in the business of articulating some sort of periodic underpinning.) Rather than dramatically monumentalize tonic, dominant, and periodic phrasing—as in the opening of the Fifth Symphony or that of the *Appassionata* Sonata—Beethoven creates in such cases a search for tonal stability. The *Coriolan* Overture (written in 1807, the year before the completion of the Fifth Symphony) provides a particularly apt example (see example 2.5).

Example 2.5. Beethoven, *Coriolan* Overture: measures 1–22.

Example 2.5, continued

The octave Cs at the outset of the *Coriolan* Overture represent an opening gambit much used by Beethoven. Arnold Schering, discussing the *Egmont* Overture, links such openings to the symbolism of fate.[21] Concerning Haydn's similar opening, in his "Representation of Chaos" from *The Creation*, Tovey remarks that the empty octave is the most chaotic thing in the whole piece (because some sort of significant chord would already represent something closer to cosmos than to

Example 2.5, continued

chaos, and a "violent and unexplained discord would . . . be a mere phenomenon of human petulance").[22] In all these cases, the stentorian octaves present a challenge and demand a reaction.

At the beginning of the *Coriolan* Overture, it is as if the music itself reacts to the thrice-reiterated Cs, for each repetition of the octave C calls forth a different chord from the orchestra. With each new chordal response the plot thickens, tensions accrue: the first chord is a consonant F-minor triad, the second a diminished seventh on $B\natural$, the third a diminished seventh on $F\sharp$. A harmonic plot of the first eleven bars would read as follows: 1) V–i (if in F minor) or i–iv (if in C minor): F minor is probably more likely at this point; 2) V–vii$^4_3$/V (if in F minor) or i–vii$^4_3$ (if in C minor): F minor is even more likely, for the C can clearly be heard as a decorated dominant; 3) i–vii^7/V (in C minor): F minor is no longer tenable, is in fact canceled by $F\sharp$, as the harmony jumps from decorating the dominant of F to decorating the dominant of C. (The rising tension of an upward fifth sequence is audible in the relation between $B^{\circ 7}$ and $F\sharp^{\circ 7}$.) Without once enunciating the tonic minor as a chord, Beethoven's opening, by bar 11, clearly calls for the dominant of C minor. And again, the listener is pulled into this coalescing drama, for each new reiteration of the Cs and each new chordal response changes the picture, adds more information. By the third chord we have a sense of harmonic orientation, if not confirmation. The tonic $^6_4$ in bar 13 is the first expected resolution, but one that occurs ironically, as a disruption of the now-growing expectation to hear another statement of the octave Cs.

That the arrival from i$^6_4$ and V onto root-position C minor at bar 15 is also undercut is something Beethoven makes clear in several ways. First, the dynamic level drops to $\boldsymbol{p}$; second, in place of the expected full harmonic resolution we hear octaves again; third, the theme stutters, repeating the same figure three times, the first two of which kick up to the fifth scale degree; fourth, the theme enters two bars too early, if we take into account the pattern set up by the first fourteen bars (2 + 2; 2 + 2; 2 + 2; 2, then theme), or, more accurately, the octaves start out sounding like downbeats and end up as upbeats, a reading that has the theme entering on a downbeat—but not an unequivocal one. And the theme itself represents no toehold on stability: after its initial stammering it rises in a petulant sequence and is impelled into the airstream of a bass descent, through augmented sixth, to V. This cadence makes a hectic and peremptory stop, for the bass voice gets there first, the full orchestra crashing in at the last possible moment. Nor does it lead to the weighty tonic arrival that we were promised earlier but is cut off imperiously and followed by the theme again, now in B♭ minor. As a result, we are compelled to follow Beethoven's train of thought "auf Schritt und Tritt"; nothing is taken for granted.

The capricious vacillation of the opening section of this overture can of course be linked to the fundamentally conflicted personality of the hero Coriolanus. What is new here is not the musical portrayal of a dramatic character but the means of such portrayal, for this opening eschews anything like a thematic representation of its hero. Instead, the very process of the music—harmonic, tonal, rhythmic, and so on—sounds as if it embodies the hero's tragic dithering.

No melody in fact establishes itself until the second theme in E♭ major. At that point the bass stabilizes, working with the melody to articulate regular four-bar phrases. Even this stability is soon to be undermined; the four-bar phrases do not complete a cadential motion in E♭ but progress in a sequential series through F minor to G minor. Be that as it may, when the second theme arrives, a significant level of stability is reached for the first time in the piece. Until the arrival of this theme, the bass line leads; with its arrival, the melody becomes the primary voice, the bass its support.

The idea of bass composition, of the bass being the leading voice, is proper to transitions, and may be said to be of contrapuntal origin. (It is often found in Schenkerian middleground analyses in the guise of parallel sixths or tenths.) In these cases, the bass voice functions as a directional line. Starting the musical action with such bass composition serves to engage the listener in a directed motion; the music sounds transitional rather than expository. Perhaps more important phenomenologically is the impression of deep-seated momentum that the bass, as the bottom-most support of the musical texture, can arouse when so moved.

II

It is clear that in the beginnings alone of heroic-style movements, Beethoven has guaranteed a high level of almost visceral engagement on the part of the listener. The openings of these pieces are treated not as stable departure points that may be moved away from (and returned to) but as destabilized states that can only move forward. The initial tonic is either not firmly established, through the use of a transitional opening or through lack of cadential confirmation, or else destabilized by making it top-heavy rhythmically (and prone to resolve to its dominant). How is the engagement inherent in such openings sustained; and how do these processes work with the underlying formal strategies of classical-style sonata form?

In an art of dramatic engagement, the climax is a powerful expedient. We have seen how programmatic analyses of the *Eroica* tend to shape their narratives around climactic passages. Marx's narrative account of the *Eroica*, which I have analyzed as an increasingly intense series of actions and reactions, offers insight into Beethoven's art of long-term dramatic suspense. At any given point the music is either building to a climax or subsiding from one, and such action-reaction cycles act as engines of dramatic engagement. In this regard, we may say that Beethoven's heroic style is highly rhythmic, for the notion of upbeat to downbeat is made into a form-building principle—but in a very different way from that propounded by hierarchic theories of rhythm. The big arrivals in this style are not so much the product of metric organization as they are that of rhythmic impulse. Large upbeats lead to large downbeats not as the main pillars of a hierarchic hypermeter but in a more directly temporal way. That is to say, such arrivals feel like temporal *events* rather than measured accumulations of time. This, I feel, gets close to why we tend to hear Beethoven as engaging us primarily at a visceral level. A feeling of motion is more readily imparted when departures and arrivals are emphatic and well removed from one another. Contrasted with the more articulated progress of regular periodicity (with more clearly defined subdivisions), Beethoven's procedure works like Peter Schlemihl's famed "seven-league" boots: not only are we moving, we are moving on a grand scale.[23]

As an example, note how the second theme of the C-minor Symphony reacts to the first theme. The horn call that announces the second theme relaxes the opening motive by transforming its clenched third into the relative composure of a fifth. At the same time, the horn serves to dissipate the heavy accents at bars 56 and 58 by echoing them in 60 and 62. The second theme area thus establishes itself in short order, by absorbing and transforming the energy of the opening fifty-eight bars within the course of one succinct phrase. Although much debate has been generated concerning the precise phrase boundaries of this theme as it unfolds,[24] no such arguments are needed to hear this entire section as a distinct rhythmic contrast to the first section: the quarter-note motion of the melodic voice; the easy rocking of the harmony, articulated in even slower half notes; the motto rhythm now reduced to a phrase marker in the bass, at the service of regular four-bar phrases—all these things make this theme feel like the ebb after a crashing wave. And, like all waves, the music soon starts to develop a strong undertow. All the parameters work together to project this developing intensity: chromaticism is introduced; the phrase rhythm breaks down via the three-bar group at bars 83–85 to two-bar groups; the bass line begins to travel upward rather than merely hold down a four-bar canvas for the melody written upon it; the melody itself becomes obsessed with a two-bar fragment of its previous statement; and the dynamics increase from p to ff. All this leads to the big downbeat at bar 94, where the final peroration of the exposition commences.

The reactive sections in the heroic style need not always be shaped as part of such a tight wave cycle. Another common strategy is the long-range buildup to a climax that reaches a ne plus ultra and then breaks off, followed by more or less new material. Perhaps the single most momentous example is that of Marx's "battle scene" in the development of the *Eroica*, where the music drives for almost one hundred bars to a shattering climax (186–279), beyond which lies the new theme. The process begins again in bar 300, where a fresh intrusion of the first theme (in C major) drives to E♭ minor and another sounding of the new theme (bar 322). The next big motion is from the arrival on B♭ in the bass at 338 to the big C♭-major fanfare starting in 362. This climax is then followed by the reactive section that eventually includes the horn call and sets up the conditions for the arrival of the recapitulation at bar 398. These sections are considerably larger than the waves of action and reaction found in the first forty-five bars of this movement. Here in the middle of the movement, the pattern of rhythmic action and reaction governs immense lengths of time. On the largest scale, the section from the new theme to the recapitulation (284–398) represents the reaction to Marx's battle scene (186–279): both sections lead to a dramatic impasse that can only be followed by a drastic change, although they do so in opposite ways—the battle by building up, the retransition by scaling down. The result is an imposing expansion of the basic syntactic formula of antecedent-consequent.[25]

The development of the first movement of the Fifth Symphony resembles that of the *Eroica* in its use of a mysteriously quiet section before the thematic return. Shunning the grandiose canvas of the latter's development section, Beethoven employs in the Fifth Symphony a much more compact design that, in its own way, is no less dramatic. Two large sections develop the first and second themes, respectively. After a new version of the opening motto (now establishing F minor), the development commences in the manner of the exposition. But the dramatic half cadence has vanished, and the reference to the first theme is here used to effect a sequential motion of rising fifths. Such a progression will almost always increase tension, as the voice-leading results in a line that rises by seconds (e.g., F—through C—rises to G). Two consecutive diminished seventh chords appear to threaten the establishment of G minor (bars 168–74) but ultimately serve as an intensified chromatic approach to the dominant of the same. (See example 2.6.)

Example 2.6. Beethoven, Symphony no. 5, first movement: key scheme of the development section.

	Use of First Theme			Use of Second Theme		
Key center:	F $\longrightarrow$ C $\longrightarrow$ G (to V of G)			G $\longrightarrow$ C $\longrightarrow$ F		
Bar:	129	146	154	179	187	195

At bar 179 a sequential treatment of the second theme ensues, and the fifth cycle is reversed, now traveling from G to C and looking to continue on in this now-easy way to F. An F-minor sonority is in fact reached in bar 196, but as a first inversion that eventually suggests, through the addition of G♭s and D♭s, B♭ minor. The entire episode from bar 195 to 240 arises from the first two half notes of the second theme, which, when weighed down with their own harmonies, detach themselves from that theme and launch an independent, sled-heavy excursion that seems headed to B♭ minor. Thus the harmonic trajectory of the sequence initiated in 179 continues on (G–C–F–B♭), albeit much more ponderously.

Any forward-moving energy that remains of this harmonic sequence is strangely neutralized in the mysterious bars that follow; no key is to be granted a cadence in this unnerving calm. At bar 210 the two-bar unit is broken down, the dynamic level recedes, and the harmony drifts into the unlikely area of F♯ minor (arrived at enharmonically through a D♭^{6} chord). Such a sound is all the more uncanny as the development up to this point has been quite conservative tonally, rarely going more than a fifth beyond C minor in either direction. The antiphonally alternating wind and string chords constitute something like the eye of a hurricane, or the uneasy respite of a battle; far from the titanic standoff implied by the similarly alternating choirs at the climax of the *Eroica*'s "battle," these chords are more like the suddenly audible respirations of a nervous soldier. Here the drama is in fact much the same as that which engendered the horn call in the *Eroica*—the absence implied by the quiet is more terrifying than any real presence could be. (We might construe the tonal circumstances figuratively here and point out that in terms of tonal relationships, F♯ minor represents the absence of C minor better than could any other key.[26]) That the entire episode grows out of an obsessive fixation on one aspect of the second theme is in itself unsettling. Moreover, the combination of such perseveration with the draining off of all sense of purpose is terrifyingly close to madness.

As E.T.A. Hoffmann notes, Beethoven goes into this passage from the flat side and comes out on the sharp side—the wind parts show both F♯ and D♭, in a curious example of notation reflecting enharmonic ambiguity. A 6–5 voice-leading pattern effects both the move into F♯ and the move from there to the dominant of C, and we can see that this whole hushed episode performs harmonic magic: the motion in fifths from G to C to F to B♭, which had traversed large expanses with much commotion, is now neutralized and returned to G (which will lead to the C-minor reprise), by voice-leading of the simplest sort—the episode thus stands as a striking example of lateral thinking (see exam-

Example 2.7. Beethoven, Symphony no. 5, first movement: measures 213–29, figured-bass reduction.

ple 2.7).[27] A prolonged diminished seventh on B (representing the dominant G) then leads to the churning repetitions of A♭ and F, which open into the return of the symphony's motto like a river into the sea.[28]

The development sections of the first movements of the *Eroica* and Fifth Symphonies heighten the eventual arrival of the recapitulation in similar ways. Both generate a tension, bordering on terror, by introducing a hushed episode fraught with the sense that something must happen. The recapitulation is thus treated as an *impending* event, with the result that this fundamental articulation of the underlying form is invested with an urgency that goes beyond that of a syntactical joint (however important), becoming at the same time a watershed event in an already heightened dramatic process. Quite simply, the recapitulation is made to seem necessary, not by convention but by the demands of the individual work. This is how Beethoven enhances, or narrates, the underlying form, making it appear as if the form develops with the developing line of the musical process. Or, at the risk of putting it glibly, this is how Beethoven transforms the syntactic into the semantic: the underlying syntax is now charged with meaning and assumes the ethical heft of human significance. We are more directly affected by a recapitulation charged in this way than by one that is dictated by convention alone, no matter what the aesthetic pedigree such convention boasts. (For the same reason, our minds will drop the loftiest metaphysical trains of thought to snatch at the merest tidbit of human interest: what avails the *ding an sich* when we hear the latest gossip about someone we know?) The dramatic potential inherent in classical-style syntax is here made maximally explicit, its formal articulations given epic significance.

In the first movement of the Eighth Symphony—a work that seems to trade on heroic gestures that are neither burdened with excessive gravity nor treated with disdain, and as such comes off something like a staging of the heroic style in a marionette theater[29]—Beethoven brings on the recapitulation as the climax of an almost seamlessly taut dramatic process reaching back to the beginning of the development. As is the case with the Fifth Symphony, the music of this development section moves forward in broad swatches of sound, this time with a descending bass (C, in bars 103–23; B♭, in 124–31; A, in 132ff.). This slowly moving pedal has the effect of a ponderous sinking into the thick of things. The thick of things happens to be the section starting in bar 143, where the main motive of the movement initiates some dramatically conceived action in D minor (reminiscent of the "battle scene" in the *Eroica*). In terms of bass motion, the sum of those three steps downward is a step upward, from the C at the end of the exposition to the D in bar 145. A sequential progression of fifths leads from D minor through G minor and C minor to F minor. Obsessive treatment of the opening motive then pushes the upper register from C to G (c–d♭–d–e♭–e–g, in bars 160 to 187), preparing the blinding arrival on A in the first violins over the return of the main theme in cellos and basses (Tovey referred to this as "noontide glare"[30]). This climactic wash of upper-register sound serves to replace the feeling of arrival we may have missed by not having the root in the bass at the outset of the recapitulation (because of the placement of the theme in the bass).

The lack of strong intermediate cadential articulations gives this development a feeling of almost unbroken intensification. There are two large sections—the first serving to lead from the exposition (using its last motive), the next to the recapitulation (using its intial motive). The joint between these sections (at bar 143) is effected by the use of an anticipation similar to those that populate the Ninth Symphony. Unlike the case in the *Eroica* and Fifth Symphonies, here the recapitulation is reached as if by an arrow shot from the end of the exposition, the climax at its outset the result of one uninterrupted flight. The lack of a reactive section, of a psychological abyss, speaks for the compactness of the Eighth Symphony and its ultimately lighter weight.

III

Despite the immediate effect of a release of long-ranging tension, Beethoven's recapitulations do not signal the arrival of stability. His use of initial thematic material that is extremely unsettling automatically problematizes the recapitulation as a return to some sort of normality. Not for a moment is the listener encouraged to let his or her attention to the unfolding events flag, for where one might expect the festivities of a homecoming Beethoven will often change course dramatically. In the first movements of both the Fifth Symphony and the *Eroica*, the recapitulation actually commences in a relaxed state, not sustaining the feeling of a strong syntactic arrival. In the Fifth Symphony, the recapitulated theme has nothing like the unmitigated urgency of its counterpart in the exposition. It is now sweetened with woodwind embellishments, culminating in the famous oboe cadenza. The fermata following this cadenza is phenomenologically different from the one in bar 21; because the phrase that follows is shorn of its hortatory A♭ and F (which we have heard in profusion just a few moments earlier), the high drama of the first violin's G leading to the A♭ and F is no longer appropriate here. Instead we hear something like a sigh of resignation; the oboe does in fact sound the high G of the dominant sonority (as the climax of a melodic line begun back at bar 254) but then descends, with a world-weary flourish, to the lesser energy level of the fifth, D, from which the next phrase—now without its exordium—continues. The oboe's line thus attenuates the native urgency of this passage; it is now relaxed enough (or perhaps resigned enough) to sing. After the intense drama of the end of the development and the arrival of the motto, the opening of the recapitulation seems to pull back from the action. This is felt not as stability but rather as a kind of breather: the important arrival of the home key and first theme is made retroactively to feel like the goal of a struggle whose intensity has made such a reprieve necessary and highly deserved.

This undercutting of intensity at the outset of the recapitulation serves once again the larger rhythmic impulse of action and reaction. A more exact reprise of the initial urgency of the exposition would not be an appropriate reaction to the intense drama generated by the development and syntactic arrival of the home key. Related to this is a feeling that the first theme has progressed to a new level, has been transformed in some way by all that has intervened; an exact reprise would undermine the experience of the development by showing that all the foregoing sound and fury has indeed signified nothing. The oboe's cadenza testifies sadly to the contrary: all too much has transpired since first hearing the opening theme, and now that theme is not so much reheard but remembered from a distance.[31] The point is that this is no mere return but rather another twist of the spiral; the emphasis is no longer on the syntactic business of sonata form but on the progressive trajectory of a linear history.

In accordance with this type of trajectory, the somewhat lower energy level that occurs right after the actual arrival at the recapitulation eventually accumulates momentum in turn and leads to another strong downbeat. The recapitulation of the *Eroica* first movement, for example, relaxes initially with a quiet, lyrically reflective excursion through F major and D♭ major, which then leads to a tremendously climactic reaffirmation of E♭ and the first theme. The action here deepens and intensifies the analogous section of the exposition. There we heard three successive statements of the first theme, the last one a tutti preceded by a big dominant. Here the paired statements in F and D♭ that follow the initial E♭-major statement usher in a dominant pedal point that, in its use of the triadic motive of the first theme, sounds like another retransition. This leads in short order to the tutti statement in E♭, where the theme is heard as an upper voice over a tonic pedal. The prominent triadic figure in this upper voice takes off sequentially and reaches the high A♭ that will prove so momentous at the very end of the movement. Here its resolution to G marks the point at which the theme again descends to the bass voice, whereupon the orchestra makes as much noise as it can. The result is a bifurcated recapitulation: the first arrival of the theme is immediately undercut tonally, setting up a second arrival with its own retransition.[32] This acts as an analogue to an exposition that was introductory in that it took pains to establish a big dominant before the tutti statement of the theme. Such a recapitulation serves the action-reaction scenario established in the exposition, and Beethoven thus ensures the continuation of an end-oriented, linear process.

The triumphant treatment of the first theme and its home key in bars 430 to 448 is hardly an understated confirmation of tonic, and it brings into question the necessity of yet more such noisy confirmation in the coda, especially since all the big arrivals in the rest of the recapitulation will be squarely on the tonic. (In fact, far from sounding initially like a continuation made necessary by an unstable recapitulation, the *Eroica* coda, by dropping without ceremony into D♭ major, deliberately undermines the stability of E♭ and gives the impression of a new beginning.) Another spot in Beethoven's recapitulations that can seem to seal the case for tonic confirmation is the cadence before the second theme. In the first movement of the *Appassionata* Sonata, Op. 57, for example, the tonic cadence that had been denied in the exposition is provided in the recapitulation at the arrival of the second theme (bar 174), thus rectifying the initial imbalance created by the lack of a confirming cadence in tonic during the first theme group. Nevertheless, this did not stop Beethoven from writing a coda for this movement that provides several opportunities for big tonic cadences. Like the *Eroica* coda, this one sets out by undermining the tonic sonority. Of course the end result of this last-minute deviation will be to confirm the tonic as conclusively as possible—this is like a typical cadential motion writ large, in that the most dissonance occurs before the firmest closure, turning that closure into something akin to a show of strength. In the *Appassionata*, a cadenzalike passage leads to the strongest cadence in the movement (bars 238–39), which in turn sparks the concluding *Più allegro*.

One begins to wonder to what degree the coda is in fact necessary to the tonal balance of the movement. For the Beethovenian coda is not simply the place where excess energy is discharged and imbalance redressed. Much of that sort of transaction takes place during the normatively heightened cadences of the second theme group in the recapitulation. And we have seen that the coda more often than not begins with a strong deviation from the tonic. This is the reason that many critics used to think of Beethoven's codas as second developments— they often seem to be setting out afresh, and they often refer again to the first theme (as in the Opp. 55 and 57 codas). In the previous chapter we explored the idea of the *Eroica* coda as a kind of second recapitulation, not of the exposition but of the entire movement. This notion combines the idea of setting out and that of finishing, of deviation and ultimate closure, for here an entire movement will be recalled, and an entire movement will come to a close. But regardless of the formal function we ascribe to the coda, the suspicion remains that the coda is in fact *not* the strictly necessary, organically and structurally inevitable continuation of that which precedes it, and that there is a willful aspect to Beethoven's codas that is of great moment precisely because it is supererogatory. What does the heroic-style coda achieve?

We may profit in this regard from another look at the coda of the *Eroica* first movement. As noted in chapter 1, the final version of the theme is that of a melody with noncadential, harmonically open-ended, four-bar alternations of tonic and dominant, made directional only by a tremendous orchestral swell. But even with this soaring thematic apotheosis, the movement is far from over. After the fourfold repetition of the theme, Schenker's *Aufwärtsdrang* again comes to the fore, as a surprise E♮ ascends chromatically, peaking in the high A♭ of bar 668. The line turns back down toward E♭ and brings on the cadential figure noted by Lewis Lockwood as "Unit C" (673–81).[33] This figure previously led to sections of extreme instability in the exposition (bars 64ff.) and the recapitulation (bars 468ff.); here it resolves this tension "at the last possible moment."[34] The grand dominant-seventh sonority that issues forth from this figure makes two giant swells before resolving at 689. The last of these brings back the springing intervals from the several retransition sections, now in the first violins. This muscular gesture no longer shakes the earth with the stride of some impatient Colossus, as it did when heard in the bass; now it too is released as an upper voice, carrying in its tremolos and impossible flights back and forth from B♭ the intensity of the entire movement all the way to the tonic resolution in 689 and beyond to the double bar. Three iterations of E♭ major close the movement, the first two forming a last upbeat gesture to the final chord—in the same manner that the opening chords brought the initial musical argument onto the stage way back in the first two bars.[35]

It is obvious that this movement isn't over until it's over. The effect of unbroken and intensified continuity all the way to the finish prompted Wagner to refer to the movement as a single melody and, as we have seen, to characterize Beethoven's music generally as melodic effusion in the broadest and deepest sense. At one point in his capacious analysis of the *Eroica*, Heinrich Schenker characterizes the musical process of the first movement as a "willed and necessary course."[36] This sustained intensity thus aids critical intuitions about the piece as a self-willed, self-generated process; the nature of its final closure makes it seem a self-consuming process as well. For what can possibly remain to be said after that type of finish? The sheer mass of the monumentalized final section, heard to move with nearly seamless intensity all the way to the full stop at the double bar, leads the listener to a feeling of absolute and unequivocal closure. This is what the coda achieves through its extravagant response to the tonal requirements of the underlying form.

Beethoven's heroic codas drive to an uttermost terminus; the music does not conclude merely because convention will have it so but because it is in fact finished, in the full sense of the word.[37] This effect is abetted by the emphatic repetition of tonic and dominant, utterly canceling all further urge or possibility for harmonic adventure. The dominant that resolves onto the final tonic (or the final tonic section) often sounds in extremis: if the preceding example of the *Eroica* is not convincing enough, the famous minor ninth chord in the coda of the Third *Leonore* Overture will brook no argument. And the tonic harmony heard at the end of such a movement and after such a dominant is utterly different from that heard at the outset. There it is often highly unstable, acting as a true opening, as something that must move on; here it is the place where all motion ceases. Beethoven more than anyone else could effect this fundamental change.

The type of emphasis enjoyed by the coda, when understood both as a fresh start in some sense analogous to the beginnings of exposition, development, and recapitulation and as a final closing, gives to the Beethovenian sonata form an overall rhythm of down-up-down-up-down with exposition, recapitulation, and coda forming the three downbeats. The rhythm of a more beginning-oriented sonata form without a heavily emphasized coda would be something like down-up-down-up. This change of emphasis is commensurate with the idea that the temporal process expressed in the heroic style is one of *completion*, starting from an initial large-scale downbeat and rounding off with a final large-scale downbeat. As was the case with the difference between opening tonic and closing tonic, the point here is that a big downbeat is again attained at the end—but here it closes the movement. The coda completes this larger rhythm, brings the process around again to something like the crisis of the opening, and closes it unequivocally. This type of closure thus works both as the teleological climax of a linear process and as the rounding-off of a cyclical formal design. The result is a fruitful conflation of linear and cyclical time, a notion I shall explore in chapter 4. By projecting this kind of double closure (and closing the movement with perhaps double the force needed) the Beethovenian coda makes this sense of total completion into one of the cardinal values of the heroic style. Such completion spreads its finality backward over the rest of the movement and comes to seem necessary, the predetermined self-consumption of a process of destiny.

An interesting exception to the soaring conclusion of the *Eroica* first movement is provided by the first movement of the Fifth Symphony. The coda of this movement is the epitome of the struggling Beethoven, for rarely does his music appear to work so hard in order to get nowhere fast. Every step is now laborious, an effect ensured by the figuration added to what are essentially descending and ascending C-minor scales (see bars 407 to 469, and especially 423 to 433 and 439 to 453, where the sequential melodic pattern requires taking three ascending steps to attain the net rise of one scale step in every other bar). An element of melodic construction that is often used as a means for a quick and effortless sprint from octave to octave, the scale here becomes an imposing staircase upon which some ponderous weight is hauled up and down, step by step.

Harmonically, the coda is held down by the additional and inflected emphasis of the subdominant (see bars 418ff., for example); otherwise facile tonic-dominant exchanges now labor to lift away from the gravity of this grim subdominant. The "triumphant" C major of Beethoven's recapitulation turns out to be the V of F minor in the coda. All the emphasis on the subdominant in the coda is a way of harnessing the energies of that shining C major, making it not a conclusive tonic but a secondary dominant. This reading of the role of tonic major and the subdominant supports Lawrence Kramer's view of this coda as a violent suppression of C major.[38] As such, the coda is more a tearing down than a confirmation, something that will then have to be dealt with rather than something that conclusively deals with something.

The excessive effort of this coda, expressed both in the violent outbursts at its beginning and end and in the belabored figurations mentioned earlier, can be heard as something like the forced assertions of bad faith. Consider the very last bars of the movement: the first theme is referred to almost nostalgically and then blasted away with far more firepower than is needed, resulting in an almost churlish display of power. This juxtaposition emphasizes the containment mechanism of closure, made to sound, at least in the immediate context, like overkill. The effect is actually one of irony, for the emphatic final bars do provide the commensurate degree of closure for the opening phrase of the movement (and the entire ensuing process); only by immediately appending these bars to a now wistful version of that opening does their requisite closure become overwrought and forced.

Perhaps the difference between this coda and the ebullient close of the *Eroica* first movement is simply that between confirmation in major and confirmation in minor. The inherent stylistic discomfort with closure in minor is here dramatized, as the C major heard so emphatically at the close of the recapitulation is dismissed by the peremptory asseverations of C minor, a key whose power is more likely to be characterized programmatically not as that of a noble cause but as that of a murderous usurper. In the realm of Beethoven's heroic style, this necessarily leaves the first movement open-ended, for it does not complete an acceptable story. The troubled closure of the first movement calls for a higher degree of closure at the level of the entire symphony. Or, as Kramer puts it, the symphony calls for "a C major that *cannot be followed.*"[39]

This is a situation almost unique to the Fifth Symphony. For it is not a foregone conclusion that works in this style are weighted toward their finales. Tovey rightly observes that "the first movement of a sonata tells a complete story which no later movement can falsify."[40] And the first movement of these works is traditionally the central concern of most music criticism; far less attention is lavished on succeeding movements. This is probably attributable to the first movement having served as the model and master trope for our general notion of how such music ought to go. Our critical and analytical resources are geared to these movements and are shown to best advantage in dealing with them. Conversely, these same systems often find little to say about minuets, finales, and slow movements. Yet the received opinion is that finales should in fact serve to close a dramatic and organically conceived process that begins in the first movement. Hence the scarcely concealed disappointment generated by many of the finales in the classical style, finales that are felt not to have measured up to the conditions set by their respective first movements (think of the finale of Mozart's G-minor String Quintet, K. 516, for example, with its history of detractors and apologists).

The Fifth Symphony is of course the most routinely touted example of a successfully unified four-movement design. And the conception of a finale as something more than the closing movement called for by convention is evident in many of Beethoven's middle-period works. One need only consider the preponderance of works from this period that link the penultimate movement with the finale, thus directly integrating the finale into a larger conception. These include the Piano Sonatas Opp. 53, 57, and 81a; the Triple Concerto, Op. 56; the Fourth and Fifth Piano Concertos, Opp. 58 and 73; the Violin Concerto, Op. 61; the Fifth and Sixth Symphonies, Opp. 67 and 68; the String Quartets Op. 59, nos. 1 and 3, and Op. 74; and the "Archduke" Trio, Op. 97. Yet the Fifth Symphony is the only one of these in which the finale explicitly and unequivocally resolves the rest of the work: Beethoven takes great pains to give it that effect by turning the end of the Scherzo into a mammoth retransition and by emphasizing throughout the work the charged relationship of C minor and C major.[41] Aiding the feeling of resolution is the ubiquitous presence in the finale of the imposing rhythmic figure of the symphony's opening—which has now lost its imperious cast, becoming part of the melody's triumphant thrust (bars 6ff.—see the brackets in example 2.8) or, in the second theme, a playful effusion. If in example 2.9 the rhythm can still be heard as a menacing pulse in the basses, any potential for threat is completely transformed by the time the second theme enters. The triplets in the second theme (see example 2.10) seem to toss the formerly fraught motive around like rice at a wedding. This pronounced transformation and resolution creates a sense in which the entire symphony takes on the self-generating and self-closing hermetic shape normatively reserved for first movements.

If the finale itself represents the closing of a four-movement process, how does Beethoven close the finale? With a coda within a coda.[42] The first stage of this design follows the harmonic agenda of a concerto cadenza. After the big $\frac{6}{4}$ arrival at bar 294 (which has the effect of drawing new breath), the next momentously articulated harmonic event is the series of dominant-to-tonic resolutions (starting in bar 312) that follow a huge subdominant prolongation and thus take on the heft of a final cadence. Yet the alternation of dominant and tonic seems unable to check its momentum and instead of closing on the tonic in 316 ends openly on the dominant in bar 317 (which serves, retroactively, to keep prolonging the dominant pedal point that was initiated at 294). This is followed by an undercutting section that continues to avoid tonic in the bass, in such a way as to gain momentum for the arrival of tonic at the Presto (362), the second stage of the coda.

Example 2.8. Beethoven, Symphony no. 5, finale: measures 1–8 (first violin).

Example 2.9. Beethoven, Symphony no. 5, finale: measures 34–43 (strings only).

Example 2.10. Beethoven, Symphony no. 5, finale: measures 44–46 (first violin).

The music is now caught in an inexorable thrust forward. Tonics and dominants rush by in a blur (tonic always leading to dominant); at 390 a hurriedly canonic treatment of the main theme sounds a hasty peroration. The emphatic $\hat{5}$–$\hat{3}$–$\hat{1}$ in the upper voice and the bass starting at bar 400 seems to signal an imminent close. Instead, another section of alternating tonic and dominant appears; finality is delayed by the upper voice, which flirts around with $\hat{5}$ and $\hat{3}$. At 416, the upper voice reaches c^3, and all is tonic from this point on. Now the tonic itself must be exhausted; it is not enough simply to arrive there. From 416 the tonic arpeggio is traversed in descent (from c^3 to c^1 in the upper voice, joined by the basses in the second half of its descent); at 420 this arpeggio is reversed in the upper voice and extended with rhythmic repercussions. At the point where the upper voice again attains c^3 (427), the basses run a faster arpeggio up to g^1 and back. This presages the move to g^3 in the upper voice, which resolves (after three bars of g^3 and one bar rest) to c^3 in 434. Thus tonic and dominant are still being articulated, but now within the tonic sonority, as scale degrees rather than harmonic entities. An aftershock of the arrival in 434 sounds at 436, creating a six-bar pattern of downbeat attacks every two bars (432, 434, 436). This pattern is repeated in 440, where its starting member is given its own double upbeat (438 and 439). The final sound is the tonic note alone, accompanied by a roll on the timpani.

Thus the tonic chord itself works through different voicings until it reaches its ultimate resolution on a bare C; its final iterations are delivered as massive hammer blows, aired out by the pauses needed to swing an engine of such magnitude. As in the first movement, the closure is again underdetermined by what has preceded it, but here the effect is more a superabundant display of youthful, renewed strength rather than an insecure display of power. The addition of the Presto makes for an astonishing way to close—here, where one would expect a grandiose and cumulative counterweight to the entire symphony, the music, by some inexplicable dispensation of energy, actually accelerates as with a surge of adrenalin. The final hammer blows are deft as well as ponderous; something like superhuman athleticism is indicated here. Again it is no surprise that the initial reactions to this music included fear.

Despite the example of the Fifth Symphony, the role of the finale is not always as simple as we are led to believe by the organicist view of end-oriented growth and progress. The finale of the *Eroica*, for example, cannot be considered to fulfill the same agenda, though it shares some of its features. In the extraordinary passage at bars 408ff., which has the net effect of a final retransition to E♭ major, issues from other movements are indeed relived. The most obvious of these include inflections from the Funeral March (in 420ff.), the strong albeit brief emergence of C♭ major in 414, reminiscent of the first movement development, and the overall bass motion from A♭ to G, which has been a major pitch story throughout the symphony. Thus Beethoven gives us one more trial by fire (or perhaps the memory of one) before the final window-rattling Presto. Like the Fifth Symphony, there is an almost numbing amount of pure tonic at the very end (the last twenty bars). Yet taken as a whole, this finale cannot be said to resolve the rest of the work unequivocally.

It can be deemed a failure in this regard only from the standpoint of the Fifth Symphony.[43] What is shocking about the *Eroica* finale when considered from this standpoint is the seeming triviality and dubious origins of its theme (the contredanse theme that is then used in a ballet and in piano variations). The unusual bearing of this theme is often treated by critics as some sort of elemental growth process, a Promethean struggle of creation from next to nothing. Most of the symphony's earlier programmatic critics were compelled to detach the finale from their programs, at best as a sort of epilogue and at worst as a non sequitur. A recent interpretation attempts to invert the problem, treating the finale not as a derailment but as the programmatic crown of the entire work.[44] But surely the discomfort of earlier critics and the belabored justifications of later critics are both occasioned by the attitude that a finale must somehow resolve the entire work. The case of the reception of the *Eroica* finale shows the depth of our attachment to the end-orientation model. This way of understanding Beethoven's musical process clearly arises from the strong instances of several of the first movements and from the four-movement design of the Fifth Symphony.

IV

We have tracked the means of engagement in Beethoven's heroic style from beginnings to codas, from invasively compelling onsets to endings that admit of no continuation. Wagner's sense of an ever-present fundamental line is supported by the musical values discussed in this chapter. These include thematic development as a way of making ever-greater stretches of music coherent and plastic (often resulting in action-reaction cycles), the captivating presence of nonregular periodic structures, monolithic treatment of harmony, overall teleological motion, extreme and underdetermined closure, and the monumentalization of underlying formal articulations. The resultant line is of course not melodic in the everyday sense of a prominent and foregrounded voice set against a background accompaniment. Instead, the entire texture is heard to participate in the fundamental illusion of melody, that of motion through time, and thus to partake of melody's sense of unfolding presence. This type of presence is one of the primary metaphors ascribed to the heroic style, and it attracts other, nonmusical, metaphors as well, notably including protagonist, Will, and Self. The melodic dimension in Beethoven's music is heard as processive self-structuring rather than thematic exposition—melody is that which must continue, and that which seems spontaneously generated. Formal articulations and arrivals thus seem internally generated, as opposed to appearing as the assignations of convention.

Beethoven's treatment of thematic material keeps this overriding sense of line, of presence, alive. For thematic material in the heroic style is often not thematic in the usual sense of a melodic theme.[45] Tovey notes how much of Beethoven's middle-period thematic material can be recalled by simply tapping out a brief rhythm and how often the same motto rhythm is used through the course of a piece to refer, with cogent economy, to the main thematic argument, often imparting a sense of thematic ubiquity.[46] Such motto rhythms permeate long sections of the music like an ever-present emblem of the thematic protagonist; they are heard as a sign of presence. Often the repetition of these motivic rhythms serves to sustain dramatic continuity—each repetition further loads the spring, and unprecedented amounts of energy are built up and released through setting up a repetitious situation that has to change, that makes change imperative and momentous (consider, for example, the end of the development section in the first movement of the Fifth Symphony, or that of the Eighth Symphony).[47] They can also serve as conduits of the overall line, agents of the whole form. Theodor Adorno comments on Beethoven's use of ever-shorter motives and mottos that "adapt themselves to become part of the pervading idea of the whole," thus reversing the view that the whole is additively constructed from building-block motives—for Adorno, the whole is now the a priori construction, and the thematic material is adjusted and adapted until it can serve that whole.[48] In this view, any attempt to account for the nature of the heroic style by referring to the type of thematic material used (in the manner of building material) is inherently limited. Beethoven is not composing with themes in the sense of exploring the developmental possibilities of some a priori, fixed thematic entity. He instead is creating the illusion of powerful motion, the realization of a large-scale rhythm. Everything becomes thematic, in the sense of bearing the principal argument, for the unfolding of such a whole *is* the principal argument.[49]

The prevailing line thus heard in the works of Beethoven's heroic style is remarkable not only for its sustained intensity but for the weightiness of its issue. Contributing to this sense of weight is Beethoven's use of surface harmonic prolongation, which has often been designated as one of his most individual style traits. Yet to conclude that by thus freezing harmony Beethoven emphasizes instead naked rhythmic impulse would be incorrect. The parameter of harmony is in no way deemphasized but rather made momentous and monolithic. The weight of an entire key area is put right onto the surface of the piece. It is as if Schenker's *Stufen*, those harmonic scale degrees that when composed out underpin great expanses of a musical work, were brought to the fore and heard in all their structural weight. The combination of a surging sense of line, or *Erguss*, with this kind of surface heaviness is perhaps the primary reason why this music is so viscerally engaging. When we perceive that something of such weight is in motion, the earth itself seems to move—all, indeed, is melody. As we shall see in chapter 4, this type of all-encompassing motion can express the solipsistic world of the hero (and of the self); when he moves, the world moves.[50] And when the listener identifies with this movement, his or her individuality seems to become universal. For the "story" of the listener/hero is not played out against a world-background, like a theme heard against a generic form; rather the emerging story seems to create, and then consume, its world.

The combination of sustained intensity and ultimate closure aids the prevailing intuition that a piece in the heroic style represents a self-generating and self-consuming process, a dynamic microcosm. That Beethoven could seemingly contain in a closed form the outbursts that characterize his heroic works is a measure of his internalization of classical formal procedure, with its predilection for an equilibrium of drama and balance. For the deep underpinnings of this tremendous energy flow are nothing other than the large-scale articulations of classical-style form. Expectations and fulfillments associated with classical-style periodic construction are played out at the largest level. The process of this internalization makes possible his freedom to override the superficial formal boundaries of the style, in order to mark the larger underlying boundaries more vividly.

Accordingly, formal closure becomes all the more pronounced and necessary. The need to control and contain the energy generated by this music is translated into the idea of musical necessity: part of the inevitability we claim to hear in these works is the perceived necessity of containing dangerous emotions that do not infiltrate the music in covert, subversive ways (as has been claimed about Mozart) but that actually serve as initial musical premises. Yet Beethoven transforms the effect of such closure from containment to culmination. The necessity of closure appears to become an inner necessity—in the sense of a fulfilling of destiny—as well as the externally applied necessity of convention. This concept of inner necessity translates much more readily into latter-day notions of musical necessity and organic unity than external determination, because the latter can seem arbitrary, whereas the former seems part of the thing itself.[51]

Paradoxically, Beethoven can make us believe in the interpretive scenario of an internally generated destiny not because he thwarts normative expectations but because he fulfills such expectations in a profound way by monumentalizing the fundamental articulations of the available forms. This reinforcement of classical syntax is what makes Beethoven's music dramatic and compelling rather than simply quirky and willful—familiar patterns are made to sound like heroic confrontations with destiny, as in the way that the hugely conceived half cadence in the beginning of Op. 67 takes the harmonic dynamic of periodic structure and realizes it with unprecedented drama. Most discussions of what is engaging about Beethoven's music depend on some notion of normative "gravity" in order to show the flight of genius; many even make the extreme claim that Beethoven broke free of the shackles of conventional forms.[52] I wish to stress Beethoven's reaffirmation of classical grammar, for I am eager to avoid the simplistic conception of Beethoven as a kind of musical Siegfried, he who smashes the toy forms of lesser men while forging those of the future. I am suggesting instead that Beethoven emphasizes the underlying aspects of classical style, increases their gravity, and turns these forms into something like mythological tropes, an operation from which they never recovered.

We can gauge the nature of Beethoven's relation with the classical style and the elements of his stylistic "revolution" from another perspective by bringing in an informed counterargument to the usual claims about what is or is not unprecedented in his music. James Webster, in his impressive study of Haydn's symphonic art, argues that many of the important musical values we associate with Beethoven, including the liberation of thematic development, destabilized openings, teleological process, and general rhetorical impulse, actually originate with Haydn.[53] Given this situation (and there is no denying it), how can we explain the fact that Beethoven, and not Haydn, became the canonic composer, the embodiment of music? The very fact that there exists a precedent for many of his alleged innovations can help uncover the basis of his powerful hold on musical history.

Because Haydn did all these things before Beethoven there must be a rather obvious reason for Beethoven's art to be perceived as a stronger and more influential force. One feels that there is more at stake in Beethoven's use of these shared features; heavier issues are set in motion and brought to a less equivocal conclusion. Haydn's art feels lighter at every turn; consequently the reigning perception is that there is less struggle and therefore less redeeming (in the fullest sense of the word) value. The "Farewell" Symphony may now replace Beethoven's Fifth as the *locus primus* of the through-composed symphony but surely not as the *locus classicus*.[54] For the story that the Beethoven work is heard to tell is more directly consequential. A glancing comparison of the finales of the two symphonies will show more than anything their utterly different natures. The Haydn finale is a masterpiece of finesse, indirection, wit, inside jokes, and plot complexities— all the paraphernalia of eighteenth-century comic literature brilliantly employed.[55] In the Beethoven finale one perceives weight, directness, seriousness, and an utter disdain of secrecy. Its effect after the Haydn is something like reading Byron after Fielding, or Hugo after Diderot. We feel more immediately the pressure of a central, and fraught, presence.

For Webster, the unprecedented radicalness of the "Farewell" Symphony lies in the permeability of individual movements, the notion that a multimovement work may in fact be through-composed. The famous D-major interlude in the first-movement development is not assimilated within that movement alone but requires the progress of the entire symphony to reveal its full significance. In this sense, the interlude is indeed a more radical intrusion than the "new theme" of Beethoven's *Eroica*, which is recapitulated within the first movement itself. Yet consider the buildup that Beethoven deploys to prepare his "new theme"; it would be hard to imagine a more dramatic impasse than that attained immediately before the onset of the E-minor theme. What remains without precedent here is the feeling that the pronounced difference of the new theme is somehow made into a necessary stage of a compelling dramatic process; it is not just a tantalizing clue of some esoteric and complex design, calling on the sensibilities of a sophisticated aristocratic audience (or the resources of an adept critic) to puzzle it out. Instead of an artful play with convention and representation, Beethoven's processes seem undisguised and experiential.

Webster's inquiry is motivated in part by the time-honored desire of a historian to discover a *terminus a quo*. In effect, Webster has located in Haydn a *terminus a quo* for many of the values of Beethoven's music we cherish most and tend to associate exclusively with Beethoven. The precedence of some of the material features of Beethoven's heroic style in the works of Haydn permits us to give a more defined shape to what is truly unprecedented in Beethoven: the sense of an earnest and fundamental presence burdened with some great weight yet coursing forth ineluctably, moving the listener along as does the earth itself. Broadly speaking, Beethoven's music is thus heard to reach us primarily at an ethical level, Haydn's primarily at an aesthetic level—and thereby hangs the tale of subsequent musical thought. The history of the reception of the heroic style is a demonstration of the depth and power of art that reaches its audience at this level.[56]

So compelling is the ethical thrust of the Beethovenian process that it carries the stamp and authority of necessity in mainstream musical thought. The extreme feeling of engagement engendered by this music has compelled analysts and critics to inscribe the musical values of this one style into their conceptions of universal musical art. Their theories were consequently designed to detect these properties, thus cutting themselves off from understanding works manifesting different values. In the following chapter, we shall trace the formative influence of Beethoven's heroic style in the work of several important theorists of the nineteenth and twentieth centuries.

Chapter Three

INSTITUTIONAL VALUES

BEETHOVEN AND THE THEORISTS

IN THE LAST chapter I explored the compelling power of the heroic style from a musical standpoint, noting that it emanates from an at times uncanny sense of presence that is linear, continuous, weighty, and inexorable and that enlists the entire musical texture in its forward progress. No longer can the listener identify with a stable backdrop of convention upon which themes and episodes play and from which they receive their foreground profiles. Now all is in motion, and convention itself seems newly generated with the processive drama of each "heroic" movement.

Through the effect of such properties and the numerous biographical and extramusical connotations surrounding them, the works of this style project as well a particularly engaging confluence of values that arose in the *Goethezeit* and that promote an integrated and autonomous sense of self. But before venturing into the nature of these largely ethical values, I would like to show how thoroughly the musical values of the heroic style have shaped the way we learn to construct Western art music. I shall do this by investigating the Beethovenian prepossessions of some of the most influential theorists of the last two centuries, theorists whose assumptions about music still form the foundation of present-day musical thought.

The unprecedented degree of phenomenological engagement generated by the works of the heroic style first found expression in the music-theoretical literature through a set of dynamic values for composition that attempt to account for what was deemed new and compelling in Beethoven's music. Chief among these concerns was the issue of form; it was here that musical thinkers like E.T.A. Hoffmann and A. B. Marx could begin to make the same claims for musical works that had been made by leading romantic critics for the literary works of authors such as Shakespeare and Goethe.[1] In these accounts, form becomes processive and organic, rather than static and mechanical. The importance of the motive as a type of seed begins to be stressed, and thematic development gains precedence as a means of achieving the newly touted aesthetic goal of a unity that integrates the greatest possible degree of variety. Sonata form emerges as the chief vehicle of this type of unity, just as the *Bildungsroman*, with *Wilhelm Meisters*

Lehrjahre as its most celebrated exemplar, had emerged within literary studies. Musical composition in this its highest manifestation began to be characterized by a thematic process of development in which every episode (and later every note) was essential to the overall design. The musical process that seems to press inexorably forth to transcendent and exhaustive closure brings about an emphasis on the notion of necessity and organic unity.

The change of critical perspective engendered by Beethoven's heroic style assisted at the birth of the musical "work." Music that was felt to be maximally engaging at the temporal level paradoxically led to an essentially spatial notion of wholeness and integrity. The phenomenological momentousness of closure in the heroic style reinforced this idea of the closed work: because of the feeling of end-orientation enforced by such closure (heard as the ultimate formal articulation, in both senses of the word—unsurpassed and final), one could not hope to interpret the details of the ongoing temporal flow of a piece without a knowledge of the whole, without a perspective that closes off the work as a whole. Repeated hearings became necessary, and critic-analysts increasingly tried to survey and judge works from the standpoint of the whole. The primacy of the closed work became the alpha and omega of musical thought.

The unequivocal (and underdetermined) closures of the heroic style also reinforced the emphasis on cadential closure as the basis of musical content and process in the work of the later nineteenth-century theorists Moritz Hauptmann and Hugo Riemann. Cadence is no longer conceptualized as the common articulating device that appears at every turn in a piece of music: it is now writ large, a master formula for closing off large sections of music—thus the switch from Rameau's notion of the cadence dominant-tonic as model for harmonic progression (by which every harmonic move shares something of the essence of the dominant-tonic move) to Riemann's notion of the dialectical cadential progression T–S–D–T as abstract background of a key center (the letters are Riemann's designations of tonic, subdominant, and dominant functions).[2] Riemann offers a prototypical closed structure as an abstract harmonic category, which acts as a complement to the abstract eight-bar period of his rhythmic theory. Certainly the increased comfort with abstraction of the later nineteenth century (whose emblematic figure in this regard must be Saussure) was conducive to Riemann's way of thinking. Yet the music of Beethoven's heroic style actually makes the theoretical weight of tonic, subdominant, and dominant audible—such a theory thus gains plausibility.[3]

Beethoven's heroic style also helped Heinrich Schenker form his own end-oriented, quasi-abstract notion of musical progression and coherence. Schenker's way of hierarchizing voice-leading is distinctly teleological—the main theoretical dominant of a composition is often conflated with the final sounding dominant; actual sounding closure becomes one with theoretical closure. More important, one can also argue that the sense of presence and line developed in chapter 2 is perhaps the chief motivating force of Schenker's *Urlinie*, as will be demonstrated in an examination of his monograph on the Fifth Symphony. The *Urlinie* is a representation of a fundamental line that maintains a continuous presence throughout an entire movement.

If Schenker was to fashion musical understanding around subsurface, prototypical motives, the type of musical thought that for convenience we may affix to Schoenberg's notion of *Grundgestalt* (basic shape) is more apt to trace the course of actual motivic content as it passes through the changing contexts of a musical process.[4] For these theorists (and here I think primarily of Rudolph Réti), such content acts in the manner of a dramatic protagonist; thematic process and developing variation are ways of expressing the intuition that great music (embodied most notably by that of Beethoven) enacts the unfolding of infinite possibilities from limited material and models a process of destiny both determined and free.

It is not my intention to present a detailed and comprehensive report on the influx of the musical values of Beethoven's heroic style into the European theory community. Instead I wish to focus on the above-mentioned strands in the history of post-Beethoven theory and analysis, each represented by a predominant figure, and each of imposing significance within our continuing tradition of thinking about music: form theory and Adolph Bernhard Marx, functional theory and Hugo Riemann, voice-leading theory and Heinrich Schenker, and thematic process and Rudolph Réti. It hardly needs arguing that Beethoven's music acts as the proving ground for all these theorists.[5] Marx championed Beethoven even during the composer's lifetime, and his theoretical conception of sonata form, perhaps his best-known achievement, is inextricably tied up with Beethoven's music.[6] Riemann turned to Beethoven's piano sonatas as a definitive demonstration of his rhythmic and harmonic theories. Schenker's monographs on the late Beethoven piano sonatas, on the Ninth Symphony, and on the Fifth Symphony reflect different stages in the formation of his theory of underlying voice-leading. And Réti laid explicit and nearly exclusive emphasis on the thematic process of Beethoven. A closer look at each of these cases will show the extent to which Beethoven's music was not only proving ground but breeding ground for these important theories and is thus fundamental in forming the primary channels through which we continue to construe musical coherence and process (or even to construct music as a medium of coherent process).

The interaction of these theorists with the music of Beethoven fulfills an axiomatic condition of theory formation in the arts—namely, that new theories tend to engage canonic artists and artworks, whereas practitioners of established theories seek to accommodate a wider range of noncanonic figures. On this latter point, just think of the innumerable articles and theses of the last twenty years in the United States that attempt, like missionaries, to bring the word of Schenker to the music of benighted eras like the pretonal Renaissance, or the posttonal twentieth century. On the other hand, when Schenker himself was forming his theory it was Beethoven to whom he turned at crucial stages.

For Beethoven is the premier canonic composer of the last two hundred years. My examination of his effect on the four theorists at issue here thus amounts to a kind of impact history (*Wirkungsgeschichte*), in which we may measure the profound impact of Beethoven's music by showing how the values of that music are in fact the values we expect of all music, the values that to a large extent guide our analytical and critical enterprise. On the other hand, we may read the history of tonal theory in the nineteenth and twentieth centuries as a form of Beethoven reception, in which we are given an index of the ways in which succeeding generations characterized the composer's music. What did each generation hear in the music of Beethoven—and why? Yet separating the impact history (Beethoven's effect on the theorists) from the reception history (the theorists' effect on Beethoven) is perhaps not even possible, for the interaction between the values of any given theory and the values of Beethoven's music assumes more the form of a circle than that of a linear, two-way street whose traffic can be measured.

I

The importance of Beethoven for the entire range of A. B. Marx's activities as critic, theorist, and pedagogue is well known and documented. Even within the composer's lifetime, Marx developed a triadic view of musical history in which the music of Beethoven formed the culminating stage, that of "ideal music."[7] Marx felt that Beethoven's music had attained the ability to portray deeply compelling "soul states" (*Seelenzustände*) as part of a fundamentally dramatic narrative process.[8] Music is thus enabled to give concrete expression to transcendent content, the ideal nature of which Marx attempted to capture in his notion of the poetic *Idee*. In an important article from the first year (1824) of his *Berliner Allgemeine musikalische Zeitung*, Marx discussed several of the heroic symphonies (the *Eroica*, the Fifth, and the Seventh) as highly engaging dramatic panoramas evincing values such as individual freedom and courage, works that in their ability to rise to such values collectively create the future of music.[9]

Marx's association of Beethoven with the spiritual values of the age of Idealism continued throughout his career, with perhaps no greater consequence than in his theory of musical form. He presents this theory within a pedagogical context, that of a composition treatise. The identification of musical understanding with compositional ability was a trend in early nineteenth-century German music theory that peaked in Marx's four-volume work *Die Lehre von der musikalischen Komposition* (1st ed., 1837–1847). Marx states directly that compositional study forms the sine qua non of musical knowledge and acts additionally as a kind of spiritual upbringing. The concept of wholeness guides his pedagogical enterprise at all stages: the student must be treated as a whole being; works must be treated as wholes; and the elements of musical language must not be artificially separated. This entails a radically new approach to teaching composition: instead of building a vocabulary of musical elements treated outside the context of actual musical utterances, Marx introduces simple (and integral) forms immediately.[10] In addition to Marx's documented reliance on the progressive pedagogical theories of Pestalozzi,[11] his pervasive emphasis on the whole is informed by the hermeneutic impulse that was already being applied to the perceived nature of Beethoven's music. As is the case with scripture, a sense of inscrutable greatness was heard to emanate from Beethoven's works, a compound of enigmatic surface and compelling monumentality. And, as I shall argue presently, the role of the critic correspondingly changed from judge to exegete.

While a concern for wholeness is unquestionably an aesthetic touchstone of the age, eagerly applied to Beethoven's music, I would argue that the exclusively Beethoven-inspired aspect of Marx's theory of musical form is its dynamic underpinning. For Marx, the basis of all musical form is the dynamic impulse of rest-motion-rest, a configuration that effects all levels of form, from a simple phrase to an entire movement in sonata form. This fundamentally ternary impulse helps establish Marx's conception of sonata form as three-part rather than binary. For now Marx can show how sonata form, with its motion-oriented middle section, acts as the ultimate realization of music's basic formal impulse.

At the local, compositional level of his theory, Marx posits two basic formal categories as building blocks for his conception of dynamic form: the *Satz* and the *Gang*. Both are, initially, melodic utterances; the *Satz* is characterized by internally generated closure (of varying sorts), and the *Gang* is open-ended motion, whose closure must be externally effected (theoretically speaking, the *Gang* could go on forever). Out of these two fundamental categories of musical utterance, Marx derives the rondo family of forms, ranging from the simple first rondo form (consisting of a theme and its repetition, punctuated by a *Gang*) to sonata form. The transitional *Gang* becomes the emblematic component of this family of forms, for all these forms consist of *Sätze* that are connected by means of a *Gang*. In contrast to the more sectionalized *Liedform* family, which includes the minuet and trio, Marx detects in the rondo family a more highly evolved "urge to advance" [*Trieb des Fortschritts*].[12]

Such a progressive drive requires a different kind of thematic material. Whereas the themes of the *Liedform* family are generally periodic, those of the rondo family are more open-ended and can assume a wide variety of configurations. This is where Marx's *Satz* becomes a flexible and much-worked category: the *Satz* is any musical utterance that generates its own closure, a closure that can come in varying strengths. As Marx's derivation through the rondo forms to sonata form progresses, firmly closed subsections start to become more open-ended (with weaker closure), and larger sections form. Thus the exposition in sonata form becomes one large section, consisting of open-ended and mutually complementary subsections, sections that in earlier rondo forms were more independent and closed. Musical form moves closer to the idea of an organism with interdependent organs.

It goes without saying that musical form did not evolve historically in the way Marx describes. Yet by starting with the simple *Satz* and progressing to fully developed sonata form, Marx can show that all form is characterized by the will to motion and the internal generation of closure. Formal articulation *is* closure; such articulation makes spirit comprehensible. This is the Idealist compact at the heart of Marx's theory of form: musical form is refigured as a willed concretion of spirit. In addition, Marx's ahistorical arrangement of forms allows him to fashion sonata form as the most effective formal solution to the underlying needs of Beethoven's style.[13] The aspect of Beethoven's style primarily accommodated in Marx's theory is that of forward motion, or the flow of energy: subsections become open-ended, and the energy courses on; strong closure (acting as a "ground") is reserved only for the end of a movement. The basic formula of rest-motion-rest is now carried out with great breadth and variety, *yet without sacrificing the coherence of the simple Satz*. In fact, Marx's theory of form could be described as a way of accounting for the feeling that Beethoven's sonata form movements, in their projection of a continuous "line," behave like a single utterance—Marx builds his derivation of forms on this dynamic similarity between the simple *Satz* and the Beethovenian sonata form.

As is the case with the work of the German Idealists, much of Marx's conceptual power is granted him by the nature of certain words in the German language. An understanding of the word *Aufhebung* ("taking up," but also "abrogation"), for example, would go a long way toward a grasp of Hegelian dialectic. For Marx's purposes, the word *Satz* could hardly be more felicitous. Dozens of meanings reside in this venerable noun; in music terminology alone, *Satz* can denote a phrase, an entire movement, or composition itself (as in *Satzlehre*). By harnessing the range of this single word, Marx can demonstrate a powerful conceit about Beethoven's music—namely, the intimate relation between thematic material and overall form, both as a nesting (local *Sätze* within a global *Satz*) and as an open-ended and culminating flow of energy (weak local closure leads to strong global closure). Like Goethe before him, wielding the all-embracing category of the *Blatt* (leaf) in his plant metamorphosis, Marx could well claim that in Beethoven's music "Alles ist Satz."[14] For Marx's *Satz* entails both local theme and global form, organ and organism. And the flexibility of his concept of *Satz* allows Marx to reconfigure musical content (thematic material) in accordance with Beethoven's new and dynamic use of it, as both closed unit and conduit.

The musical content that can inform such a process is now conceived of as a form of potential energy, of *energeia* rather than *ergon*. Marx stresses the idea of thematic economy, arguing against the proliferation of different ready-made themes (which he often hears in Mozart) in favor of a concentration on the "depth and energy of one or two ideas."[15] These ideas are called motives and are treated by Marx as seeds. (The characterization of motive as seed was, for Marx, more a suggestive metaphor than the basis for an analytical method; as we shall see, the emphasis on motivic analysis was reserved for later generations.) In Marx's notion of thematic energy and economy we see the implementation of one of the reigning aspects of the Beethoven paradigm in musical thought: form becomes a dynamic process through which purposefully limited thematic content can then develop and grow. As such, form is the life process of thematic content, and thematic content lives the life of a dramatic protagonist: the musical work becomes a subject.

Marx analyzes portions of over twenty of Beethoven's piano sonatas in the course of volume 3 of his composition treatise. He claims that he is interested in showing the deep coherence of these works, and his method is to consider the individuality of each work as a highly characteristic realization of the underlying form. Each sonata movement bears a relationship to the general form as a specific case to a general law.[16] Apparently capricious mannerisms are shown to be logically engendered by invoking the dynamic interrelationships of formal categories, such as the complexly ramified relationship of *Hauptsatz* (first theme, or first theme group) to *Seitensatz* (second theme, or second theme group). Marx's analytical procedure stands in striking contrast to the usual methods of analysis in the early nineteenth century. Rather than label the components of a static structure (as Logier does, for example, in his 1827 *Musik-Wissenschaft*, where he identifies the keys, themes, and periods of a Haydn string quartet and adds an analytical fundamental bass[17]), Marx moves through the piece from left to right, justifying compositional decisions at each stage.

A brief look at a Marxian analysis of a movement from a Beethoven piano sonata will demonstrate how this works. Consider the opening of the first movement of Op. 31, no. 1 (see example 3.1).[18] Marx notes that the generally spirited yet flighty character of this opening affects (and effects) compositional decisions throughout. The first eleven bars initially appear to form a *Vordersatz* (antecedent phrase) that closes on the dominant, here realized with a full cadence rather than the more normative half cadence. This phrase consists of two different motives: the first of these (bars 1–2) has the character of spontaneity, quick to arise and quick to disappear. It can give rise to a *Gang* but not to a *Satz*. Thus it must break off, so that a motive that can be built into a *Satz* may appear (this motive Marx designates as the main motive). Yet breaking off the opening motive suppresses that motive, while the *Satz* that follows moves prematurely to the key of the dominant. Hence the first motive must reappear, followed in turn by the main motive. Marx explains the transposition to F by invoking the impulsive character of the whole; setting the repetition in G or even in the dominant, D, would compromise that character. (We shall see in what different fashion Riemann justifies this move to F.) In the next section (12–30) the main motive is given more space, and it overshadows the first motive to such a degree that the latter finally spills forth in an intensified and extended fashion in bars 30–45. This passage is a true *Gang* for Marx; he notes that it is brought forth by the opening motive and its subsequent suppression.

These first forty-five bars are thus construed as a form-generating opposition between a *Gang*-engendering motive and a *Satz*-engendering motive, between the will to motion and the will to closure. Each phrase is understood to call forth the next in some way. The opening *Gang*-like motive must be interrupted by a more suitable motive. This leads in turn to a premature arrival on the dominant, which must be

Example 3.1. Beethoven, Piano Sonata in G major, Op. 31, no. 1, first movement: measures 1–113.

Example 3.1, continued

Example 3.1, continued

Example 3.1, continued

counteracted by a surprise transposition to F. The increased suppression of the initial motive brought on by the expanded treatment of the main motive and its return to G major instigates the explosion of energy in the *Gang* of bars 30–45. The categories of *Satz* and *Gang* in this movement are distinguished in terms primarily of behavior and gesture rather than pitch and rhythm—note, for example, that Marx does not choose to point out the blatant rhythmic similarity between his two motives (the sixteenth-note upbeat). The compositional logic of Beethoven's highly individualized music unfolds here as a narrative drama of oppositions.

A higher-level opposition is that of the *Seitensatz* to the *Hauptsatz*. This opposition is part of the dynamic nature of the underlying form. For the *Hauptsatz* is said to determine the type of *Seitensatz* used and in so doing may be considered as the main determinant of a work's content. But Marx also characterizes the *Hauptsatz* as incomplete and in need of complementary completion by the *Seitensatz*. What used to be thought of as a given theme is now somehow incomplete, even though it determines what follows. Here we can see the beginnings in the theoretical literature of the notion of self-generating form and the primacy of opening material. An active first theme requires a reactive second theme that forms its necessary continuation. Such a relationship is miles away from the simple idea of theme and contrast, for here the first theme determines its own contrast dialectically; in this sense it becomes (or it wills) its own contrast. Understanding the relationship between *Hauptsatz* and *Seitensatz* as a dynamic one rather than a formal/sectional one allows Marx to account for the way in which the sonata-form movements of Beethoven's middle period tend to start in a state of imbalance, sometimes not becoming stabilized until the second theme group. And Marx can do this without sacrificing the material primacy of the opening *Hauptsatz*.

In the case of Op. 31, no. 1, Marx claims that a firm and cohesive *Seitensatz* is required in order to complement the impulsive and fragmentary *Hauptsatz*. He makes much of Beethoven's use of B major for this important section and is understandably concerned to justify this exotic key. His first move is to explain why the more normative dominant key, D major, was not used. After the premature cadence on D in bar 11 and the long *Gang* of bars 30ff., D major has been imprinted to such a degree that its return in the second theme would forego all freshness and vitality (the fact that we would now consider both these uses of D as denoting not D-as-tonic but D-as-dominant-of-G does not enter into Marx's thinking—most tonicized chords were felt to represent a modulation in early nineteenth-century German harmonic theory). Marx then claims that the next best choice would be D major's relative minor, B minor.[19] But a minor key would not correspond to the capricious and lively character of the *Hauptsatz*—thus B minor is transformed to B major.

Marx supports his notion of a doubly removed substitution key by pointing out how the music, as if in remorse for the passed-over keys, quickly turns both to B minor (74ff.) and to D major (79–80). The closing theme makes the point once more, ending in B minor but including a two-bar reminiscence of B major. Thus the initial urge for a major key is not forgotten, while the nearer keys of D major and B minor assert their right to be heard. It is here that we can see Marx invoking the notion of a normative underlying formal process subject to highly individual realization. The use of an unusual key is justified in terms of a substitute relationship to an underlying harmonic norm, here implemented in a manner suited to the impulsive character of the opening (and determining) material.

Marx's account of the link in this sonata movement between *Hauptsatz* and *Seitensatz* is also of interest, as it furthers the drama of oppositions begun in the *Hauptsatz*. Again Marx first attempts to explain why the music does not fulfill a logical expectation, in this case, why it does not initiate the *Seitensatz* immediately following the half cadence on D that ends the *Gang* in bar 45 (in the manner, perhaps, of what Robert Winter has dubbed the "bifocal close"[20]). To do so, argues Marx, would be to allow that long *Gang* to overpower the primary constituent of the *Hauptsatz* in the mind of the listener. Hence the main motive must again appear and have the last word, locally prompted as in the beginning by its opposite, the *Gang*-like first motive. It is thus the *Satz*-like component of the *Hauptsatz* that must serve as transition to the *Seitensatz*; the underlying predilection to use a *Gang* as transition is satisfied in this case by the figural elaboration of the F♯ in bars 64–65.

In his analysis of the musical events of this exposition, Marx constantly stresses the interrelationship between underlying form and individual process. Yet he does not chart the coherent individuality of the realization of underlying form in terms of motivic relationships; instead we are told of thematic character, of stability and instability, motion and closure. Weak closure invites the continuation of similar content, whereas strong closure invites contrasting content. Marx's analyses read like flow charts: each step in the musical flow draws on the next; each step solves a problem and creates a new one.[21] The underlying form is not a mold into which the composer pours musical content. Instead, a set of dynamic propensities is realized in different ways according to the nature of the material.

Such a conception of form works to define the way in which the music of Beethoven's heroic style is heard to project itself. For Marx, the fundamental nature of musical form is not structure, or balanced repetition, but motion. Marx's family of rondo forms embodies motion through the use of the *Gang*; its highest manifestation, the sonata form, makes continuous motion possible by loosening internal articulations and by giving over an entire section to the *Gang*-like property of pure motion (the development section, which, in Marx's derivation, is the most highly developed evolutionary stage of the first rondo form's connecting *Gang*). The development section also replaces the main contrasting section in the higher rondo forms, thus making for more coherence—a great variety of content can now be related to a single set of materials (the *Hauptsatz* and *Seitensatz*).

Heinrich Christoph Koch's late eighteenth-century view of musical form makes for an instructive point of comparison.[22] Koch saw musical composition as the inspired creation of what he called the *Anlage*, followed by the mechanical working-out of the rest of the form. Koch's *Anlage* consisted of the main thematic section of a piece and was the only aspect of the piece that was the product of inspiration. Since it was felt that the invention of melody simply could not be taught, the brunt of the pedagogical emphasis fell on the subsequent working-out of the materials of inspiration, the craft of putting together musical forms. Koch's work thus stands at the crossroads between the notion of the artist as artisan and burgeoning theories of the artist as creative genius. In contrast to Koch's dichotomous portrayal of musical composition, Marx posits an inherently incomplete theme that determines the way the underlying form is carried out. The entire working-out of the form now becomes the product of inspiration. Koch's concept of a theme as a closed entity that acts as the highly articulated seat of some primary affect is now transformed into a mode of *energeia* with loosened articulations that determines a highly dramatic process of interaction with a dynamically conceived underlying form. Of course, Koch was modeling his conception on the da capo aria, and Marx was concerned with sonata form. Yet this fact is in itself revealing. Marx's work shows that by the mid-nineteenth century the sonata form had become central to the theory of musical form—the values of musical composition were now those of sonata-form composition.

It would not be difficult to show that with his flexible categories of *Satz* and *Gang*, and with his somewhat vague notion of unfinished business or potential energy, Marx is determined to justify anything Beethoven does (perhaps I have already shown it). Yet this motivation alone must be deemed singular in the early nineteenth century and then increasingly representative as the century progressed. For now the musical work is clearly making demands on its critics, as opposed to critics making demands on works. The prevailing attitude toward Beethoven is also clear: that his works displayed deep coherence despite apparent surface incongruities was an article of faith for musical thinkers like Marx. His understanding of such local peculiarities was aided by an appeal to a dynamic conception of form or to the demands of an overriding poetic *Idee*. The old Enlightenment credo, so succinctly expressed in Pope's Essay on Man—"All discord, harmony not yet understood. . . . Whatever is, is right"—is here transferred to the organic musical work. Theorists would now justify individual works through analysis, with the result that their theoretical demonstrations would ultimately appeal to such works rather than to nature or to reason or to some generalized notion of praxis. And the premier model for the coherent musical work was (and still is) the heroic-style sonata form movement by Beethoven.

In Marx's Idealist formulation, Beethovenian sonata form becomes the essential basis of all form, the *telos* that all lesser forms portend. The musical values he inscribes in his compositional theory include the idea of sonata form as the highest manifestation of the aesthetic desideratum of unity-in-variety, and motion as the primary impetus of sonata form (and thus of all form). The emphasis here is on the dramatic, temporal aspect of musical art, most cogently embodied in the highly engaging works of Beethoven. And the concept of theme has changed, in order to empower this type of focus: theme now implies form-determining potential energy. Basic categories of musical utterance, *Satz* and *Gang*, are designed to function as types of dynamic impulse, either closed or open-ended. The implication is that a musical work is a flow of energy that is articulated through a series of formal sections that act as conduits. The final cadence grounds the current and closes the work unequivocally. The emphatic codas in Beethoven's heroic style, as we have seen in chapter 2, clearly convey this impression of a closed flow of energy, self-gathering and self-consuming.

II

If Marx's work offers a temporal and dynamic representation of Beethoven's music, the focus at the end of the nineteenth century was to shift to the idea of the work as a totality that could be conceptualized more profitably as a spatial entity. This new emphasis is nowhere so apparent as in the theoretical and analytical work of Hugo Riemann. As a convenient starting point for charting the contrast between Riemann and Marx we may take Riemann's cardinal objection to Marx's work, namely the category of the *Gang*. We find the following definition of Marx's *Gang* in Riemann's *Lexicon*: "In Marx's composition treatise the *Gang* is the opposite of the *Satz*; it is a formal fragment without any distinct caesurae. The concept was a crutch, because Marx did not penetrate the problems of periodic construction sufficiently enough to be able to explain more complicated configurations in terms of a unifying principle."[23]

Riemann's unifying formal principle is the eight-bar period, which he treats as an abstraction with which to classify every bar of a musical work. Given such a starting point, it would be hard for him to see that the *Gang*, as a second formal category, was of fundamental importance for Marx, that it had more the character of breakthrough than "make do." Riemann's incommensurability with Marx's form theory is revealed even in the first sentence of his definition, where he calls the *Gang* a fragment of form. This clearly implies that the *Gang* is part of a spatial conception that can be broken down in analysis. For Marx, the *Gang* is the very emblem of musical motion, the bearer of the dynamic formal impulse. In Riemann's view of Marx, the *Gang* is what's left when the rest of the content is classified into periodic structures by an analyst unequipped to account for nonliteral periods.

Riemann's encounter with the Marxian *Gang* is doubtless a standard case of a theorist asking an earlier theorist the same questions he himself is interested in, and is thus not particularly shocking as an example of incomprehension. Yet his complete miscasting of what constituted a theoretical breakthrough for the earlier theorist reveals how far he has moved from the dynamic standpoint of a Marx. The fundamental aspect of form is no longer a dynamic impulse but a complete protostructure, a microcosm. Lotte Thaler refers to Riemann's agenda as the transposition of temporal impressions into spatial representations, necessary for the comprehension of a musical work as a totality.[24] The emphasis is still on the wholeness of the musical work—but whereas this wholeness was acknowledged as a single dramatic utterance by Marx and represented as such in his derivation of sonata form from the single *Satz*, Riemann transfers the idea of wholeness to a theoretical construction and then indirectly applies it to the musical work. For him, a whole work is one in which all the content can be accounted for in terms of whole protostructures.

Riemann's prototypical eight-bar period is the result not only of the historical prevalence of such a thematic structure in the common practice period but also of a theoretical generalization about the rhythmic nature of music. (This mix of actual praxis and theoretical generalization in the creation of an analytical/theoretical metalanguage for music is not unique; it is, in fact, a standard condition of such discourse.) Riemann's theory posits an opening upbeat and end accent as music's basic rhythmic structure. In terms of the eight-bar period, this means that the first four bars act as upbeat to the last four bars, that the cadence in bar 8 answers that of bar 4. Within each four-bar group, the last two bars provide a cadential answer to the initial pair. Thus each bar of the eight-bar period has a function: 8 is final cadence, 4 is medial cadence, 7 and 3 are penultimates, and 1–2 and 5–6 are the initial pairs to which the cadential pairs form an answer (see example 3.2).[25]

Example 3.2. Hugo Riemann's eight-bar period, after Ivan Waldbauer, "Riemann's Periodization Revisited and Revised," 339.

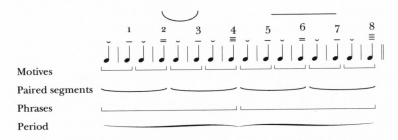

Riemann's functional theory of harmony bears an important resemblance to his rhythmic theory in the use of a quasi-abstract category with which to classify musical content. The complement to Riemann's rhythmic prototype is his harmonic prototype, the progression of tonic, subdominant, dominant, and tonic functions (T, S, D, T).[26] All surface harmonic entities either fulfill one of these functions directly or act as variants of one of them. Decisions as to which function is being represented are often made on the basis of the prototypical ordering: Ss tend to follow Ts and precede Ds, and so on. Riemann's fundamental progression was influenced by Moritz Hauptmann's more or less Hegelian dialectic of tonal harmony: an initial tonic, which can be a dominant (to the subdominant), and which leads to a dominant, is transformed into a final tonic, which can have a dominant, and which is led to by the dominant. As we saw in chapter 2, the inherent drama of this cadential syntax becomes to a large degree the overarching tonal drama of an entire movement in the heroic style, heard as the transformation of opening tonic into closing tonic. Opening tonic and closing tonic are two clearly different things: the former is unstable, developmental, inchoate; the latter is stable, conclusive, and fully determined.[27] In addition to this fundamental transformation, the general tendency of Beethoven's heroic-style music toward the monumentalization of tonics, subdominants, and dominants may well have provided an intuitive support for Hauptmann's (and then Riemann's) idea.

Like the eight-bar period, Riemann's harmonic prototype is a complete structure unto itself, a key-defining progression that lays the groundwork for a conception of a tonal work as a large-scale realization of a key center. The fundamental insight is that a musical work is the extensive (i.e., temporal) product of a closed system that enacts a dialectical process. Riemann's theoretical prototypes attempt to represent this insight. As we shall see, a behaviorist model of perception lies behind Riemann's use of closed-system prototypes: the theoretical listener takes in closed units, and only by so doing can such a listener gain a purchase on the entire work. Paradoxically, the work itself is now open (the number of periods is not specified), while the system embodied by its components is closed; this very nearly reverses the terms of Marx's theory, where the work represents a realization of a closed dynamic form, while its components (*Satz, Gang*) are open to any number of possible deployments.[28]

The use of abstract categories gives Riemann considerable analytical power. To see his theory in action, as well as to keep alive the comparison with Marx, it will be useful to consider Riemann's analysis of the opening section of Beethoven's Op. 31, no. 1 (see example 3.3).[29]

The analysis is divided into periods, shown by Roman numerals above the staff. This excerpt contains three such periods. The numbers in parentheses below the staff denote the position that the following bar represents in the prototypical eight-bar period. Harmonic functions are denoted by letters, and key changes are announced by an equals sign that shows either the two concurrent functions of a

Example 3.3. Analysis of Beethoven, Piano Sonata in G major, Op. 31, no. 1, first movement: measures 1–45. From Riemann, *L. van Beethovens sämtliche Klavier-sonaten*, vol. 2, 327–29.

common chord (as at bar 8) or the relationship of a new key to the old (as at bar 11, where the new tonic F is explained as the lowered third of the old tonic D).

Note first that those sections that were deemed to be *Gänge* by Marx are now duly classified as periodic structures. The opening motive is an incomplete period that Riemann refers to as a *Vorhang* (opening curtain). Although this motive is only a lead-in to the period that extends from bar 3 to bar 11, Riemann claims that it acts as the seed (*Keim*) for all the material of the movement. He isolates two components of the motive to support his claim: the sixteenth-note upbeat figure and the last seven sixteenth notes of bar 2 (which he characterizes as a sevenfold upbeat). Whereas Marx saw this first motive as creating a fundamental and form-generating opposition with the following motive, Riemann sees it as insignificant formally but all important materially, as the source for the movement's motivic/thematic content.

How does Riemann deal with the transposition to F in bar 11? Remember that Marx considered it as an alternative to either the tonic G or the dominant D, an alternative made appropriate by the work's impulsive character. Riemann's functional analysis leads him to point out in his prose commentary that the entire section from bar 3 to bar 30 is a multitiered installation of the tonic G, which first establishes its dominant (bar 11) and then its subdominant (bar 22). At each stage of this process, a tonic becomes a subdominant (G becomes IV of D; F becomes IV of C; and, closing the circle, C becomes IV of G). Riemann lauds Beethoven's ability to demonstrate the higher unity of the key by presenting it as the synthesis of its two constituent dominants. His gloss of this feature includes a direct reference to Hauptmann's dialectic: "[Beethoven's] contemporaries surely must have been astonished by this practical demonstration of the coherence of the main key as a higher unity of its two dominant keys, a demonstration that waited half a century for a Moritz Hauptmann to define it theoretically."[30] What for Marx was an appropriately quirky dynamic chain of events, motivated by the alternating suppression of two opposing and irrepressible motives, becomes for Riemann a calculated and virtuosic demonstration of harmonic coherence. Note also that Riemann's conclusion is strictly analytical: it could only be made retroactively from the standpoint of the entire section.

The long passage from bars 30 to 45, Marx's culminating *Gang*, is analyzed by Riemann as a period with a reiterative 7 and 8 sequence. Riemann shows that this passage ultimately emphasizes the dominant rather than the tonic when he switches the assignment of bar 8 midway through the passage from the tonic to the dominant (achieved by the equivalence 8 = 7 before bar 36). He thus reacts to a subtle but important change in the cadential weighting of the passage by which the dominant becomes the chord of resolution and the tonic the dissonant chord.[31] Beethoven achieves this change deftly, by the introduction of a chromatic passage leading to D. Marx's blanket concept of *Gang* knows of no such rhythmic/harmonic subtleties. In addition, Riemann's use of the number 9, which at first blush seems to serve as an ad hoc device invoked to account for the extra bar that results at bar 44, also touches on a subtle rhythmic aspect of this passage. The last of the two-bar groups of 7–8 ends at bar 43 and is followed by another bar of downward driving arpeggio. Riemann prepares the designation of 9 in bar 44 by offering 9s as alternative readings for the last three pre-8 bars. Another shift is implied here, as the 8s change from final bars to penultimate bars that somehow still maintain the priority of final bars (final bars with echoes). This shift coincides with the onset of the arpeggios. We are here asked to consider the pre-8 bars as post-8 bars, as bars appended to the previous 8 rather than leading to the next 8. Beethoven's sforzandi thicken the plot, falling in bars 40, 42, and 44 (all the 9s in Riemann's analysis). Clearly Riemann's classification of rhythmic functions opens up many new questions about the rhythmic nature of this passage, questions left unaddressed by Marx's category of *Gang*.

Riemann's commitment to revealing the complex details of Beethoven's rhythmic practice aligns well with his general notion of musical hearing: "Since hearing music means constructing ever larger configurations in the memory from small subsections successively offered to the ear, is it even possible to ascertain the correct overall lineaments when one proceeds from the wrong subsidiary members?"[32] This observation points up the difference between Marx's and Riemann's views of musical understanding. For Marx the whole is in view at all times, both as a spiritual principle and as a single formal impulse in the process of realization. For Riemann, the larger form is built up of smaller limbs, each of which needs to be comprehended in a detailed way if the large design is to be understood. This conception reflects Riemann's emphasis on the cognitive basis of musical understanding, on the way the listener processes musical information. Riemann liked to think that his work was moving away from what he called *Formenwissenschaft* (the science of forms) to a more empirical and psychologically informed investigation of actual musical content.[33] The differing standpoints of Marx and Riemann may be compared to rationalist and behaviorist views, respectively, of the linguistic speech act. For Marx, an underlying dynamic form acts as a product of artistic reason that can be concretized in infinite variety. His readings depend primarily on a left-to-right perusal of the music from the standpoint of the compositional decision-making process; the unfolding music is compared at each stage with the expectations generated by the underlying form and is said to realize that form in ways that differ in accordance with the type of thematic material. Riemann's left-to-right perusal is more strictly an act of analysis, and its terms are those of the listener's cognition, not the underlying and overall form. For Marx, the whole is synthesized, his left-to-right approach compositional; for Riemann, the whole is analyzed, his left-to-right approach cognitive and listener-oriented.

We are now in a position to see how Riemann's work makes possible an important turn in the history of Beethoven analysis, and thus of music analysis in general. For Riemann's functional prototypes are measured in terms of human cognition, as intelligible units, rather than in terms of an overall underlying form. The prototypical dimension remains, but it has shifted from the global and spiritual to the local and perceptual. *As a result of this situation the unity of a musical work begins to be expressed in terms of the content of motives rather than a controlling poetic* Idee. Because the closed work is now thought of in spatial and largely synchronic terms, the unity informing such a work is no longer that of a dramatic narrative with a concomitant unfolding form. Taking its place is a conception of motivic unity, in which musical content resembles genetic material whose presence can be demonstrated throughout the work. No longer is the individual work's relationship to an underlying dynamic form the basis of both its unity and its individuality; now the relationship to underlying form is one of taxonomical classification of constituent elements, and the piece's unity and individuality are discussed in terms of motivic content. From here it is but a small step to the Schoenbergian notion of the *Grundgestalt* and Rudolf Réti's subsequent work on motivic cells and thematic process. But it is hard to imagine any of this motive-oriented work becoming so prevalent, so central to our analytical discourse, without the musical example of Beethoven, especially in works like the Fifth Symphony.

For Riemann, the motive itself is the primary unit of individual musical concretion; he conceived of it as the fundamental synthesis of expression and artistic formation, inclusive of all the elements of music, "a piece of what happens in music" ("ein Stück musikalischen Geschehens").[34] In addition to its vivid encapsulation of Riemann's sense of what a motive is, this combination of a spatial metaphor with a temporal one ("a *piece* of what *happens*") neatly sums up his entire perspective. For it would be a mistake to think that Riemann banished the temporal domain from his analytical methodology, exclusively favoring the spatial. The temporal is instead abstracted, reconfigured in the form of his harmonic dialectic as well as in the form of his rhythmic model: temporality is captured in a *Stück*. Whereas Marx focused on the entire work as a temporal utterance characterized by motion, Riemann sees the work as a structure built of temporal units, harmonic and rhythmic. These prototypes are schematic translations of a temporal impulse, and the work is a spatial collection of concretized prototypes. Temporality is thus "in the genes" but not explicitly in the overall *Gestalt*. Riemann's conceptualization of the eight-bar period shows most pointedly his manipulation of the temporal element: the numbered categories of classification, the basis of Riemann's taxonomy, transform the results of temporality (the various openings and closures of a period) into spatial placeholders. His theory converts, like a calculus, Marx's dynamic impulse of rest-motion-rest into a binary system based on the iamb, on upbeat and downbeat, tension and release, question and answer.[35]

Riemann's fashioning of the local structures (the eight-bar period and the TSDT cadential progression) of the Viennese classical style as fundamental prototypes of tonal music represents a tacit urge to promote that style as the essential basis of Western music.[36] The binary logic of his rhythmic theory (which I believe is related in principle to the basic dualism of his harmonic theory) could be said to reflect the classical style's prevailing compositional logic and the source of much of its drama—namely, its use of paired and balanced phrases, a local rhetorical polarity matched at the global level by the tonal polarity of tonic and dominant.[37] Thus one could reasonably argue that it is not Beethoven but the classical style itself—and its canonic masters Mozart and Haydn—to which Riemann is reacting. Yet Beethoven's music is clearly the object of demonstration after demonstration of Riemann's new analytical methodology—one need only cite the exhaustive three-volume set of analyses he published of all the Beethoven piano sonatas, even including six sonatas from the Bonn period. (Riemann's only comparable effort was his set of analyses of the preludes and fugues from Bach's *Well-Tempered Clavier*, and these were not carried out in the same detail.[38]) If Riemann's underlying motivation is not, as is Marx's, to show what is new in Beethoven but rather to show what is universal, this only indicates the changed perception of Beethoven's music from an emblem of music's future to the embodiment of music itself. By showing how his theoretical ideas could be applied to Beethoven, this most individual of composers, Riemann was serving a cherished assumption: that the engaging individuality of this composer is in effect indicative of the highest degree of universality.

III

It is a distinct temptation to impose an explicit narrative direction to this précis of Beethoven's influence on German music theory by introducing the work of Heinrich Schenker as a synthesis of the preceding dichotomy of Marx and Riemann. For Schenker seems committed both to conceiving the musical work as a surveyable (spatial) whole and to understanding the work as a single directed utterance. His theory shares with Riemann the modern penchant for abstraction, with the consequential difference that Schenker's abstract prototype is coterminous with the whole work. Schenker also felt that by expressing his prototype not as a numbered or lettered schematic but as a rudimentary musical (specifically, contrapuntal) utterance, he had arrived at the first theory of music that takes seriously the notion that music is first and foremost about itself.[39]

Schenker's *Ursatz* (see example 3.4) offers an elegant conjunction of two dimensions of the musical process developed in his theoretical work: the fundamental line (*Urlinie*) and the prolongation of harmonic areas (*Stufen*). These two dimensions are literally counterpointed, and an entire movement can now be represented as the linear elaboration of a single sonority. The phenomenon of voice-leading is absolutely fundamental to this conceptualization of the musical work; for Schenker, voice-leading mediates the vertical and horizontal aspects of tonality.[40]

Example 3.4. Heinrich Schenker's *Ursatz*.

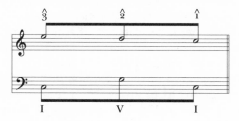

Schenker uses metaphors connected with counterpoint and with melodic embellishment to describe the process by which his prototypical background utterance may be said to generate the foreground that is the musical surface: working through a series of ever more complex layers (*Schichten*), elementary background configurations take on melodic diminutions (embellishments) such as passing tones and neighbor notes; voice-leading progressions familiar from species counterpoint are heard to underpin and control the melodic exfoliation at each level. Schenker characterizes this process of generation, from background to foreground, as a form of inspired improvisation available only to the musical genius. The theoretical conceptualization of a musical work as an utterance whose coherence at any given moment depends on the informing presence of an underlying prototype (Schenker's term *Ursatz* is clearly meant to resonate with Goethe's *Urpflanz*) is thus treated metaphorically as a form of musical composition: the musical genius improvises diminutions on basic contrapuntal motions. In other words, Schenker describes the theoretical motion from background to foreground in terms usually reserved for the compositional motion from beginning to end (left to right). Such a conflation should not come as a surprise in a theory that holds that music is about itself—theoretical abstraction thus becomes another form of music composition, and, indeed, Schenker liked to consider his way of thinking to be more an art than a theory.

Schenker's *Ursatz* represents the musical masterwork as the contrapuntal prolongation of a single sonority. Yet this is no open-ended prolongation. As is the case with both Marx and Riemann, Schenker assumes that closure is theoretically prior, in the sense that it dictates the terms of his conception—the musical masterwork moves toward closure, it completes a motion. Musical content is deemed a product of this motion, arising in the form of potentially dramatic digressions and retardations of a fundamentally goal-oriented traversal.[41] Hierarchically speaking, earlier events are theoretically dependent on later events. This perennial conception of the musical work as a one-way process, complete and unequivocally closed, surely finds its *locus classicus* (if not its *locus solus*) in the heroic style.

But apart from the issue of the theoretical weight of closure, I would like to argue that Schenker's concept of fundamental line is closely linked to Beethoven's music, and that the Fifth Symphony in particular helped shape that concept. Schenker's monograph on the Fifth Symphony originally appeared in serial fashion in his journal *Der Tonwille* (1921–24; the articles on Op. 67 appeared in 1921 and 1923). It was later published as a whole in 1925.[42] The monograph marks an important station in the transformation of Schenker's conception of musical motives, *Stufen*, and the fundamental line. In his earlier monograph on the Ninth Symphony (1912), motives are treated like dramatic protagonists and supported by *Stufen*. Consider example 3.5, in which Schenker isolates a string of motives from the first theme of the Ninth Symphony, each with its attendant *Stufen*.[43] These *Stufen* appear to be mapped onto the surface motives. In his later theoretical work (from *Der Tonwille* through *Das Meisterwerk in der Musik* to *Der Freie Satz*), motives become more prototypical as they are enlisted in the service of the fundamental line. In addition, they now seem to support *Stufen*—

Example 3.5. From Schenker, *Beethovens Neunte Sinfonie*, 8.

they often prolong a single *Stufe* or link *Stufen*. The Fifth Symphony monograph (with its incipient delineation of the *Urlinie*) falls at the crossroads where these two distinctly different conceptions of the relation of motive and harmony meet. On the one hand, the fundamental line is heard in direct relation to the surface motives, and in fact helps define the boundaries of those motives (we shall see that this is the case with the opening motive). And on the other hand, sections of the fundamental line start to become more prototypical, linking or prolonging *Stufen* by outlining intervals of a fourth or fifth, and are more often manifested as descending segments.[44]

Schenker's first lance of the monograph breaks against the received opinion that the initial two pitches, G and E♭, constitute the basic motive of the first movement. Instead, he claims, the first four pitches (G, E♭, F, D) form a four-bar motive (see example 3.6). In Schenker's *Urlinie-Tafel* we see that the four-note motive is really a two-note descent from E♭ to D. Schenker believes that his proposed *Urlinie* provides the most convincing argument for this position: to construe the initial G and E♭ as the motive would be to admit a one-note motive. Thus the fundamental line is here employed to define the boundaries of a surface motive.

Example 3.6. From Schenker, *Beethoven V. Sinfonie*, supplement, figure 6.

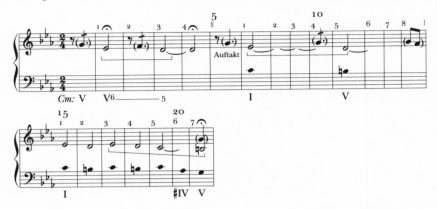

With this two-note descent in hand, Schenker can go on to demonstrate a kind of organic proliferation in the next long phrase. The first part of the phrase (bars 5–10) makes an audible connection to the opening by repeating the two-note descent in a prolonged version; this descent now connects and articulates the tonic and dominant *Stufen*—we thus hear *Stufen* being prolonged through the agency of an elemental motive as if in a made-to-order demonstration of the concept of motive and prolongation. There follows an extension of the two notes to a four-note descent that also links tonic and dominant *Stufen* and gives a direction to the phrase by making the dominant its goal. In addition, Schenker's graph shows the foreshortened intensification in bars 15ff. of the Eb–D motive. This motive truly resides just below the skin of the surface; playing Schenker's graph up to the half cadence in bar 21 makes this abundantly clear.

Schenker then derives the *Urlinie* content of the entire movement from this initial growth of a four-note descent. In another and very different sort of graph he shows how the rest of the movement consists primarily of descending stretches spanning fourths and fifths, at different hierarchical levels (see example 3.7). The language in Schenker's description of this figure is powered by organicist metaphor: "Being indeed the very first formed expression of the creative imagination, against which the . . . *Urlinie* of [example 3.6] is already a kind of initial realization, this figure shows clearly how the two germinal tones of the motive even strive for a merger with still more tones, up to the nodal points of the fourth or fifth."[45] A kernel motive strives to grow into the span of a fourth or fifth. And in terms of compositional process, a formulaic version of the entire movement is born in the creative imagination and is then initially worked out as the *Urlinie* of Schenker's *Urlinie-Tafel* before becoming the piece as we know it. Here the

Example 3.7. From Schenker, *Beethoven V. Sinfonie*, 6.

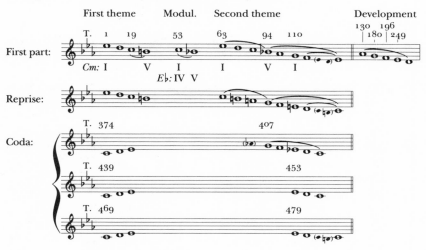

idea of a closed whole presenting itself to the inspired composer is given a concrete correlate. What was exciting to Schenker in this instance was the way in which he could show how the opening motive, when conceived of as an *Urlinie* seed, could engender a coherent whole. He thus continues to honor the notion of surface motive as seed of a left-to-right growth process. Yet on the other hand, the physical arrangement of the graph in example 3.7 points to a differently conceptualized coherence: a series of motivic parallels are located within a paradigmatic chart roughly equivalent to those used in structuralist analyses. Such a presentation implies a synchronic view of the piece. Thus the left-to-right coherence of the Beethovenian motive-as-seed is juxtaposed with something like the background-to-foreground coherence of Schenker's later theory. This tension is crucial, for it shows Beethoven's privileged position in Schenker's thought: it is with Beethoven that Schenker takes his *Urlinie* across the threshold from particularity to generality.

A glance at Schenker's *Urlinie* graph for the second theme group shows that his *Urlinie* segments are already somewhat more abstracted from the musical surface than was the case with the opening twenty-one bars (see example 3.8). The positing of a descending *Urlinie* articulated in spans of a fourth allows Schenker to connect the second theme to the first, as a variant in the relative major—both are descending fourths starting on E♭ but ending with different versions of B (B♮ for the first theme, B♭ for the second). Thus he claims that the B♭ of bar 62 in the second theme actually stands for a d^1, forming a covert step of a second from the E♭ of bar 60.[46] This second then grows, as in bars 1–21,

Example 3.8. From Schenker, *Beethoven V. Sinfonie*, supplement, figure 6.

to a span of a fourth, whose ending tone B♭ (bar 66) was forecast by the B♭ that represented the d¹ in bar 62. The B♭ of bar 62 is thus both substitute and foreshadow, acting as an index of the transformation of E♭–D–C–B to E♭–D–C–B♭ by sounding the new boundary pitch of the transformed motive almost immediately after its first pitch.

Here again we see that this analysis stands at the crossroads for Schenker. A concern for showing subtle relationships between intrawork motives is mixed with a concern for showing how the musical surface is a diminution of prototypical underlying and generative motives. The *Urlinie* enables Schenker to demonstrate the organic unity of first theme and second theme. And yet at the same time, he observes the transformation of *Urlinie* motives in accordance with the exigencies of the form (i.e., the way in which E♭, D, C, B is transformed to E♭, D, C, B♭, in order to reflect the modulation to the relative major). This latter observation is more in keeping with a conception of the different themes as variants, or diminutions, of more prototypical material. In his later analyses he of course prefers to continue along these lines, to show how the analyzed piece relates to a prototypical background; less emphasis is placed on intrawork motivic coherence. But given that the prototypical spans of the *Urlinie* are very much part of the surface motivic content at the beginning of this movement, it is not entirely surprising to find the prototypical merging in this way with the idiosyncratic throughout the rest of the analysis.

Schenker's treatment of the development section shows explicitly the bifurcation of his *Urlinie* motives to both surface and background. The first three of the five different *Urlinie* steps of the development, as represented in example 3.7, correspond to clearly demarcated sections of the development and are not as aurally apparent on the musical surface. Yet between these steps Schenker locates connective ascending fourth spans. For example, the G of bar 180 is connected to the F of 196 by two such spans (see example 3.9). The F of 196 then leads to the E♭/D at the head of the recapitulation through two more fourth spans (see example 3.10).

Example 3.9. From Schenker, *Beethoven V. Sinfonie*, supplement, figure 6; and 12.

Example 3.10. From Schenker, *Beethoven V. Sinfonie*, 12.

It is clear that Schenker locates spans of a fourth or fifth both within the same phrase and as higher umbrella structures. These spans are thus becoming more abstract and prototypical even in the course of the same analytical discussion; the workings of the *Urlinie* in Schenker's reading of the development section are of a different hierarchical order than is the case in the exposition and recapitulation.

Schenker's prose account of the development reflects a shift of the music's dramatic protagonist from surface thematic material to subsurface *Urlinie* material. Thus, for example, the drama of the passage from bar 196 to the recapitulation is translated by Schenker into that of a compelling interplay of the upper voice (which is realizing the *Urlinie*) and a middle voice (see example 3.11).

The upper voice attains a D in bar 221, at which point it begins to die out (this D is a passing tone in service of reaching the *Urlinie* E♭ in bar 249). In the midst of its demise, the listener (according to Schenker) is startled by the sudden outcry of a variant of the first theme (bars 228ff.), heard as a middle voice. The upper voice D is as yet unmoved by this outburst, and Schenker remarks that it is dying even while the middle voice is calling for a new beginning. Only after the middle-voice hammer blows of bars 240–48 have sounded can the upper voice die and be "resurrected" as the all-important E♭ signaling the return of the opening material. The music thus plays out a drama of the *Urlinie*, which is heard to undergo a death and transfiguration.

This very passage—especially bars 209ff.—has long been a locus of the uncanny for the symphony's critics;[47] its uneasy quietude and remote key area lend it an aura of unnatural calm, as in that patch of sea known as the horse latitudes, where all wind stops. Schenker's description of the death and resurrection of the upper line captures something like this feeling but translates it into the drama of the *Urlinie* and its course through the piece. What remains constant is the perception that something dramatic has transpired; only the terms of the drama have changed. The tonal remove attained by the passage, which had been the point of dramatic fascination for E.T.A. Hoffmann and others, is in fact downplayed by Schenker as a straightforward— albeit chromatic—contrapuntal solution to the problem of leading from the IV *Stufe* in 196 to the V *Stufe* in 229 (see example 3.12).

Thus Schenker gives the sense of a dramatic scenario to his *Urlinie*, while leaving the "explanation" of the passage to his uncovering of an underlying version of normative contrapuntal and harmonic syntax. (And again we sense a mingling of theoretical aims.)

In this particular analysis, the *Urlinie* has assumed the burden of motivic development, both as the bearer of intrawork motivic significance and as the vehicle for the type of dramatic characterization

Example 3.11. From Schenker, *Beethoven V. Sinfonie*, supplement, figure 6.

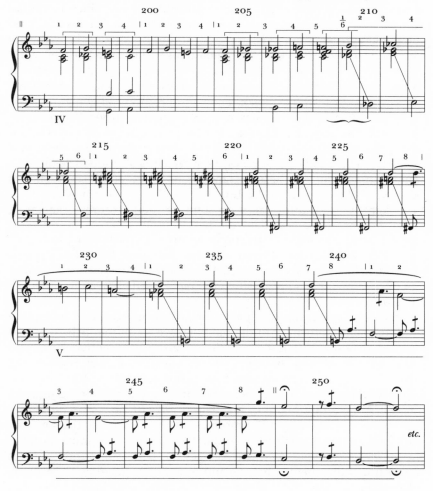

Example 3.12. From Schenker, *Beethoven V. Sinfonie*, 12.

normally reserved for discussions of motivic process. Yet in addition it also stands for the quasi-abstract principle upon which extensive sections of the musical process may be based. Indeed, Schenker's paradigmatic representation in example 3.7 argues for a more abstract view of motivic unity than is the case either in his earlier or in his later work: different hierarchical levels are here commingled, represented at the same theoretical level.[48] The distinction between surface motivic generation as a left-to-right phenomenon and prototypical generation as a back-to-front phenomenon has not yet been established theoretically. But while this may be read as a constitutive tension of Schenker's *Tonwille*-period analytical methodology, it need not be construed as a flaw in an eventually perfected system. What is at issue instead is the unique co-existence of these two modes, as a sign of the confluence of Schenker's theory of voice-leading and Beethoven's heroic style. Thus Schenker's voice-leading takes on some of the inexorable generative thrust perennially detected in the heroic style, whereas Beethoven's music is shown to embody the types of motivic parallelisms so important to Schenker's later theory. On the one hand, Schenker's quasi-abstract *Urlinie* appears to construct the analysis, to make its particular discoveries possible. On the other, the piece itself appears to construct the *Urlinie*.

This latter point, that the piece constructs the *Urlinie*, needs some reinforcement. Returning to the opening, we recall that Schenker had claimed that his *Urlinie* helped discover the real motive here—but could we not suggest that the opening four bars in fact discover the *Urlinie*? Of course such a question seems fatuous in light of later Schenkerian method, for it goes without saying that opening motives suggest some type of *Urlinie*, just as a priori *Urlinie* conceptions suggest ways of hearing opening motives. Yet in the case of this analysis the distinction is crucial, because there are as yet no a priori forms of the *Urlinie*—so where did Schenker get the *Urlinie* that then clarifies the nature of the opening motive and proceeds to generate the motivic material of the rest of the movement? From the opening motive.

Returning to Schenker's *Urlinie* graph (example 3.6), we note a curious feature of that motive—namely, Schenker hears it as a 6–5 appoggiatura over the V *Stufe*, effectively separating this initial form of the motive from its immediately subsequent forms, which are heard to connect tonic and dominant *Stufen*. Schenker justifies this reading by pointing to a later instance of the opening motto (bars 398ff. of the coda), where it sounds against a bare G in the bass. But this interpretation is odd, because it makes the E♭, the first tone of the *Urlinie*, into a dissonance (relatively speaking) and implies that the subsequent D is in fact the structurally prior tone. And this would then suggest that

Schenker's two-note *Urlinie* motive is actually a one-note motive (D). Given the nature of Schenker's subsequent *Urlinie* segments and their harmonic support, his interpretation of the initial motive is extremely problematic. Why could he not simply assign two *Stufen*, tonic and dominant, to the opening motive? This, it seems to me, would be the obvious thing to do if the *Urlinie* (of bars 5ff.) were truly to reveal the nature of the opening motive, as Schenker claims is the case. What does he gain by hearing the motive as underpinned by a single *Stufe*?

Quite simply, Schenker gains a voice-leading rationale for the descent of E♭ to D. By not assigning the E♭ a tonic harmony, Schenker makes its descent a case of contrapuntal necessity; a consonant E♭ would have no inherent need to descend. His claim about the motive encompassing all four notes (as a diminution of two underlying pitches) is thus supported not in the same way as the rest of the *Urlinie* (as a prototypical line connecting consonant *Stufen*) but rather by local voice-leading considerations. But only when so isolated does the motive need this sort of justification. Schenker treats the opening motive as a disembodied descent; his *Stufe* designation is about that descent. In other words, the opening motive is treated as the true beginning of the piece, from which issues all else. Otherwise Schenker would not need to explain its descent in a way different from that of its subsequent appearances. He attempts to justify his posited E♭-to-D *Urlinie* descent without recourse to what follows—the explanation for this descent is not found later; instead it is shown to inhere in the opening motive itself. What this means is that it is the opening motive, and not the subsequent *Urlinie* of bars 5ff., that is primary for Schenker. The opening does not function as the first tone of the *Urlinie*; instead it acts as the self-inhering motivic seed of the *Urlinie*, a seed whose primary characteristic is urgent descent.[49]

And I would argue further that if the opening motive of the Fifth Symphony in some sense engenders the *Urlinie* of the first movement, it also goes a long way toward generating the concept itself of the *Urlinie* as Schenker would henceforth employ it. Consistent with his already established notion of melodic fluency, Schenker was at pains to demonstrate that the true motivic action in the movement consists of stepwise motion.[50] Yet how much of his later theoretical conception of prototypical *descending* linear motion and prolonged *Stufen* was, so to speak, handed to him by this very opening? Can we not hear, in the two emphatic fermatas of the opening, Schenker's *Urlinie* in its barest form? And does the slow harmonic rhythm of the first twenty-one bars not offer an actual sounding demonstration of prolonged *Stufen*?

Either this piece was made to order for Schenker's way of thinking, or Schenker's way of thinking was made to order for this piece. Yet either/or misses the mark here, for this is clearly both: Beethoven's compelling surface influences Schenker, while Schenker appropriates that selfsame quality for his *Urlinie*. Think what Schenker gains from this. His *Urlinie* is here made palpable, for it becomes identified with the inexorable thrust of Beethoven's line. Thus Schenker attempts to validate his theoretical concepts by appropriating one of the most engaging openings in all of music as a direct demonstration and sounding confirmation of his ideas. The Fifth Symphony quite simply makes Schenker's *Urlinie* more compelling: Schenker borrows Beethoven's inexorability for his own purposes, and we see another way in which the redoubtable opening of this symphony works itself into our collective musical consciousness.

While I should not hope to prove in any positivistic sense that Beethoven's Fifth Symphony was formative for Schenker's concept of the *Urlinie*, I shall at least point out that the work was certainly on his mind when he began to formulate his notion of the *Urlinie*: in his first extended discussion of the *Urlinie*, which appears in the introduction to his 1920 monograph on Beethoven's Piano Sonata Op. 101, Schenker refers the reader to his forthcoming essay on the Fifth Symphony.[51] It is thus tempting to suggest that Schenker was aware of the formative effect of the Fifth Symphony for his theory of the *Urlinie*. In the Op. 101 analysis itself, apart from the introduction, the word *Urlinie* appears only once, as a synonym used interchangeably with other terms denoting either a linear presence or a fundamental presence or both, such as *Linie*, or *Ur-Idee*, or *Ton-Urreihe*. It is only in the introduction (surely written afterward) that Schenker promotes the term *Urlinie* to its status as an umbrella concept. And Schenker's use of the concept of fundamental line in the Op. 101 monograph is not troubled with the different hierarchical levels of his Fifth Symphony analysis. Perhaps the greatest analytical triumph of the Op. 101 monograph is Schenker's demonstration that the Adagio lead-in to the sonata's finale has as its own *Urlinie* a more covert version of the *Urlinie* of the first movement's theme. Like the Fifth Symphony analysis, the fundamental line is employed in this instance to demonstrate inner thematic unity, and Schenker succeeds handsomely when he can show a relationship that obtains between movements. Yet there is little trace of the type of generalization of the *Urlinie* that was to begin in the Fifth Symphony analysis.[52]

Shortly after his analysis of the first movement of the Fifth Symphony, Schenker started using the caret markings that were to distinguish all subsequent portrayals of the *Urlinie* and that are clear signs of a more generalized and abstract conception.[53] Thus the Fifth Symphony analysis is the first to be written fully under the rubric of *Urlinie* analysis and yet is prior to that concept's more generalized applications. Again we are tempted to ascribe to this analysis a formative influence on the *Urlinie* concept. But it is ultimately unimportant to locate the exact point of origin, the specific weight of influence: whatever the actual genesis of Schenker's idea of *Urlinie* (he himself claimed it was the result of an epiphany[54]), the Fifth Symphony offered him a powerful confirmation. Since the Fifth Symphony had long been touted as the premier masterwork of organic coherence, the fit between its sounding surface and Schenker's theoretical generalizations must have felt like the best evidence imaginable for his ideas.

Schenker's use of the Fifth Symphony demonstrates once again the circular relationship that obtains between Beethoven and the theorists: it is never clear whether the theory is made to fit the music or the music is heard to fit the theory, and it is ultimately beside the point to attempt such a determination. In fact, the Fifth Symphony monograph represents the quintessential manifestation of this situation, for its theoretical tension between left-to-right coherence and back-to-front coherence makes it a uniquely situated interface between the construction of Beethoven's music in terms of a new theory and the construction of a new theory in terms of Beethoven's music (i.e., in terms of the prevailing general construction of Beethoven's music). The tension between these types of coherence could not stay in a state of equipoise for very long; in his later work Schenker clearly opts for back-to-front theoretical generalization. What remains, however, is the fact that Beethoven is most definitely on the horizon when Schenker initiates the shift from interpreting musics to interpreting Music.

Schenker was quick to begin identifying the presence of an *Urlinie* with the presence of compositional genius and organic life in the musical work. In the introduction to the Op. 101 monograph he claims that "knowledge of the *Urlinie* is the surest way to promote knowledge of the genius."[55] There he also associates the *Urlinie* with the human soul: "Just as [the soul] travels with a human being from cradle to grave, so too the *Urlinie* goes along from the first tone to the last."[56] The *Urlinie* is the spark of life, that which is born at the outset of the work and dies only at the very end. Here, then, is a theoretical concept that defines the musical masterwork as a living process, in which a musical line is kept alive from beginning to end. It can hardly be a coincidence that this concept came to fruition with the music of Beethoven's heroic style (we again remember Wagner's account of Beethoven's symphonic music: "Everything becomes melody, every accompanying voice, every rhythm, even the pauses").[57] Schenker's metaphor of the soul is another, acutely romantic, version of the presence felt by other critics in this music.

But Schenker was not concerned with just the linear course of a musical work. The spatial conception of the closed work was too much with him for a wholesale return to a largely temporal understanding of musical process. In 1925 he wrote that "the *Urlinie* makes possible this miracle: that the great artist embraces with the same care that which is nearest as well as that which is most distant. . . . In the face of his love for the whole, a love that issues from the *Urlinie*, everything in the work is equally close."[58] Here the *Urlinie* is the means to a syncretic grasp of the piece: the point is not so much the temporal traversal of the *Urlinie* (the left-to-right perspective of the listener) as the fact that it alone touches all points of the piece. The *Urlinie* thus becomes a uniting presence as well as the standpoint from which the composer can comprehend the work as a whole.[59] And as Schenker continued to develop his notion of *Urlinie*, eventuating in the concept of the *Ursatz*, his living musical line became increasingly prototypical, its life no longer that of the temporally unfolding musical work but that of the quickening into extensive presence of an intensive background protostructure. Thus the emphasis shifts from a metaphorical view of the perceived temporality of a musical work to a metaphorical view of the creative process: the developing line of the finished work becomes the developing work in the mind of genius. Schenker's change of emphasis from the track of the listener to the act of creation inscribes into musical theory the romantic view of the artist as a rival Creator (a view that is nowhere so evident as in the nineteenth century's glorification of Beethoven). For the artist is now fully a hero; the analyst a high priest— and genius the ambrosia either possessed or divined. The descending lines heard by Schenker in the opening of the Fifth Symphony may well be the fault lines of this crucial shift, marking the place where Beethoven's music becomes Music's fate.

IV

About a decade after the death of Schenker, the Serbian-born emigré Rudolph Réti (who was trained in Vienna) developed his theory of thematic process as a direct result of an intensive study of the works of Beethoven. The theory enjoyed a brisk yet brief reception, and is now often mentioned only in a negative sense. Yet the techniques of motivic analysis that Réti employs have become commonplace, and the type of motivic parallels his analyses uncover are still convincing—if only when we discover them ourselves. Within the historical trajectory of post-Beethovenian tonal theory we are currently tracing, it is possible to see Réti's theory as a way of returning to the Marxian temporal standpoint of understanding Beethoven's dramatic process while maintaining something like Schenker's more modern strain of structuralist organicism.[60] And as we shall see, Réti also returns to the idea that the analysis of musical works can communicate extramusical spiritual values.

Réti begins his study of Beethoven piano sonatas (*Thematic Patterns in Sonatas of Beethoven*, 1944–48, published posthumously in 1967) with the following words: "Every musical composition of a high structural level contains several motivic cells from which its structure is formed. These cells need not necessarily be identical with the concrete motifs. In some compositions the cells may not even be visible in their literal form. The motifs, and subsequently the themes, are developed from the cells; the cells, however, usually represent the essence of the motifs rather than the motifs themselves."[61] The emphasis on structure is explicit—musical works worth analyzing exhibit a high structural level. Such structures are formed with quasi-abstract pitch cells, which represent the essence of actual musical motives. (In a footnote, Réti explains that the cell is to be thought of not as generating the motif but rather as a privileged variant of the motif, one "which represents the shortest extract of a motif, its contour."[62]) By invoking the metaphors of cell and structure, Réti merges the biological with the architectural, in the characteristic fashion of twentieth-century notions of organicist structuralism. Also at play here is the idea that these cells may not be visible (in their literal form) and may thus need the instrumentality of analysis, like a kind of microscope, in order to be discovered. Such a conceit invokes images of modern science as well as modern depth psychology.

It is important to keep in mind that Réti's cells are not actual motives but nonrhythmic, ordered collections of pitches. This explicit separation of rhythm and pitch may well be a direct inheritance from Schoenberg, but not specifically from his notion of *Grundgestalt* (basic shape). As Carl Dahlhaus has pointed out, the principle allowing the separation of these parameters can be abstracted from Schoenberg's (twelvetone) compositional technique. Dahlhaus also observes that such a principle appears in brusque contradiction with the Beethovenian motive, which presupposes the indivisibility of pitch contour and rhythm.[63] Here Réti can be seen to continue the Germanic theoretical tradition of mixing abstraction with music, in the service of a musical metalanguage: the operative abstract category, in this case the "prime cell," is also to some degree a musical utterance. Yet there is no little irony in the observation that what motivated the intuitive supposition of such prime cells—namely the compelling pervasiveness of the actual Beethovenian motive—has now been largely attenuated in Réti's

Example 3.13. Réti's list of motifs from Beethoven's *Appassionata* Sonata, Op. 57. From Réti, *Thematic Patterns in Sonatas of Beethoven*, 102–3.

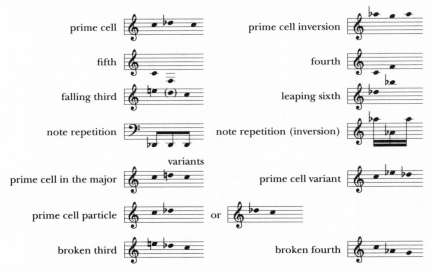

To this list must be added the two particular features:
　Arpeggio motif: referring to the characteristic of broken chords
　Appassionata rhythm: referring to the rhythm of the beginning.

peculiarly twentieth-century reconfiguration of what constitutes material primacy in a piece of Beethoven's music. Interestingly enough, Dahlhaus himself, though at times seeming to speak from beyond this tradition of associating musical process with abstraction, remains strongly within it: supporting August Halm's (and Adorno's) notion that Beethoven's thematic material is in the service of the overall form, he claims that Beethoven often transferred "the 'real' thematic material from the surface of actual melody and rhythm to a lower 'submotivic' stratum, consisting of more abstract structures."[64] But whereas for Dahlhaus, Beethoven's abstract thematic structures are almost always engaged in some sort of dialectical process with a piece's formal functions, Réti treats his prime cell simply as organic material manifested throughout the piece, while also characterizing it as a dramatic subject undergoing transformation and resolution.

　The prime cell in Réti's analysis of the *Appassionata* Sonata, for example, is the three-note unit C–D♭–C. This he finds at many different levels in the piece: it appears directly on the surface; it controls the first two phrases; and it can be heard as governing the symmetry of all three movements (this last is the type of observation for which Réti has

Example 3.14. From Réti, *Thematic Patterns in Sonatas of Beethoven*, 103.

Example 3.15. From Réti, *Thematic Patterns in Sonatas of Beethoven*, 104.

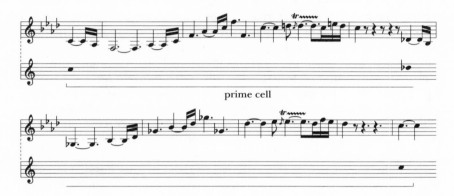

been discredited, for it involves mixing two slightly different pitch categories that just happen to form the prime cell: he hears the prominent fifth scale degrees in the outer movements as interacting with the tonic D♭ of the Andante). In addition to this prime cell, Réti identifies several variants of it, two other important cells, and several other recurring features, including note repetition, the "arpeggio motif" (any occurrence of broken chords), and the "*Appassionata* rhythm" (the rhythm of the opening theme) (see example 3.13).[65] The various themes in the work are analyzed and shown to contain patterns of the important cells. Réti's analysis of the opening theme is shown in example 3.14, with brackets marking the presence of cells. Réti then jumps to the next level of structure and demonstrates that the first three phrases are organized around the prime cell (see example 3.15).

But not only is Réti concerned with the ubiquitous presence of a limited number of fundamental motivic cells; he is also keen to demonstrate that these cells undergo a transformation and resolution through the course of the work.[66] In the case of Op. 57, the original prime cell

C–D♭–C is transformed in the Presto coda of the finale into F–A♭–G.[67] Réti derives this Presto variant from a variant in the first movement: B♭–D♭–C♭. Transposed to the level of F, this variant would read F–A♭–G♭. But because the new variant in the finale expresses tonic and dominant it requires a G rather than a G♭. This transformation thus reflects the harmonic resolution of tonic and dominant while at the same time merging the prime cell with the cell of the third, another primary element in the work. For these reasons, Réti claims it as an example of architectural resolution. Such a resolution forms for Réti the realization of a work's inner force, a force manifested in motivic elements.

In Réti's view, analysis has neglected this inner force, being too concerned with what he calls the outward force.[68] This latter force affirms and articulates the more primary inner force, through the operation of grouping. Groups are delineated by motivic differentiation, thematic resumption, or cadential harmonization, all of which serve to make the inner shaping of a composition recognizable. Réti clearly identifies the spiritual dimension of music with this inner motivic force: "An adequate evolution of these motivic elements enables the inspired composer to merge his structural ideas with spiritual and emotional ideas. This is heard dramatically in the motivic resolutions in the music of Beethoven."[69] With this, Réti explicitly locates the merger of structure and spirit in the heroic style of Beethoven. The presence of this inner force then becomes a general criterion of musical greatness: "The great composers, from the classical period right up to our time, develop their compositional shapes primarily from the inner structure, though they often affirm this inner shaping through an outward grouping, so to speak."[70] Again we see that an aspect of composition perceived to be fundamental to Beethoven's heroic style—the presence of an inner entelechy, concretized in motivic processes—is installed as the basic measure of musical artistry.[71]

In Beethoven's music, structure emerges from a process of motivic transformation and becomes a spiritual phenomenon.[72] The spiritual dimension of the musical work thus assumes a distinctly teleological and narrative presence, for Réti thinks of thematic process as an "architectural plot" in which motifs and themes are progressively transformed and led to a resolution. This plot, as the "innermost artistic idea" of a musical work, "makes all the shapes of a composition a part and expression of one higher unity."[73] Réti shared none of Schenker's qualms about the extramusical scenarios that are often invoked metaphorically as aids to understanding the unifying "idea" of a composition. In fact, he explicitly attempts to link such metaphors with analysis, just as he links spirit with motivic structure: "Once we succeed in comprehending music in its innermost thematic mechanism, the structural and esthetic-dramatic content of music becomes incomparably more transparent."[74] In his analysis-*cum*-interpretation of the Fifth Symphony, which appeared in his later book *The Thematic Process in Music*, Réti shows what such a merger would entail.

The first part of Réti's analysis again locates several fundamental motivic contours within the opening bars and then shows how the main themes of each of the succeeding movements manifest the same material. He next addresses the opening motto of the work and attempts to chart its progress through the entire symphony in terms of the "spiritual allegory" of Fate. For this purpose, the motto is analyzed into two components: the "beat motif" (the threefold repetition of a note) and the "hook" (the interlocking of two falling thirds). Striking examples of threefold repetitions from the rest of the symphony are then adduced, to show that the spirit of the beat motif pervades the entire work (see example 3.16).[75]

Only after he has thus shown the pervasiveness of the basic materials does Réti proceed to a reading of the piece's spiritual progress. The first phrase of the piece, reaching the half cadence in bar 21, represents an unusually quick evolution from tension to resolution. Réti interprets this premature resolution as an audacious turn of the hero toward happiness in the very face of the Fate motive. With the onset of the following bars, the hero sadly learns that there is no shortcut to

Example 3.16. Threefold repetitions in Beethoven, Symphony no. 5.
From Réti, *The Thematic Process in Music*, 171.

victory. Here the hook is felt, as the $A\flat$ and F interlock around the sustained G of bar 21. The rest of the movement, claims Réti, represents this same impetus: "The attempt to build a straight, optimistic course . . . which . . . is invariably threatened by some inexorable grim reality."[76] This grim reality is musically expressed by the presence of beat motif and hook. Réti's lengthy discussion of the first movement closes with the would-be jubilation of the coda's "victory march" facing a reversal in the final bars—the resolution of the conflict cannot be allowed to happen in the first movement.[77]

The Scherzo furnishes the turning point for Réti. In a critical judgment that must be unique in the history of this symphony's reception, Réti claims that the Scherzo's theme, despite beat motif and hook, "is an enunciation of utter optimism, of almost unbounded joy of life."[78] He "allegorically" concludes that although we cannot evade the predestined law of Fate, we can triumph *through*, rather than in spite of, Fate.[79] The Scherzo thus serves as a huge upbeat to the finale, wherein beat-motif and hook no longer hinder the jubilation but actually enrich it.[80]

Réti hears the theme at the Presto, in the finale's coda, as a crowning resolution to the entire process of the symphony. Here the work's opening motto is now made straight: the four notes of the motto are transposed and played without the interlocking hook (see example 3.17).[81] Réti refers to this as the "coda theme" and shows how it plays out, near the end of the coda, the contour of the finale theme (see example 3.18). "This," claims Réti, "is indeed the great resolution of the Fifth Symphony. At last, the idea to which the work strove from its beginning has become reality in this triumphant thematic combination."[82] (Characteristically, Réti locates his resolution in an abstract pitch contour: in his view, the symphony's goal is not the transcendent assimilation of the rhythmic beat motif but that of the pitch-motivic

Example 3.17. From Réti, *The Thematic Process in Music*, 188.

Example 3.18. From Réti, *The Thematic Process in Music*, 189.

a. Coda theme

b. First finale theme

"hook.") Réti's enthusiasm over the radiantly resolved thematic process of the Fifth Symphony prompts him to exclaim in his peroration that "a work of musical art is determined by laws so strict, logical and organic that it becomes in itself an allegory of all creation. And it is through this *inherent* allegory that an eternal bond between musical shapes and the human world is sustained."[83]

The notion of music as inherently allegorical allows Réti to bolster interpretive extramusical readings with the material evidence of his thematic process. In the case of the Fifth Symphony, the symbol of an assimilated Fate is linked to the motivic process of the work and becomes its essential idea: the symphony itself, through a long and arduous process, learns to assimilate, joyfully, the fateful opening motto. As Réti concludes, "The symbol ... given by the composer himself in a title, text, or any other form ... can often illuminate the whole structural horizon and help us to understand the most profound connections."[84] Réti now invokes the interpretive, extramusical dimension to clarify the material dimension; that is, the "esthetic-dramatic" reading now seems primary, and the thematic dimension is applied as evidence thereof. It is no longer clear whether the motivic process or the ethically tinged interpretive intuition is the starting point of a successful analysis. This is important, for it indicates that the two have indeed merged and are no longer separable. And I would argue further that Réti thus makes explicit the fundamental condition of all Beethovenian theory and analysis—the ethical and the material dimensions have never been separated, no matter the amount of rhetoric expended on insisting that they have.[85]

Elsewhere Réti identifies the symphonic theme and its process with a hero and his exploits, thus generalizing the experience of the Fifth Symphony to include all symphonic art:

> We compared a symphony's theme to the hero of a dramatic play who is led through the vicissitudes of his fate to the solution of his life problem. Seen thus allegorically, the first and last movements could be thought to constitute the actual drama, wherein the central idea is developed, while the other movements represent episodes which take the hero through different events and environments. Yet, as throughout all these different events we encounter the same hero, *the theme*, these sections, too, become organic parts of the work's artistic whole. The new environments influence the "hero," who in turn influences them, and the final outcome is the result of this interplay, both in a symbolic and in a technical, that is, thematic sense.[86]

Thematicism is explicitly touted as the heroic aspect of music, and we are returned to something like Marx's view, combined with a twentieth-century enthusiasm for latency, for that which lies below the surface, ensuring an extra dimension of profundity. The sense of self modeled by Beethoven's heroic style is now made compatible with the newer Freudian view of the human psyche.

We have surveyed the work of four influential theorists whose theories about the nature of music share a circular relationship with the music of Beethoven. Individually they represent unique stations in the history of Beethoven reception; collectively they provide an ongoing measure of the impact of Beethoven's music on institutionalized ways of thinking about music in general. Throughout the trajectory of their work the intuition of unified coherence in Beethoven's music is never abandoned, but the manifestation of that coherence is variously expressed. We may characterize the path of this trajectory generally as progressing from poetic intuition to quasi-scientific evidence. Marx matched his controlling poetic *Idee* with a dynamic view of underlying form (aided by the loose but flexible categories of *Satz* and *Gang*), a view that works well with the notion of an end-oriented dramatic program. The later theorists in our survey all felt they were dealing with harder evidence, whether it be taxonomical classification, or an embedded *Ursatz*, or latent thematic cells. The acceptability of the evidence is dictated in all cases by the leading intellectual models of each generation: for Riemann, these were natural science and taxonomical method; for Schenker and Réti, depth psychology and structuralist analysis.

All these theorists characteristically deal in abstractions, yet each matches what he hears on the surface of a Beethoven work with the essential basis of his abstract prototypical unit. Beethoven's music acts not only as the privileged form of concrete evidence for each theory but also as the nearest concrete equivalent to the quasi-abstract notions of Marx's *Gang*, and his fundamental formal impulse of rest-motion-rest; of Riemann's cadential dialectic and the primacy of the motive; of Schenker's *Urlinie* and Réti's thematic resolution. Thus Beethoven's music fulfills an Idealist compact with post-Beethovenian tonal theory, for it provides the place where the ideal and the real merge. Translated into the essentialist norms of these theories, Beethoven's music is heard as the voice of Music itself.

Tonal theory has been listening almost exclusively to Beethoven and, more specifically, to his heroic style. The musical values of the heroic style—thematic/motivic development, end-orientation and unequivocal closure, form as process, and the inexorable presence of line—are preserved in the axioms of the leading theoretical models of the last two centuries. Beethoven's music even survived the turn to nontonal musical analysis because of the continued interest in thematic process, touted as the common bond of the great German tradition from Haydn to Schoenberg.[87]

Yet for all this continuity, it is undeniably true that each generation projects onto Beethoven's music a somewhat different aesthetic concern: for Marx, Beethoven's music realizes the spiritual ideal of music history by means of a dramatic and morally uplifting process centered on the musical theme as protagonist; for Riemann, it realizes the classical ideal to which all Western music allegedly aspires, and it does so without sacrificing subjective individuality; for Schenker, it realizes the heroic ideal of the musical genius and the essentially linear utterance of the musical masterwork; for Réti (and Schoenberg before him), it becomes the highest exemplar of thematic process, the apex of motivic saturation and the integral artwork. And we might also remember that for Adorno (and Dahlhaus after him), it plays out, like no other music, the essential Idealist dialectic of subject and object. Thus Beethoven becomes something akin to Gary Taylor's vision of Shakespeare, as sketched in his wonderful study *Reinventing Shakespeare*, in which each age is seen to appropriate the great artist for its own ideological ends[88]—with the crucial difference that in the case of Beethoven reception all the views adumbrated here still resonate; none has become so outlandish as to be unthinkable. This is because they are not generated by rival ideologies after all. The combination of these values—spiritual import, subjective expressivity ultimately grounded in classical rationality, dramatic impulse, coherent integrity, dialectical process, and the possibility of transcendent heroism—is manifest in a moral and aesthetic view of the self that flourished overtly some two hundred years ago in German culture and is evident in expressions of that culture ranging from the depiction of individual heroism in the dramas of Goethe and Schiller to Hegel's ultimate aggrandizement of the self. It is to these values that we must now turn.

Chapter Four

CULTURAL VALUES

BEETHOVEN, THE GOETHEZEIT, *AND THE*
HEROIC CONCEPT OF SELF

> Einem gelang es—er hob den Schleier der Göttin zu Sais—
> Aber was sah er? Er sah—Wunder des Wunders—
> sich selbst.
>
> (To one it was granted: he raised the veil of the goddess of
> Sais. And what did he see? He saw—wonder of wonders—
> himself.)
>
> (*Novalis*, Die Lehrlinge zu Sais)

I

BY ANALYZING tonal music with the analytical tools and theoretical assumptions we have inherited from theorists such as Marx, Riemann, Schenker, and Réti, we implicitly claim that Beethoven's music most closely resembles the way music ought to go. The perennial hardiness of this imperative leads one to believe that it is motivated by more than the bare fact of the music itself. I would like to suggest that the homogeneous reception of this music, its long reign as a musical ideal, is due largely to our continued subscription to the subject-laden values of the so-called *Goethezeit*, or Age of Goethe (allowing this capacious designation to house the German Idealists as well).[1] These values form the ethical bedrock beneath the often abstract reckonings of Beethoven's music that we surveyed in chapter 3.

Fundamental to the worldview of the *Goethezeit* is an ennobling and all-embracing concept of self. The emerging "forms of the romantic imagination" (to use M. H. Abrams's expression) are based on the rhythms and scenarios of the individual self, such as birth and death, personal freedom and destiny, self-consciousness, and self-overcoming. In Germany these currents swelled to create a new intellectual ethos, merging an incipient cultural nationalism with the apotheosis of Self, a merger instrumental in lending that nationalism the imprimatur of universality. Beethoven's heroic style has been heard not only to instantiate these values of self but to give them unimpeachable expression.

It is hardly a secret that Beethoven's music has consistently been judged to be expressive of the primary features of the modern Western concept of self, such as the self as a spiritual or moral entity, the constitutive autonomy of the self, the possibility of self-transcendence, and the fundamental condition of struggle. In chapter 2 we examined some of the phenomenological bases for the prepossessing engagement this music compels in its listeners. What needs additional emphasis here is the fact that the nearly unanimous consensus positing the toil and triumph of the self (and of humankind) as the principal subject of Beethoven's heroic style argues not only for the engaging dramatic realism of his music but also for the suitability of mortal travail itself as *the* subject for music felt to be so unarguably sublime. In the mid-nineteenth century Thomas Carlyle wrote: "[The] struggle of human Free-will against material Necessity . . . calls the Sympathy of mortal hearts into action, and . . . is the sole Poetry possible."[2] Carlyle's quaintly capitalized nominatives form a compact equation of the metaphysical, ethical, and aesthetic—one that has been heard in the music of the heroic style. Instead of portraying the ineffable bliss of some remote paradise, Beethoven's music has been felt to express the temporal machinations of our own sublunary realm (*ici-bas*), the plight of humanity in its uphill struggle for freedom—and yet it brings to this human narrative the sublimity of the beyond (*au-delà*). We can thus hear this music as another, and indeed fundamental, expression of an age characterized by the centrality of Self.

For the age of Goethe, Kant, and Hegel was a watershed in the history of humanism. Man once again became the measure of things, as the Enlightenment's vaunted faith in metaphysical reason gave way to a perspective decidedly *sub specie humanitatis*. Yet humankind was not merely thought of as the highest terrestrial link of the Great Chain of Being, as an abstract placeholder in a continuum encompassing all the world and beyond. The emphasis was switched from man's place in the world to the world's place in man. Kant taught that the world we know can be understood only as the product of our own categories of thought, thus making epistemology the starting point of any reasonable philosophical investigation. And Hegel construed the science of truth and of human history as a world-sweeping dialectical process based on that of human self-consciousness. The progress from Kant to Hegel consists of nothing less than the transformation of human cognition from a radically limited interface with reality to the origin and destiny of all reality. (In other words, that which was confined to putting a distinctly human construction on a forever unknowable reality now constructs—in the strong sense—that reality.) The *Weltseele* of German Idealism is the non plus ultra of anthropomorphic imperialism, the ultimate expansion of one's sense of self.

The renewed power of Christianity played no small role in confirming this orientation toward the self. Its influence was quite explicit for the early romantics in Germany: Novalis dreamed of a new Europe, a spiritual community united through Christianity.[3] Several famous men and women of German letters either converted to or returned to Catholicism.[4] Nietzsche later seized on this affinity and was fond of ridiculing the Idealist philosophers as "Tübinger theologians."[5] Yet the romantics responded to Christianity primarily as an aesthetic force. In France, for example, Chateaubriand argued for the poetic authority of Christianity in his *Génie du Christianisme* (1801), a book that was an instant sensation and remained highly influential.[6] Two aspects of Christian thought were fundamental to the emerging romantic worldview. First was the Christian conception of history as a one-way, goal-oriented linear process, which can be understood in terms of the life of the individual self. History no longer repeats itself in the endless cyclical iterations and metamorphoses celebrated throughout non-Christian mythology: here there is only one apocalyptic process, one master cycle, consisting of Creation, the Fall, and Redemption. More important for our purposes than the formal analogy between a human life and the life of the Christian cosmos is the interface between the will of the individual and the all-embracing cycle: Christianity provides for a mythology of the self. An individual's redemption is now possible through his or her own agency; one can create one's own future.

Yet the process of realizing this newly conceived potential is attended by intense tribulation. At times the struggle itself is glorified as the fundamental condition of Western, Christian humankind—its saving grace, in fact, if we are to take at face-value the ending of Goethe's *Faust*.[7] The power to engage in this worthy struggle, to create one's own destiny, was celebrated over and over again in the most popular German dramas of the *Goethezeit*, usually expressed as the heroic quest for freedom. Yet, contrary to the way that Beethoven's music will be heard to express this quest, for Goethe there is no such thing as arrival; man must keep metamorphosing, for this is the way of nature. "We must not seek to be anything but to become everything." Goethe's famous words can stand as a motto for his age. The emphasis on an endless process of becoming puts the eventual redemption promised by Christian eschatology into an impossibly remote perspective. Schiller's "sentimental" artist is one who imperfectly aims at that distant ideal, rather than one who perfectly portrays present reality (the "naive" poet). Actually getting there would be antithetical to romantic thought. Like magnetic north, the pull of a distant ideal provides a constant point of orientation; arrival at the North Pole would confuse the compass needle.

Two other aspects of this force of Becoming are raised in Goethe's work. The first involves the attraction—like a moth to a flame—of the self to symbolic rebirth, to a remaking of oneself (an act envisioned in the well-known injunction "stirb und werde," or "die and become," from the poem emblematically titled "Selige Sehnsucht" ["Blessed Longing"]). Thus the self is now empowered to incorporate cyclical metamorphoses—previously regarded as suprahuman and even supratemporal—within its own mortal trajectory, rather than conceive that trajectory as a stage in some larger cycle: the rhythm of mythological history instead becomes a useful metaphor for the spiritual growth of the individual. The other aspect of Becoming stressed by Goethe has to do with the way he conceives of the interface between the individual and his or her destiny. One does not have an unlimited control of one's destiny; one must steer a course strewn with obstacles. This image was so vivid for Goethe that he used a striking formulation of it from his earlier drama *Egmont* to close his autobiographical work *Dichtung und Wahrheit*: "As if whipped on by invisible spirits, the sun-steeds of time sweep the light chariot of our destiny along, and the most we can do is to maintain courage and calm, hold the reins tight, and steer the wheels to right or to left, here avoiding a stone and there avoiding a plunging crash. Where we are headed, who knows? We hardly recall whence we came."[8] We are creatures of time, pulled inexorably onward. Yet we hold the reins and can act courageously.

In the wake of Rousseau and the great revolutions in France and America, the freedom to hold one's own reins was deemed—in a justly famous formulation—an unalienable right.[9] The winning and maintaining of this freedom creates much of the dramatic impetus in the highly influential stage works of Goethe and Schiller. Characters like Götz von Berlichingen, Karl Moor, Egmont, Wilhelm Tell, and the Marquis von Posa captured the popular imagination for generations with their call for freedom. In one of the most revered speeches in the whole of German theater, Schiller's Marquis von Posa pleads with the Spanish king for freedom of thought (*Gedankenfreiheit*); the last breath of Goethe's Götz carries the word *Freiheit* across the stage. The values of the free self quickly became enshrined in a literary movement that earned the status of *Klassik* even while its progenitors were still alive—and just as the works became classic so too did the values they projected. For these dramas serve to ennoble the human situation Goethe portrays with his image of Fate's runaway chariot. Man becomes a hero: he hazards a course of action, persists, and sometimes triumphs. There is a reason to hold the reins.

Many of the heroes of German classical drama earned their popularity in no little degree simply by being recognizable humans in identifiable situations. The typical hero of German classic drama is a conflicted hero, a man invested with both a set of values worth dying for and a domestic situation worth living for. In accordance with the ethical mandate of Christianity, the basis for heroic decision must come from inside the hero himself, not from the gods or from nature. The relevant model for heroic action was less Achilles than Hector, the hero who by attempting to protect his family (both his immediate family and the extended family of Troy) risks the end of their protection (namely, his life).[10] Achilles, son of a goddess, knows no such human encumbrances. The mythic saga of the hero is thus brought closer to everyday human existence: heroes are now fathers, sons, brothers, and lovers. As a result we can feel the weight of their decisions; the arena of heroic consequence may be no larger (and no smaller) than one's own hearth and home.[11] A striking case is provided by Schiller's *Wilhelm Tell*, where the struggle for the freedom of Switzerland is accomplished through the defensive actions of a father—Tell's actions on behalf of his country are both triggered and conditioned by his role as a protective father.

We can say all this more economically by stating that the hero of the *Goethezeit* is a self-conscious hero. He is aware of the full ramifications of any aggressive course of action, aware of his time and his place and of all the appurtenances of self. His course of heroic action is characterized by a rhythmic pattern of contemplation and activity—no deed without consideration; no consideration without a deed. (Egmont is an exception to this, as we shall see presently, and this may well constitute the fundamental flaw of his character.) This rhythm is mirrored for Goethe in his theory of plant metamorphosis, as the alternation of progressive and regressive stages of growth in the spiral trajectory leading from seed to fruit (and back to seed again). And it forms an operative dialectic in the *Bildungsroman*, a genre that began to flourish in Germany at this time and that typically involves the spiritual evolution, through a series of vicissitudes, of a central character. In *Wilhelm Meisters Lehrjahre*, the most influential German *Bildungsroman* of the age, Goethe captures the charged and consequential equilibrium of the polarity of act and reflection with the aphorism "Thought broadens but lames; action enlivens but limits."[12] The hero of German classical literature lives between these poles. He both enacts and sees himself enacting, and thus bears the weighted wrap of self-consciousness, *the* human condition which was to become fundamental to German Idealism's concept of reality and its history.

For the dialectical process proposed by Fichte and brought to a culmination by Hegel is at bottom a description of human consciousness. Consciousness is not a timeless quality that can ground a deductive enterprise. It is rather a product of its own motion through time; Hegel gives it a constitutive history. The recognition of this motion forms what Hegel calls his "method of scientific truth." Such truth can no longer be grasped by the abstractions of mathematics: for Hegel, that which is fixed is dead.[13] Consciousness is portrayed as a self-determining process, and the philosophical method that encompasses it can no longer take the form of an externally applied syllogistic logic.[14]

Hegel's proposal to change the basis of philosophical method from syllogism to dialectic is momentous. The basis of truth is wrenched from its secure and timeless realm and made to take its chances in the arena of human temporality. Philosophical understanding, if it is not to remain external to its object of study, must go through the same temporal stages as that which is being understood; a motion, a process, a history must be experienced. No longer a revelatory sideshow, Truth is that which is unfolded through us ourselves in the here-below. And its life is one of process and change, like the life of humankind. Metaphysics is transformed from the power of Reason comprehending (and controlling) an external world to the quest of Spirit to know itself, a quest envisioned in terms of the rhythms of human experience.

The problem of thought attempting to understand itself drives the narrative in Hegel's *Phenomenology of Spirit* through its successive stages up to and including the goal of absolute knowledge. Near the end of this process the spirit is heavy with its history; through the process of coming to know what it is, it has sunk into what Hegel calls the "night of its self-consciousness." But its existence will be reborn into the targeted state of absolute knowledge (of itself), from which it will have to traverse once again the stages of its history, only now from a higher stage of awareness. Presumably it is this second traversal that Hegel himself performs in the *Phenomenology*. Here the goal has been reached: "History comprehended [die begriffene Geschichte] . . . builds the reality, truth, and certainty of the throne of absolute spirit."[15]

Unlike the endless process of becoming that underlies and informs the poetics (and ethics) of Goethe as well as the yearning reach of Schiller's sentimental poet, Hegel's system is closed—the self generates and culminates its own destiny. And not only is the goal not projected into an inaccessibly remote future, it is in fact attained in the very present by Hegel himself, through his system of thought. More-

over, the goal itself is fundamentally constitutive for the entire historical process: the intermittent stages attain their full meaning only when
the whole is known. Note the strict opposition between the closed and
self-directed motion of the Hegelian subject and the course of destiny
as envisioned by Goethe. Goethe's hero can manage only a brief tenure
at the reins of a blindly galloping process that knows not whither it
tends ("Where we are headed, who knows? We hardly recall whence
we came"). But Hegel's subject encompasses the entire process; it
knows where it is going precisely because it knows where it has been.
Goethe's present moment appears as a flashpoint illuminating a continuum of vanishing perspectives; for Hegel the ends of the continuum
backlight the present moment. In what follows I shall argue that in
Beethoven's heroic style both these standpoints are possible, their co-
existence not only plausible but essential. And in thus arguing that the
Beethovenian standpoint underlies and unites these two vitally influential views of human possibility and destiny, I will be tempted to go
further and to suggest that the heroic style does indeed sound the
deepest keynote of its age.

II

> Und keine Zeit und keine Macht zerstückelt
> Geprägte Form, die lebend sich entwickelt.
>
> (And neither time nor force can ever break
> The finished form that growing life will take.)[16]
>
> (*Goethe*, Urworte. Orphisch: Dämon)

Like the philosophical systems of the post-Kantian generation, the musical works of Beethoven's heroic style register as closed systems, self-
generating, self-sustaining, and self-consuming. The musical process
manifested in the heroic style is heard to share a similar sense of progressive development toward an immanent and transcendent telos. In
attempting to account for this perception, critics and analysts have
concentrated on the nature of Beethoven's thematic material: instead
of the presentation of a fully formed theme that enacts a standard formal type, Beethoven is credited with the use of subthematic abstraction (Dahlhaus), or de-individualized thematic material (Adorno), or
thematic cells (Réti), all in the service of a processive form that seems
to develop as a result of the exigencies of the thematic material.[17]

Beethoven's music is thus heard to embody the form of artistic mimesis newly privileged in the late eighteenth century: the imitation of

natura naturans, or the process of nature, supersedes that of *natura naturata,* the product of nature. Such an emphasis also reflects the way views of the self and human nature had changed by 1800. Many of the literary and dramatic works of the eighteenth century present human nature as a collection of fully formed types, hence, for example, the allegorical names of characters in writers like Fielding (e.g., Mr. Allworthy) and Goldsmith. Such fixed characters guarantee the predictability that loads the comic mainspring of much eighteenth-century comedy, as witnessed by the resurgence in that century of the comedy of situation.[18] That characters could genuinely change and develop is more the province of the emerging genre of the *Bildungsroman;* there the characters are initially presented in forms analogous to the way that Beethoven's heroic-style themes are heard—incipient, malleable, and, above all, transitive.

As we have seen in chapter 2, the phenomenological basis for this type of progressive evolution in Beethoven's music entails a flexible and often far-reaching rhythm of action and reaction, downbeat and upbeat. Each large-scale downbeat releases tension and feels well earned, metaphorically marking an ongoing cycle of setback and fresh resolution, struggle and triumph. As David B. Greene argues, the feeling of arrival in Beethoven (and generally in the classical style) can take on the same temporal envelope as a decision freely made, based on what has gone before but in no way exclusively determined by it.[19] This exercise of free choice, conditioned but not controlled by the past, fully justifies the phrase "fresh resolution": the momentous arrival resolves past conflicts while fostering resolve—understood as the conviction that constructively "fresh" choices can (and will) be made. Greene's view of temporality in Beethoven (and his view of music as a metaphor for temporality) makes plausible the ready identification of musical theme (or, at least, musical process) with a human protagonist. The sustained experiential intensity of continuous renewals felt throughout a sonata-form movement in the heroic style can be heard as a metaphor for the stations of a hero's progress.

Such a process corresponds not only to the Idealist dialectic of oppositional conflict but also to the typically conflicted nature of the self-conscious hero of German classical drama, living between the polar forces of deed and reflection. As we have seen, all the programs for the first movement of the *Eroica* Symphony surveyed in chapter 1 are characterized by a polarity between active and passive elements. Critics and analysts variously fashion these elements as husband and wife, hero and troops, will and contemplation, or downbeat and upbeat. The arrival that is both solution and fresh beginning marks a Hegelian motion; the fresh beginning that is soon complemented by a reflective state satisfies the condition of a Goethean polarity as well. Beethoven's upbeat prolongations, such as the buildup on the dominant of $B\flat$ in bars 99–109 of the *Eroica* first movement exposition, share with the regressive stage posited by Goethe's plant theory the same feeling of winding the spring for the next progressive leap.

Perhaps the most consequential form of this polarity for later musical thought is that which became attached (primarily through A. B. Marx) to the perceived duality of first group and second group in sonata form. Variously expressed as *männlich/weiblich*, aggressive/passive, and productive/receptive, the opposed categories of this polarity play ubiquitous parts in early nineteenth-century German aesthetics, appearing in various more or less closely related versions, such as Wilhelm von Humboldt's essay on the fundamental *männlich/weiblich* polarity of artistic production, Goethe's notion of *Anschauung* and *Tat*, and Schiller's *Formtrieb* and *Stofftrieb*. The two sides form a polar tension felt to be necessary for the production of balanced (classical) works of art, and it can be no coincidence that this polarity was heard in (and projected into) classical-style sonata form. The prevalence of this kind of intellectual construction in nineteenth-century thought may help explain the dominance of the thematic view of sonata form, a theory that eclipsed the harmonic view of the eighteenth century.[20]

To get to a yet deeper point of contact between Beethoven's heroic style and the intellectual impulse of the *Goethezeit*, we must consider the implications of Beethoven's merger of the drama of thematic development with an underlying generic form. As we have seen, the pervasive sense of thematic development informing the musical process of an entire movement gives that process a linear, teleological thrust. In fact, Beethoven's enhanced sense of drama entails a new relationship between theme and form: the form no longer serves to present prestabilized thematic material but rather becomes *a necessary process in the life of a theme*. This identification of theme and form allows the form to appear to develop as the theme develops. (It is interesting that this conjunction of theme and form can be described—without contradiction—in exactly the opposite terms: the theme is now a function of the form, the whole.[21]) By thus heightening the sense of temporal drama already inherent in the underlying syntax of sonata form, Beethoven brings about a new and powerful realization of the form, one that befits the spirit of his age. For now the theme as subject truly appears to create its own objective world (its form), thus musically embodying one of the principal conceits of German Idealism.[22] And this is all the more extraordinary, for the form that seems to develop before our ears is not a fantasialike, one-time-only construct but a familiar and generic one. This illusion can thus act as a potent realization of the

Idealist subject-that-creates-the-world, for the subject is creating this, our familiar, world. The necessary is made to seem free, and, by extension, our shared human condition is made to seem heroic.

In a strong sense, the heroic concept thus projected in Beethoven's music can be said to resolve (or combine) conflicting contemporary manifestations of the heroic. In his classic study *The Byronic Hero*, Peter Thorslev notes the essential tension in the character of what he calls the "Romantic Hero of Sensibility": the urge to be subsumed in a greater organic whole struggles against the urge to be passionately individual and self-assertive.[23] In Beethoven's heroic style, both urges are satisfied: the passionately individual is made to sound as a larger organic universality.[24] This is because the passionately individual self, which is heard to be projected by the music, *is all there is*: one does not hear a world order against which a hero defines himself—one hears only the hero, the self, fighting against its own element.[25] Thus the "superclosure" effect of the "organically unified musical masterpiece": there is no world beyond the piece, no fading horizon, no vanishing point of perspective. All is in the piece, and the piece is all; all is now. The feeling provoked by this music is one of transcendent individuality, of merger with a higher world order in the name of Self. This effect is identical to that enunciated in the Idealist trajectory of Hegel's phenomenology, with one overwhelmingly important exception: Beethoven's music is heard and experienced; it is a concretion with a degree of compression and concentration that Hegel's philosophy could never hope to reach.

The final stage of this self-generating process is brought about by the all-important Beethovenian coda. In chapter 1 we recorded a tendency in the programmatic reception of the *Eroica* to treat the coda of the first movement as something like an epic retelling of the events of the rest of the movement. The implication is that the coda reaches a standpoint somehow beyond that of the "present tense" embodied by the foregoing music. The coda is heard as the goal of the movement, a goal outside of the process itself yet paradoxically part of it. Critics from our own century tend to regard the Beethovenian coda as the locus for unfinished business; again the implication is of a higher, more cumulative stage from which the rest of the work is surveyed and completed. Images of transcendence, apotheosis, and utopia attach themselves to this perceived culmination, for the coda seems actually to arrive at the transcendent state promised by the Idealist vision of history and supported by the ethos of Christian eschatology, seems to signal both salvation and completion. Beethoven's codas thus suggest the realization of a future in the actual present—the future is heard to materialize as both future and present.[26] This also contributes to the perception of the closed and self-consuming work, for the whole history of time is contained in one process.

The tendency to hear Beethoven's music in this way was abetted by the important shift in early nineteenth-century music criticism to the standpoint of the whole, a shift arguably brought about as a response to this music. In the case of Beethoven, repeated hearings were now deemed necessary for a complete understanding of any of his works. Making sense of the local complexities of this music depended on knowing the entire process, for an inherent destiny is projected back onto the idiosyncrasies of Beethoven's themes by the way they come to be consummated in the coda. The music is heard to be about thematic process and development; the full understanding of a theme waits upon a knowledge of its eventual outcome. The Beethovenian *telos* is not just an end but an end accomplished (which is in fact the definition of *telos*). In the music of Mozart and Haydn, endings seem more a matter of convention; there is less sense of inherent closure in the material. In Beethoven, such inherent destiny is made manifest.

Letting the ending thus influence the way the story is told and understood makes the Beethovenian heroic-style sonata form akin to one of the fundamental narrative forms of the nineteenth century. As is the case with Hegel's *Phenomenology of the Spirit* (as interpreted by M. H. Abrams), this narrative can be composed only from the standpoint of its conclusion. Thus the works of both Hegel and Beethoven resemble the method of the first-person *Bildungsroman*, such as Dickens's *David Copperfield*. A developmental process is surveyed from the knowledge of its completion.[27] In *David Copperfield* this higher standpoint manifests itself in the tone with which foregoing events are related. Early references to ill-fated characters, for example, are often ironically marked with the author's knowledge of that fate.[28] In fact, the narrator's standpoint in these cases is fundamentally ironic, and it is no less so in the case of Beethoven, as we shall see presently.

But despite an overall teleological similarity, the Beethovenian coda turns his form into something resoundingly different from most manifestations of the literary *Bildungsroman*. This disparity registers in the perception that the coda brings the process around again to something like the conditions of its opening. Often the coda begins with a fresh start of the thematic material of the opening and then develops that material, hence the now obsolete view of the Beethovenian coda as a second development section.[29] But here the tonal center of the beginning has been transformed: the tonic harmony heard at the end of a Beethovenian coda feels utterly different from that heard at the outset of the movement, though it is materially the same.

As noted in chapter 2, the type of emphasis enjoyed by the coda, when understood both as an independent formal section in some cases analogous to the exposition, development, and recapitulation and as a final closing, gives to the overall dynamic design of Beethoven's heroic sonata form a rhythm of down-up-down-up-down, with exposition, recapitulation, and coda forming three large-scale downbeats. This dynamic pattern is commensurate with the idea that the temporal process expressed in the heroic style is one of completion, starting from an initial large-scale downbeat and rounding off with a final large-scale downbeat. As is the case with the difference between opening tonic and closing tonic, the point here is that a big downbeat is again attained at the end—but here it closes the movement. The coda's overall rhythmic function of a large-scale closing downbeat brings the opening downbeat to a higher stage, in the manner of a spiral trajectory. In so doing, Beethoven's heroic style projects what we might call the underlying rhythmic impulse of its age.

For the entire age finds itself at a crossroads: preoccupations with consciousness, memory, and a sense of history are met by a renewed emphasis on the "eternal return," the mythic time of cyclical death and rebirth. These two temporal forces, linear time and cyclical time, create an equilibrium that results in the underlying temporal design of much of German romanticism: the spiral journey, where a progressive sense of linearity is superimposed on a cyclical course. This pattern can also be viewed as the romantic restyling of Christian history, wherein the path of redemption leads from a prelapsarian golden age to a future golden age—past and future merge mystically. The work of M. H. Abrams has shown the extent to which this design permeates the literature, criticism, and philosophy of German and English romanticism. The circuitous journey is the path of Hegel's dialectic, the building block as well as the grand design of his philosophy of spirit; it is the individual hero's journey in Novalis's *Die Lehrlinge zu Sais* and in Hölderlin's *Hyperion*; it is Man's journey in Kleist's superbly magical essay *Über das Marionettentheater*. Not only does the music of Beethoven's heroic style number itself among these romantic effusions, it manages to sound the common themes of both the German *Klassik* (as represented by the dramatic heroes of Goethe and Schiller) and the age of Hegel, while borrowing some of its musical rhetoric from the spirit of the French Revolution, through the influence of postrevolutionary French symphonic music.[30] In one of his better-known *Athenäum* fragments, Friedrich Schlegel identified the three defining tendencies of his age as the French revolution, Fichte's *Wissenschaftslehre*, and Goethe's *Wilhelm Meister*. That a music joining these tendencies could ever materialize is the stuff of romantic utopian fantasy. That it in fact did materialize, and only some few years after Schlegel's declaration, has been the stuff of our own fantasy, for in it we hear the apparent proof of an aggrandizing metaphysics of self, the ultimate music of the modern post-Kantian world, and an abiding hedge against the nameless terrors of an indifferent universe.

III

In order to deepen our view of the relationship of the heroic style to the culture of the *Goethezeit*, and to resist the too easy temptation to characterize the relationship simply as a kind of homology, it will be revealing at this point to turn to a case where Beethoven's music is a direct response to another cultural product of the age, namely, Goethe's *Egmont*.[31] Comparing the effect of Beethoven's *Egmont* Overture to that of the drama that was its inspiration will sharpen our perception of the distinctive voice of the heroic style, the voice that sets it apart from other forms of contemporaneous cultural expression. Among other things, we hope to arrive at a more sophisticated understanding of the function of the Beethovenian coda and how it acts as a particularly conspicuous locus of the uniquely narrating presence of this music.

In Goethe's play, Egmont is a popular and charismatic prince of a Netherlands province sharply oppressed under Spanish dominion. His compelling force of personality and ability to live in the moment make him the admired friend of all his subjects. As he reveals to his beloved Klärchen, he deeply resents the dissembling and spiritually numbing political roles that he must assume, much preferring the openness he enjoys in her company. Through an inability to heed the warnings of his pragmatic friend William of Orange, Egmont becomes the political prisoner of the duke of Alba (minion of the Spanish throne), characteristically speaks his mind on the subject of freedom, and is subsequently sentenced to death for the crime of treason. While waiting for his execution he falls asleep and has a vision of Klärchen, allegorically costumed as Freedom. She assures Egmont that his death will inspire the provinces to fight successfully for their freedom. He then wakes to the sound of military music and is led offstage to the scaffold, whereupon Goethe calls for the music of a "Victory Symphony" to accompany and succeed the closing of the curtain.

One of the troubling aspects of Goethe's play is the rather peremptory and forced transformation of Egmont from a self-involved "active force" (to invoke Karl Philipp Moritz's term[32]) to a public symbol of political freedom. The Egmont we follow through the play is a man fetchingly engaged in the moment at hand, disdainful of his friends' overweening concerns with the past and the future and blind to the threatening machinations of power—this is decidedly not the profile of a political maven. Egmont simply did not possess much political clout before his death; this is made clear by the townspeople's notable reluctance to come to his aid after his imprisonment, despite their love for him.

Instead, the psychology of the drama hinges on the relationship of Egmont and Klärchen. In good classic form, Goethe structures the drama around a central scene involving these two characters, a scene that Nicholas Boyle has recently dubbed a theophany.[33] Critics from Moritz on have underlined the importance of this scene; it represents the maximal flowering of Egmont's forceful individuality and of Klärchen's receptive nature, a moment of true fulfillment that can only be followed by death.[34] Thus the transformation of Egmont into a hero symbolic of political freedom at the end of the play has left many of its critics cold, not the least of whom was Schiller.[35] For Goethe's ending has the effect of shifting the center of gravity of the drama from the bloom and subsequent demise of an active force (the plight of such an individual in a political setting[36]) to the death of that force as the signal of future political glory. What Goethe's ending suggests is that Egmont becomes an important symbol for freedom only through his death, that Egmont the individual becomes Egmont the public symbol only after the drama itself is over.

It seems that Goethe himself was at something of a loss to put this transformation across. In any event, it is highly revealing that he called for a Victory Symphony to suggest the apotheosis of his hero and the triumph of liberty. It can almost appear that he made the best of a bad job by appealing to the power of music to effect his eleventh-hour transformation of Egmont from compelling individual to political martyr. He thus uses music when he wants to suggest a future outcome directly, without the denotative *longueurs* of language or stagecraft. Yet this is not his only way of using music in the play. Music suggests the death of Klärchen[37] and accompanies Egmont's vision of freedom. And there is no little irony in the fact that it is another sort of music that wakes Egmont from his epiphanic vision (and its music) to grim reality, namely, the military music of the approaching guard. This threatening music reminds Egmont of his own military service, and he transforms the drums calling for his death into a call to freedom and glory: "How often that sound has summoned me with free step to the field of battle and of victory! How lively my comrades strode to the path of peril and of fame! I too am about to stride forth from this prison to an honorable death. I die for the liberty I lived and fought for, and to which I am now a passive sacrifice."[38] One can imagine the drama ending here, with the ironic and paradoxical use of a music that can simultaneously suggest both ultimate oppression and ultimate freedom, thus leaving us one last time with the renewed impression of Egmont's ability as an active force to transform the reality around him.[39]

But this is not how the drama ends. How, then, are we to hear the required Victory Symphony? Surely not as stage music, for that was the role of the military music. Instead we hear music as something like an outside agency, telling the future course of events. But this is no mere epilogue, particularly with Beethoven's music. Goethe must have suspected that music could do more than just paint a picture of the future, that through its special immediacy it could in fact create the future right then and there. This is potentially a stunning dramaturgical move, for the tragic emotion associated with Egmont's execution is immediately subsumed by the music, as by fiat, into one of glorious consummation. Among other things, it demonstrates, indeed thematizes, music's sheer dramatic power, its perceived role as a medium transcending words, and even actions, in its ability to suggest: the sudden ending of the action on the stage (enforced by the ultimate showstopper, the death of the lead character) emphasizes the music as "music" rather than as accompaniment. Music literally takes over where drama ends. And as music, the Victory Symphony is asked to effect an astonishing transformation, to achieve an instant, and culminating, apotheosis. (The drama per se had reached its own culmination with the dream scene, a reflection of that central scene so important to Moritz.)

Music's ability to achieve closure and consummation is thus appropriated by Goethe when he needs a similar result for his drama.[40] His appropriation serves to thematize this aspect of music. It is revealing that the music Beethoven used to mark this closure in the play also serves as the coda of his *Egmont* Overture, for this suggests that his coda can create closure even without any preceding music logically connected with it—the coda is thus treated like a disembodied *telos*, as free-floating closure, waiting for something to close. (Of course, we would presumably remember hearing this music as the coda of the overture when we meet it again at the end of the drama and would thus make a logical connection, but the Victory Symphony is still detached from any immediately relating music.) But what is the effect of this music when heard as the actual coda of the *Egmont* Overture? What kind of closure does it achieve in that context? And how does Beethoven's overture compare to Goethe's drama as a dramatic process?

The overture has an outwardly simple design: a slow introduction leads to an Allegro with two prominent themes; this section serves as the exposition of a compact sonata form, whose recapitulation is followed by the triumphant Victory Symphony. It is commonly thought that the Victory Symphony coda bears little relation to the rest of the overture, thus acting as an analogy to Goethe's ending (having the function, if not the character, of an epilogue). Dahlhaus, for example, argues that the lack of motivic relations between the Victory Symphony and the rest of the overture separates the former from the latter in a manner that mirrors the form of Goethe's drama.[41] As we shall see, however, Ernst Oster finds the motivic relations that Dahlhaus denies, triumphantly asserting the thematic integrity of the entire overture and the paradigm of motivic development.[42] And Martha Calhoun has shown how the Victory Symphony acts as the harmonic goal of the overture: much of the end of the recapitulation is in $D\flat$, and the return to F right before the coda is not only a weak arrival but is radically cut off (with Egmont's head, if one credits the usual programmatic reading of this moment).[43] Calhoun goes on to interpret Beethoven's overture as a subversive text to Goethe's drama, in that it neglects the personal drama of Egmont and Klärchen and overemphasizes the—in Goethe's version only implied—victory of the Dutch over the Spanish.[44]

It is hard not to hear Beethoven's coda as a culminating outcome of the overture, regardless of the lack of an explicit thematic link signaling the culmination of a thematic process. For one thing, the coda creates its own dramatic process by beginning with a dramatically intensified pedal point on the dominant. (It is interesting to observe that Beethoven pares this pedal point down to two bars when used as the Victory Symphony. Evidently the point there is to get to the climactic music as quickly as possible, whereas the coda to the overture needs more dominant preparation.) Its climactic resolution is both harmonic (resolution of C^7 onto F) and modal (transformation of F minor to F major). Whereas Schiller has criticized Goethe's ending for being a *salto mortale*, a tumbler's leap from dramatic decorum into the world of opera, Beethoven's ending, even without the usual thematic integration of a heroic-style coda, is heard as no such fatal inconsistency. Perhaps the overture is a little closer to drama than to symphony, just as Goethe's play is a little closer to opera than to drama, but its symphonic features are consequential. Thus Calhoun is right about the subversive nature of Beethoven's *Egmont* when compared to Goethe's;

because the music of the drama's apotheosis acts in the overture also as the harmonic closure of the preceding music, what is only a political afterthought in the drama appears to become the whole story in the overture. In Goethe's play there is no comparable sense of something within the play generating its own closure; indeed, its end arrives *ex machina*, and there are too many other issues (like the fates of Ferdinand and Brackenburg) that find no ultimate resolution.

On the other hand, the claims of music are different from the claims of drama, and any comparison of the two is by nature problematic: in music, the force of closure is more straightforward and self-contained. There is more closure in the very syntax of music than could ever be achieved in a drama; the only dramas that come close are full-blown comedies, in which everyone gets married off at the end, and fullblown tragedies, in which everyone dies. In fact, we could even argue that there is no closure in any other art form—or any other form of human activity—that satisfies quite like a final cadence in tonal music. No other art form can manage anything like the trick of ending with the material conditions of the beginning—on a strong beat and with the tonic harmony—and yet with the opposite effect of closing rather than opening. A weak version of such a thing can be claimed for the "frame story," or for the use of frame in visual art; but in these cases, the frame itself is just that, a frame, and is not a fundamental condition of the entire work. (The frame of the musical experience is, as Edward T. Cone has argued, silence.[45]) And there is no closure in music quite like that of the Beethovenian coda. Beethoven monumentalizes the inherent phenomenological effect of cadential closure in such a way as to ratify resoundingly the burgeoning theories of organic wholeness and the art work as closed system. More important, closure becomes culmination, and music is conceived of as a developmental, end-oriented process.

Our eagerness for this culmination scenario is such that we are ready to read all Beethoven's codas in this way and to assume that extroverted closure of this sort automatically means inner organic growth. As mentioned earlier, Ernst Oster attempts to save the problematic coda of the *Egmont* Overture through the use of a motivic analysis reliant on Heinrich Schenker's theory of underlying voice-leading. Oster reveals that a key motive in the introduction and Allegro, a descending fourth, is inverted triumphantly in the Victory Symphony section. His analysis reflects the common obsession with Beethoven's heroic style: the close association of thematic—or in the case of Oster, motivic—material with a dramatic protagonist. In Oster's analysis, the motive of a descending fourth "frees itself from tragic somberness" and "emerges victoriously" as an ascending fourth.[46] Oster himself takes on a triumphant tone when he reveals previously unnoticed motivic connections between the coda and the body of the overture; now the overture can fit the paradigm. It seems the process we want to hear in the *Egmont* Overture is singleminded and teleological, despite Beethoven's setting it up as an overture with victorious coda. This is the way we tend to interpret all Beethoven's heroic pieces, and although it works grandly for some (like the *Eroica* and the Fifth Symphony), it is hardly the whole story for others.

For what is the effect of the *Egmont* coda? How does Beethoven present his major key resolution? This is not simply a case of the major key triumphantly superseding the minor.

Consider first the way he projects the most distinctive feature of F major in this context, namely the pitch A, its major third (see examples 4.1a and b). Beethoven gives this A the most garish treatment imaginable: it is initially heard at the top of the texture marking all the strong beats (it is the goal tone of the dramatic upward sweep that coalesces over the introductory dominant pedal point), making its point with the penetratingly shrill voice of the piccolo. This repetitive harping on A, as the signal of F major, has an effect more brassy than grand, more insistent than commanding. And this without even mentioning the most obvious aspects of this passage: the rhythmic foreshortening, where the same figure is heard twice as many times in the second two bars as in the first two (295–98), its "horn-fifth" harmonization, and the high-register string tremolos. All these elements go beyond boisterous to something less buoyant and certainly more forced, reaching a kind of tantrum of joy.

In the next section of the coda, starting in bar 307, some of the chromatic tones from F minor ($E\flat$ and $D\flat$, along with $F\sharp$), instead of being gloriously transformed and assimilated, are neutralized, made to serve the brutish cheer of a banal cadential progression repeated over and over, with every fourth step landing once again on the tonic. Of course the orchestral build-up of this progression is the greater part of the glory here, yet it is just this combination—orchestral crescendo and harmonic banality—that creates the special atmosphere of this coda, its blunt assertion of culmination. Can all this enforced bluster really give us the same feeling of triumph as, say, the ending of the third overture to *Leonore*? The piccolo line at the very end is an ironic emblem of our reception of this coda, for it can be heard both as a shrill accompaniment to the generally hollow feeling of the festivities and as a summation of the story of the motive of the fourth so crucial to Oster—thus the piccolo is simultaneously the locus of the coda's culminating force and that of the ironic undermining of that culmination (see example 4.2).

Example 4.1a. Beethoven, *Egmont* Overture: measures 287–99.

Example 4.1a, continued

Example 4.1a, continued

Example 4.1a, continued

Example 4.1a, continued

Example 4.1b. Beethoven, *Egmont* Overture: measures 307–17.

Example 4.1b, continued

Example 4.1b, continued

Example 4.1b, continued

Example 4.2. Beethoven, *Egmont* Overture: measures 341–end.

Example 4.2, continued

This brings us close to a disturbing ambiguity lurking in Beethoven's heroic codas. The culminating act of a thematic drama is attended by, indeed effected by, conventionally unpromising gestures made monumental: the banal is raised, indeed apotheosized. We recall that the coda of the *Eroica* first movement features a version of the theme that would appear impossibly banal if heard at the outset of the movement but that serves splendidly as the ultimate monumentalization of the theme. Are we being told that all such consummation is underwritten by banality, and thus can represent but a fool's paradise? Or are we only ready, here at the end of an engaging and continually intensifying process, for the grand simplicity of the truly important, the truly sublime? That we are hard pressed to answer these questions, or even to distinguish with confidence between cases in which the banal is inflated into the monumental and those in which the monumental is deflated by the banal, signals the presence of a fundamental irony.

On the other hand, it is tempting simply to assert the privilege of naiveté for the *Egmont* coda—Beethoven splashing around in the sounds of triumph, reveling in the major third and the pleasures of an unproblematic dance around tonic. But there is no critical gain to be had from asserting naiveté and leaving it at that; I would argue instead that Beethoven's coda is ironically poised between naively enacted celebration and the narration of celebration. There is a sense that we are being told about closure even while we are closing, that the artifice of rhetoric and the sincerity of enactment are two sides of the same thing. In other words, Beethoven's coda is not just closing; it is commenting on the act of closing by overemphasizing and monumentalizing the features—harmonic, thematic, and sonic—of musical closure.

This irony of simultaneous enactment and narration is made possible only when the Victory Symphony is used as a real coda. In the setting of Goethe's drama, the Victory Symphony simply enforces closure; within the overture, the Victory Symphony can be heard both to culminate a musical process and to enforce closure ironically, in the way it is made to culminate the preceding music. Goethe's drama only appropriates music, using it as a sign of closure and consummation; the same music when heard in Beethoven's overture expresses a much richer state of consciousness, in which culmination is simultaneously enacted and narrated. Thus the *Egmont* coda, by nature of its dual provenance in the drama and the overture, can serve as a heightened case of an important aspect of all Beethoven's heroic-style codas: they are similarly underdetermined in relation to what has preceded (too much closure for the preceding music) and overdetermined in regard to their own means (all the parameters work together and to such an extent that the actual closure is overdetermined). As such they strongly narrate the form, not only culminating the movements to which they are attached but standing apart from them, adding "The End" to their respective stories in such a way that one leaves the experience convinced that "The End" is more than some arbitrary cutoff point: it is actually present, in potentia, from bar 1. The process of narration and the story being told become one.

IV

> Mit dem Selbstbewusstseyn sind wir also nun in das einheimische Reich der Wahrheit eingetreten.[47]
>
> (Through the consciousness of self we have now entered the native realm of truth.)
>
> (*Hegel*, The Phenomenology of the Spirit)

The claim that Beethoven's heroic-style music simultaneously enacts and narrates needs to be worked out carefully here, for it leads to a larger claim that will be instrumental in showing not only how this music expresses the deeper agenda of its age but why it continues to inform our musical thought at a fundamental level, namely, the claim that Beethoven's music successfully models human self-consciousness. The works we have been concerned with enact an affirmative model of the development of self while projecting a sense of awareness of the full course of that development.

That Beethoven's music is at all a form of narrative can no longer be lightly assumed; thanks to the work of Carolyn Abbate we are now concerned less with the idea that music represents a sonic encoding of some narrative plot than with the act of narration itself and the diegetic distance from the story that it implies.[48] Abbate has claimed that music has few instances of this sort of diegetic distance, and that these are found chiefly in the operatic literature.[49] And it no doubt seems counterintuitive that the "composer's voice" in this music—perhaps the most extroverted in all of music—should be heard as that of a distanced narrator. Yet I would argue that in works like those of Beethoven's middle period, the internalized use of sonata form makes possible this effect of narration.

This is not the same as saying that the narrative thrust of such movements is in the manipulation of the standard plot of sonata form; rather the "standard plot" of sonata form has now become an underlying dynamic pattern whose security in the minds of composers and listeners allows it to accommodate and carry inflected realizations. These may include the heroic quest, or the cyclical eternal return, or the pastoral, or parodies of any of these. In other words, whereas composers like Haydn arguably narrate by means of the superficial features of sonata form (ordering, etc.), wittily playing with the outward features of convention and presenting the same story again and again with different tellings, Beethoven treats the form as an underlying dynamic capable of supporting different stories (heroic, etc). If Haydn narrates sonata form itself, Beethoven narrates through sonata form. He has internalized it to the point where its reality lies not at the level of formal ordering but at a more underlying level of dynamic pattern. This is the gist of Beethoven's relation to classical style: the conventions of sonata form are now deep enough and strong enough to contain an unprecedented level of drama. As I claimed in chapter 2, he can thus overrun the superficial boundaries of the style, in order to mark the larger underlying boundaries more emphatically. When he marks these boundaries with his own incomparable drama (as in the case of the *Eroica* horn call, or the famous parallel harmonies at the outset of the coda to that movement) he is in effect narrating them, for such moments rise above the musical texture and assert the presence of Beethoven's unique and unmistakable voice, now heard to speak across the present moment, telling of things like imminent return, or glorious consummation.

The heroic journey, or quest plot, heard in the *Eroica* first movement is projected through a sense of ever-present line but also, and more important, through a series of crux points that enunciate and narrate the form. The outset of the journey is marked by an exposition that is unstable and developmental; the famous C♯ of bar 7 has always been treated as a crux that speaks of future events. Thus this section is clearly marked as a beginning, as music that demands continuation. The crisis point of the journey is marked by the huge climax and supremely reactive "new theme" in the development section. Return home is marked by the famous horn call; thanks to the dramatic reduction of the musical texture and the horn call's incantatory whisper, the recapitulation is heard to impend and becomes a highly dramatic resolution. Renewal is suggested by the softened voice apparent in the beginning of the recapitulation—carried by the *dolce* horn and flute solos and the enchanted tonal juxtaposition of F major and D♭ major (the result of a very different treatment of the opening C♯)—which then leads to a climactic thematic statement in the tonic. Apotheosis, the final stage of the journey, is marked by the parallel harmonies announcing the coda. All these crux points, while appearing on the surface as striking disjunctions, mark the nodal points of the underlying form as stations in an archetypal heroic journey.

But the real heft of the heroic style does not simply reside in this act of narration through crux points of a now underlying and dynamic formal impulse but rather obtains in the perception that this same act of narration has the immediacy, or presence, of enactment. The perceived presence of a pressurized linear trajectory belies the notion of diegesis and tends toward enactment itself. And yet the very presence of such a line indicates a way of telling the form—the form is now secure enough to act as a ground over which an energetic sense of line could run from a beginning through a middle to an end without the danger of becoming an open-ended process so idiosyncratic and willful as to be uncommunicative. Thus the engaging quality of the heroic style, with which we have been concerned throughout this study, perhaps resides ultimately in the music's special status as both a telling and a presence or enactment. I would like to refer to this quality as a "telling presence."

For here Beethoven is poised impossibly at both the internalization and externalization of the forms of the classical style. Form in this music appears to develop as the processes of the thematic surface develop—sonata form is projected not as a matter of external convention but as the product of inner generation; it is fully internalized, made part of the genetic entelechy of the music. This accounts for Adorno's observation about the merger of subject (thematic dimension) and object (formal dimension) in Beethoven's middle-period music. And yet the extrovert voice of this music speaks from outside the formal process, across that process, or of that process. This is perhaps most perceptible at the coda, as we have seen, but can be heard throughout a movement as that pressurized utterance that tells of beginnings, middles, and ends. This voice is both a distanced, narrating entity, speaking from a place beyond the moment-by-moment temporal enactment of the music, and the very sound of that music's ongoing process. It is both the voice of Goethe's chariot, pulled by the steeds of Time, and of Hegel's realm of absolute knowledge, imagining those steeds and their journey.

Thus Beethoven's heroic style merges the Goethean enactment of becoming with the Hegelian narration of consciousness. The merger of internalized and externalized sonata form was probably conceivable only at the historical moment inhabited by Beethoven. After Beethoven, sonata form could no longer be internalized in the same way, and it became a more externally adopted process, the mark of a classicist sensibility.[50] And before Beethoven, the form was perhaps not yet fully internalized, in the sense described in the preceding, where it could become more an underlying dynamic than a surface procedure. Sonata form in the hands of Haydn or Mozart, with its tempered combination of drama and balance, plays well as a product of German classicism, where these concerns are otherwise most notably apparent in the superbly constructed dramas of Schiller. But Beethoven's use of the form accentuates the drama of "becoming" while introducing the Hegelian perspective of a narration of a completed history, and thus brings together the underlying concerns of a larger period of cultural time, the period I have loosely designated as the *Goethezeit*.

The ultimate and abiding effect of this simultaneity of enactment and distanced telling, of story and narrator, is one of irony. Of course, all three of the great classical-style composers, Mozart, Haydn, and Beethoven, project an ironic presence, for they share, as a given, the self-conscious use of the conventions of sonata form. In Haydn the listener is teased by witty commentaries on his or her expectations. Ironic distance flickers most spiritedly at the joins and ends of the form—in false recapitulations, trick endings, cadencelike openings. Mozart's irony lies in the way convention is made into rare beauty, the banal and transparently everyday made profound, marmoreal, distant.[51] In what is perhaps the ironic tour de force of the eighteenth century, Mozart's *Così fan tutte*, the screw turns even further. Here beauty seems to countenance deceit, or, put more strongly, to be the very countenance of deceit. What could be more heart-stoppingly exquisite than the farewell trio in E major, whose gentle waves seem to lap at our souls from some great communal sea of human sorrow and hope? And yet it is here that the author of the basest of deceptions, Don Alfonso, sings as beautifully as the rest.[52]

The irony in Beethoven's heroic style is paradoxically less noticeable because it is in fact more a fundamental condition of the music, less a scrim than the stage itself. His merger of enactment and narration reveals a deep kinship with the irony of the German romantics: when the self becomes all-consuming, such that the world is henceforth defined in terms of the self's rhythms (or musical form is defined in terms of the life of a theme), there is yet a distance from one's self when that self is so conceived, a systemic irony always aware that one is, after all, narrating oneself. Of course such irony sometimes breaks out crassly, revealing a chasm between the author and his work, unstringing all sense of identification, as in the comic appeals to the audience in Tieck's *Verkehrte Welt*, which deliberately destroy the suspension of disbelief, or in the stupefying juxtapositions of sublime and grotesque in Beethoven's late music. This type of heavy-handed irony is often styled as romantic irony proper.[53] But the more pervasive irony of this period rests in the simultaneous assumption that the world is all that the self is (to pervert Wittgenstein's fine formula) and yet that one can stand apart from this master narrative, in fact, must stand apart from it in order to narrate it, or even to be aware of it. This is why the trope of narration plays so well in studies of nineteenth-century culture: the very act of self-awareness, of self-consciousness, is a type of narration. And all such narration is fundamentally ironic.[54]

The telling presence of Beethoven's heroic style—the narration that somehow enacts, the enactment that somehow narrates—gives this music its special place as the deepest keynote of the *Goethezeit*. For the quality of a perspective simultaneously subjective and objective allows the heroic style its particular presence as a modeling of ironic self-consciousness, while the narrated projection of an end-oriented process both linear and cyclical (and thus spiral) expresses the ethos of the self as hero—whether as an individual realizing a personal destiny or as the cosmos coming to know itself. The great and defining experiment of the age of both Goethe and Hegel was to model human consciousness in this way. Beethoven simply does it best.

Chapter Five

BEETHOVEN HERO

> Mit Tönen kann man die Menschen zu jedem Irrtume und
> jeder Wahrheit verführen: wer vermöchte einen
> Ton zu *widerlegen*?
>
> (With music one can seduce others into any error and any
> truth: who would be able to *contradict* a tone?)
>
> (*Nietzsche*, Fröhliche Wissenschaft, §106)

I

PRESENCE has been the fundamental metaphor applied to Beethoven's heroic style from the beginning; at issue is the feeling that when one listens to Beethoven's music one is in the presence of something more than music. I have argued that this presence is essentially a telling presence, that the music projects the voice and authority of a narrator but also the compelling sweep of an enacted narrative. Reception tradition has generally focused on the enactment of narrative in these works. Programmatic interpretation constitutes only the most explicit acknowledgment of this propensity, and it represents one of the cardinal ways of accounting for the sustained intensity of Beethoven's line, by giving it the causal tug of an often familiar, and even mythically potent, plot. Other less explicitly representational narratives include latter-day notions of fundamental line and structure as well as thematic process and resolution. Beethoven's telling presence is the common denominator throughout the entire reception history of his music.

At the outset of this history, the element of voice predominates over that of narrative. E.T.A. Hoffmann hears a transcendently authoritative voice, issuing from the "spirit realm" and inspiring awe and fear. This voice sings to the romantic soul and awakens within it an endless longing. A. B. Marx hears the Beethovenian presence as that of a transcendent *Idee*, an ideal essence that is more concrete than Platonic, that must unfold and take on temporal life in order to be understood. The voice begins to narrate. Specifically, Marx claims in effect that this music speaks of what is highest and deepest about humanity (such as the human spirit's quest for freedom), and that it is distinguished from earlier "sentimental" music insofar as it expresses universal states of soul rather than personal feelings.[1] Beethoven's voice thus assumes a distinctly moral force; with Marx we pass from the ethos of romanticism to something closer to that of the Biedermeier. Wagner heard a philosophical depth and motivation in Beethoven's symphonic works; one of the characters in "Ein glücklicher Abend" imagines that Beethoven takes up and organizes the plan of a symphony in accordance with a specific philosophical theme before he consults his fantasy in order to invent musical themes.[2]

Our own century has all but eschewed the transcendental trace Beethoven left in the nineteenth century. (Réti's work stands as a rule-proving exception.) Instead, Beethoven's voice is heard either to encode a message from another medium or to stand above (or below) the surface of the music as a metamusical commentator. Representing the first of these positions, Arnold Schering believed that each piece encodes a specific and unique literary source. His so-called literary keys purportedly unlock Beethoven's musical works, in the name of interpretation. Whatever one feels about the dubious hermeneutic grounding of Schering's assumptions concerning musical meaning and the role of the critic,[3] one gets a sense from his work that Beethoven was so secure with the underlying formal procedures of his style that he could tell different stories more readily than previous composers—hence there could be heroic narratives, antiheroic narratives, buffa escapades, and so on. In recent years this propensity to tell sonata form in varying ways has been read rather differently. Carl Dahlhaus and Ludwig Finscher have argued that the predominant feature of Beethoven's so-called "new way" is the appearance of a metastylistic agenda.[4] Introductions take on some of the functions of expositions and vice versa. Second themes seem more themelike and expository than first themes. Developmental passages may appear in any section of the form. Instead of telling stories from the literary medium, Beethoven's voice is heard to tell about music itself, commenting specifically on its formal functions.

As do all commanding figures in intellectual history, Heinrich Schenker combines various signal trends of his age within one sweeping vision. His theory shares features of Schering's work and adumbrates aspects of Dahlhaus's thought. Like Schering, he conceives of Beethoven's music as having an essential meaning that can be discovered. "Finally, after years of misguided hermeneutic fantasies, I am about to reveal the true content of this work": we would have no trouble attributing these words to either Schenker or Schering; both have said many versions of the same thing. (Whereas Schenker may be said to merge aesthetic meaning with essentialist theory, Schering merges aesthetic meaning with history.[5]) And like Dahlhaus, Schenker grants to Beethoven a metamusical voice; as we saw in chapter 3, he hears the Fifth Symphony tell about the *Urlinie*, about the fundamental presence of line with which he would henceforth identify and characterize all musical masterworks. The Fifth Symphony thus enunciates the primal plot for all great music. Nor has the authority of that symphony diminished in the work of Rudolph Réti; there it dictates a master scenario of thematic development and resolution. The power of this plot moves Réti to declare that music thus acts as an "allegory to all creation."[6]

It is clear that all these critics and analysts hear this music speak of different things, depending on their own intellectual predilections; yet they all hear the music as indeed saying something beyond itself, and are all equally caught up in the effort to determine what that might be. In chapters 2 and 4 we started to explore what it is in the way we take in Beethoven's heroic-style music that establishes its telling presence. We concluded in chapter 2 that it has to do with a sustained line heard to be both weighty and inexorable, initiated with an exhortation, continued with wavelike momentum, and concluded with monumental asseveration. In addition, there are moments in the music that I have called crux points (like the horn call in the *Eroica*), which seem to introduce an extra dimension, standing above the musical landscape in something like supratemporal space. The voice vivifying these moments acts both as an uncanny incursion and as a key stage in an unfolding process, often narrating an impending return or conclusion. In the case of the heroic-style coda, the sense of an ending is both rhetorically narrated and phenomenologically enacted: we feel both an oratorical peroration and the culmination of our own journey with the piece.

As I argued in chapter 4, this combination of narration and enactment models self-consciousness, merging the aggrandizing impulse of German Idealism with the dynamic polarity of Goethean speculative empiricism. It also helps us understand why this music plays to one's sense of self: an external presence is simultaneously heard as an internal presence.[7] Yet the external presence heard in the heroic style is one of imposing authority, often inspiring the sense of awe associated with the sublime. Consider again the opening of the Fifth Symphony, or of the *Eroica*, or that of the *Egmont* Overture, or the *Coriolan*. These openings are all classic instances of an authoritarian voice: they assume the tone of exhortation, of imperious command. Why do we identify with this transcendental presence? Why has it become so closely associated with our sense of self, as opposed to remaining forever remote, as a revered, or even feared, other? If I may be allowed a dialectical resolution, I would suggest that the music manages both to model the self and to inspire the awe due to the sublime. The effect of this music on the listener goes beyond being seized by an overmastering presence, which is a typical eighteenth-century way of describing the experience of the sublime. Instead it demonstrates, far more convincingly than Hegel, that the developing self can indeed be a thing sublime, that the rhythm of individual struggle can become the rhythm of the *Weltall* (the cosmos) and vice versa. This constitutes the fierce joy of this music, its apparent proof of the Idealist conceit that solipsistic self-absorption can in fact be a way to construct and experience one's relation to all things else. The heroic style offers a concrete locus of the merger of the individual and the universal; as such it has been granted the talismanic power of a philosopher's stone.

The self thus appears to partake of universal experience. But this is no meditative *unio mystica*, no dissolution of the ego; if anything it is a celebration of the ego, a universalizing of the ego. The experience of Beethoven's combination of uncanny voice and heroic trajectory takes the listener beyond the musical raptures of a Joseph Berglingen, beyond passive intimations of infinity. The music instead seems to animate and empower its listeners; its role may be compared to that of a Homeric god inspiriting the being of some mortal warrior on the plains of Troy. The god becomes a mortal; the mortal becomes a god— and the listener experiences an *aristeia*, a crowning moment of triumph and exaltation. One becomes literally enthused, flushed with the interiorized presence of the sublime. Within the context of the *Goethezeit*, and, by extension, of the entire modern era, the presence within the heroic style amounts to a theophany in the Age of Self.

The self is made sublime, the sublime given a history. For the vaunted wholeness of the heroic-style work is not just the inhering integrity of a self-sufficient object, or of an objectified, sufficient self. Wholeness is instead a result of *completion*, the result of an all-consuming temporal process brought to unequivocal closure. Other music of this period (or of any period) rarely gives the same feeling of the utter exhaustion of its means. The phenomenological feeling of unequivocal closure leads the listener to infer material exhaustion of the composition—nothing else could possibly remain to be said. At first blush, this type of closure may seem to work against an identification with the temporal life of the self, for one can never be directly conscious of one's own existence as a self-generating and self-consuming process. Instead we tend to imagine the self as a subject characterized by an inhering integrity in the face of external changes, a self that was somehow always there and always will be there. The heroic style engages the listener at this level (that of the inherent self moving through temporal existence) and then allows him or her to experience this subject as having a definitive beginning and end, as self-sufficient completion. This is precisely the force of this music, the warrant of its sovereignty in the aesthetic sphere. Through the process of identification offered by this music, the self can be directly experienced as a whole; it identifies with and experiences a culmination that is not open-ended, that leaves no loose ends. Thus the self is made to seem universal; the self and its progress is all there is. In addition, the trajectory of such a self is definitively closed and therefore inviolate. Wholeness and closure have long formed the very definition of the aesthetic experience and of our ethical view of ourselves—this is why organicism is really an ethical position. And it can be no surprise that music—and this music in particular—became both the exemplary aesthetic experience and the exemplary expression of the unmediated self.

It is important to keep in mind that Beethoven's heroic-style music, throughout these many years of its hegemony, has not been thought of primarily as some sort of musical analogue to contemporaneous conceptions of a dynamic and all-encompassing self. Yet uncovering the values this music shares with other cultural expressions of the *Goethezeit* yields more than an academically motivated exercise in historicist analysis; indeed, it leads to an understanding of a constitutive moment of the entire reception history of the heroic style. The persistent and profound influence of this one style on the history of musical thought, its status as the embodiment of Western art music, expressed through the imposing theories whose first principles are based on it, came to pass because a particularly compelling concept of self was animated by Beethoven's music and through it seems ever renewable. The experience of this music has been primarily an ethical experience. How else could it have assumed pride of place in the musical-theoretic thought of the next two centuries? How else could it have come to stand for Music itself? The investment that the musical community has made in Beethoven's music is not one of aesthetic predisposition so much as one of ethical faith. This music has remained attached to the experience and integrity of self in a way that other contemporaneous expressions of the self (such as German classical drama and Idealist philosophy) have not.

The Viennese classical style in general has been associated throughout its reception with an affirmative ethical worldview. Critics often describe the classical symphony as if it were a public oration, an appeal to the better nature of humanity. James Webster links the rhetorical power of the classical style to "deep ethical concerns" and attributes both rhetoric and ethos to the profound coherence of the style: "[Haydn's influence on Beethoven] also encompassed the art of projecting strong rhetorical impulses and deep ethical concerns (which

Beethoven had from the beginning) in musical works which simultaneously exhibit the greatest craft and the profoundest coherence—which generate their rhetoric and their morality precisely by means of that coherence."[8] The effect of the classical-style symphony on a large audience is perhaps analogous to that proposed by Schiller for the theater. In his essay "Die Schaubühne als eine moralische Anstalt betrachtet" (1784) he regards theater as the most effective way to convey a moral education; the audience is united in sympathy, and something like universal brotherhood is felt. This would come to be particularly true for Beethoven's symphonic music, which, when understood as a moral force unmoored to a specific dramatic situation, seems an even more potent way to perfect a universal moral education: its lack of specificity coupled with the monumentality of its expression lend it the aura of universality. If the classical-style symphony registered originally and primarily as an ethical statement, Beethoven's symphonies were to make that statement unimpeachable.

The ethical dimension of this music, or of music in general, has tended to lose its overt expression in the work of critics and analysts of our own century. Precisely because such ethical content is felt so universally, so "vulgarly," it was readily perceived as the lowest common denominator of the music's influence. Thus the values of self we have been enumerating became submerged to the point of being literally beneath notice. But because of this, they have assumed an unspoken, unquestioned, and no less fundamental place. Through their translation into the theoretical values of tonal music or of the tonal masterwork, they in fact continue to control the discourse surrounding not only these works but most others. Thus in this one venue, in the ways we configure musical coherence, we have never abandoned the defining values of the modern self concept, those of the *Goethezeit*. Their translation into more acceptable analytical and critical metalanguages is not a matter of resuscitation, of sustaining life in the hopelessly moribund—if anything, these values are even stronger now in their controlling role as the unquestioned a priori conditions of the way we tend to construct the musical experience.

Why has this valued concept of self found sanctuary in our ways of musico-aesthetic thought? We may find an answer in the role accorded to music since the romantic age: namely, that music is a form of communication beyond, or at least apart from, speech. Music is thus a safe language for our now secret concept of self—by claiming that music cannot speak, we can let music say what we no longer feel comfortable putting into words. What now seems an unfashionable emphasis on self and freedom in a drama by Schiller can stir us still in a Beethoven symphony. Safely removed from speech, music allows us to escape to older, more comforting notions of the centrality of self. These notions take on the feel of preverbal truths, fundamental and secure from question. We keep them alive like old religious beliefs; they are like the *lares* and *penates* of the ancient Romans, the household gods to whom we have recourse when all the words of the day have been spoken. Music can absorb our innermost projections of self, can permit us to continue to construe selfhood as heroism, existence as quest. The values of self instantiated by Beethoven's heroic style have long been outmoded philosophically, shucked away as the absurd wrappings of what is now thought to be an absent center. Our continued acceptance in the musico-aesthetic marketplace of such defunct philosophical currency is an indication that such currency still buys us something we value, something no longer dreamt of in our philosophy.

II

Beethoven dem Helden

(To Beethoven the hero)

(*Dedication page of Schenker's analysis of the* Eroica *Symphony*)

The story of the overcoming self is a powerful underlying force in the way we have come to construct not only Beethoven's music but all of Western tonal music. It seems we want our music to go somewhere, to complete a process, to integrate theme and form, subject and object, and to strive forth to a momentous and necessary conclusion. Although the heroic style quickly became a master trope, it is only one of the stories Beethoven tells.

As a striking example of similar means leading to very different ends, compare the opening of the Fifth Symphony to that of the Sixth. Motivic development and repetition are foremost in both; both start with a thematic motto followed by a fermata on the dominant; the basic motivic rhythm is similar (three eighth notes leading to a downbeat); and both use mostly tonic and dominant, prolonging each of these in turn. But it is the overwhelming differences that one notices: while the Fifth exudes tension, the Sixth is all relaxation.

The rhythmic motive of the Fifth Symphony is not deployed melodically, as it is in the Sixth. By isolating the rhythm in the opening motto and then subdividing the following phrases into units constructed of the same rhythm, the music of the Fifth profiles the motive as a charged rhythmic event. The opening four bars of the Sixth, on the other hand, develop the motive over a soporific drone, creating a melodic envelope that broadens into a yawn on the half cadence. At the very outset, then, the antithetical character of the two movements is unmistakably established: if the Fifth is a call to action, the Sixth is a call to inaction, an invitation to daydream.

In the harmonic world of the Fifth, tonic and dominant prolongations become powerful monolithic poles, opposed yet mutually determining. By contrast, the prolonged harmonies in the Sixth Symphony feel like slow, relaxed breathing. Tonic and dominant give way to one another; they are not driven to the other pole, as in the Fifth Symphony. These two so very different effects illustrate the range of expression made possible by the fundamental harmonic polarity that underlies classical-style form and syntax.

Finally, motivic repetitions in the Sixth Symphony do not build tension as they do in the Fifth. Those of bars 16 to 25, for example, swell and subside dynamically, but unlike the waves of tension and release throughout the exposition of the Fifth, there is no harmonic arrival at the top of the swell. In general, climaxes in the Sixth Symphony are those of plenitude rather than of arrival or the attainment of a peak. Even the arrival of the first movement's recapitulation is wholly in character with this relaxed treatment. At the culmination of a retransition pedal point on the dominant, the static C (in oboe, horn, and first-violin tremolo) rubs twice in succession against the repeated crest (B♭ and D) of a sequentially ascending line of melodic tenths (this is the only pronounced dissonance in the entire movement). On the third crest of the line, the C resolves retrogressively into a B♭ subdominant harmony, while the tremolos and general rhythmic agitation stop abruptly: this combination of events immediately saps any forward momentum that may have collected in the dominant pedal, or in the development as a whole. The subdominant is prolonged for four bars and then settles onto the tonic F, giving the return of tonic the relaxed feeling of an amen cadence rather than of charged release. Compared to its counterpart in the Fifth Symphony, the entire movement is a miracle of stylistic control; similar elements result in a radically different *Stimmung*. Whereas the Fifth Symphony galvanizes the dramatic potential of classical-style syntax, the Sixth Symphony attenuates that potential, finding in the same syntax an opposite effect.

But we have effectively marginalized works like the "Pastoral" Symphony. As Joseph Kerman notes, even nineteenth-century critics preferred the Fifth Symphony as their premier exemplar of program music, neglecting the much more explicitly programmatic Sixth.[9] Our perennial odd-even parsing of the Beethoven symphonies clearly assigns the weight of value to the odd numbers, while the even numbers seem to be involved in an act of decompression, or in a Goethean regressive stage collecting energy for the next great dramatic leap. In fact, our way of narrating the succession of Beethoven's symphonies bears a close resemblance to the narrations of the *Eroica* first movement discussed in chapter 1, where extended upbeat sections are heard as reactions to active downbeat sections. Not only do we privilege those works that behave in the manner of the heroic style but we have allowed that style to control the way we regard the totality of Beethoven's symphonic oeuvre.

The usual assessment of Beethoven's even-numbered symphonies illustrates yet again how the heroic style has come to dominate our discourse about Western art music. In fact, "dominate" is not even a strong enough word, for it implies that there are real, albeit lesser, alternatives. Yet in this case, even the alternatives are dictated by the heroic style. Everything is either in the manner of the heroic style or not in that manner. Take the case of Schubert. From Theodor Adorno to Carl Dahlhaus and Susan McClary, Schubert's music is consistently characterized as non-Beethovenian rather than as Schubertian. We can hardly begin to talk about Schubert in any other terms: Schubert is non-processual rather than processual; reminiscent rather than goal-oriented; the sense of self projected by his music is permeable rather than autonomous, or feminine rather than masculine, or "gay" rather than "straight."[10] The heroic style controls our thinking to the extent that it dictates the shape of alterity: it is the daylight by which everything else must be night. (Thus it plays well in gendered analyses as the demonized phallocentric standpoint that defines the realm of feminizing musics. These musics simply display the binary opposite of each term of the Beethoven paradigm. With such a model we seem not to have progressed beyond Adam's rib in the way we conceptualize the feminine in tonal music.)

Beethoven's heroic style, while musically representing something like destiny, itself became the destiny of music. Ever since the appearance and widespread acknowledgment of E.T.A. Hoffman's Beethoven criticism and Bettina von Arnim's wishful thinking, the critical tradition has made of Beethoven a hero, a true emancipator of music.[11] Music can now express the higher concerns of the human spirit and not merely its feelings or affects. Music can now speak to the common man of his tribulations and triumphs and not merely to the aristocrat of his ennui and diversions. For Wagner, Beethoven is the great redeemer, he who "speaks in the purest language of all peoples" and through whom "German spirit delivers the spirit of man from profound disgrace."[12] In an abiding conflation of artist and artistic creation, Beethoven himself becomes the heroic miracle, the demigod;

through him, musical art not only gains the expression of human heroism but becomes an engine of deliverance.

Like the great myths, the Beethovenian heroic-style sonata form assumes a place as one of Western culture's master plots. This led subsequent generations of composers and other musical thinkers to treat sonata form more as an ethos than as a method. The attachment of this particular musico-formal procedure to an ethical position severely alters the way other forms are viewed. As a particularly telling example of this, remember the way in which the Beethovenian sonata form acts as the crowning form in A. B. Marx's *Formenlehre*: it is the motivating *telos* of his derivation of all other available forms. These other forms are treated as problematic stages in a process of internalization that leads the budding composer to the form felt to manifest most directly and cogently the musical values of the classical style and, with them, the ethical values of the age. Marx's pedagogical program enlists Beethoven's music (and thus music in general) in the all-important agenda of *Bildung*, a process concerned primarily with the aesthetic and ethical development of self.[13] And just as Marx made Beethovenian sonata form the culminating form in his theory of forms, he made Beethoven represent the culminating stage in his three-stage view of the history of music. For Marx, Beethoven's *Eroica* Symphony initiates a new age of "ideal music," effectively defining—by closing—the cycle of musical history. Thus Marx treats Beethoven as a Hegelian *telos*: only from the vantage point of the end of history can History begin.

It is indeed the *Eroica* Symphony that first won for Beethoven the laurels henceforth accorded to "The Man Who Freed Music." Wagner's protagonist in "Ein glücklicher Abend" explicitly names Beethoven himself as the hero in the musical action of the *Eroica*, and few of us would pester Wagner's claim that the music of this symphony represents an "unerhörte Tat." Through this "unheard-of deed" Beethoven was understood to assume sovereignty of the realm of instrumental music, to become the defining force of Western musical history. Like Wagner, Heinrich Schenker also fancied Beethoven as the hero of the *Eroica*—hence the dedication of his analysis of the *Eroica* to "Beethoven the hero." Schenker's formulation of Beethoven's compositional logic as a "willed and necessary course" ("gemusster wie gewollter Weg") forms a classic definition of the hero: the hero's will becomes necessity.[14] The Greek hero Achilles serves as a ready embodiment of this definition. In the *Iliad* he controls, indeed becomes, the fate of his companions; he is a man yet descends from a god; he is almost invincible; and his rage motivates the action of the entire story.[15] His very name is symbolic of his way of being: Achilles is he who brings *ákhos* (anguish) to the *laós* (troops).[16] Achilles' will becomes necessity for the troops, much like any other force of nature. For Schenker, Beethoven's will becomes musical necessity. The work of the hero is inevitable work; it represents the work of destiny.

Although we have made Beethoven into an Achilles figure, this is not the hero of Beethoven's heroic style with whom generations have identified. That hero is closer to the Trojan Hector, who, as noted in chapter 4, is a father, son, and husband as well as the protector of his homeland. We can more easily identify with his trials and tribulations, for they are our own. Thus in these two figures, Hector and Achilles, human hero and demigod, we may discern the difference between Beethoven's Hero and Beethoven Hero. Doing so may make us more pointedly aware of the ironic interaction between the values instantiated by Beethoven's heroic style and the way in which Beethoven has been installed, through the implicit tenets of our reigning analytical methodologies, as the godlike hero of Western art music, a force of history whose will becomes musical necessity.

The components of the value system that Beethoven's music has come to represent include the central position of man as an individual and the corresponding emphasis on selfhood and self-consciousness, as well as the epistemological change from fixed truth to dynamic truth, as witnessed by the burgeoning influence of Christian eschatology (linear history with a telos), the importance of individual freedom (the ability to create one's own future), the romantic emphasis on becoming, and the change in philosophical method from syllogism to dialectic. In accordance with these values, Western tonal music has been conceptualized under the following normative conditions: music is an individualized process; a musical theme is *energeia* rather than *ergon*, resulting in an emphasis on thematic development (presence of a developing subject); form is the dynamic life process of a theme rather than a fixed a priori schema that must be enacted; closure is unequivocal and usually achieved through a coda that acts as both *summa* and apotheosis.

In making these values paradigmatic, Beethoven reception treats Beethoven himself as the subject of his heroic-style works, bringing him through a similar trajectory of struggle and renewal to a point of apotheosis at which he becomes the destiny of music. Thus the celebration of self implied by the Hector-like subject of the heroic style becomes a form of hero worship, or hero cult, when projected onto Beethoven. The hero we identify with becomes the demigod we serve. One result of this is that analysis and criticism are motivated by a kind of ethical compulsion: one *must* now show how musical works are integral and inviolate, self-generating and self-sustaining systems. In its extreme form, this compulsion dictates that one must demonstrate the necessity of every last note in terms of intrawork conditions.

This is a troubling demand, one that would never be imposed on any other art form (with the possible exception of a short poem). Joseph Dubiel expresses doubt about one's motivation in doing such analysis: "Why anyone would want to respond to a highly esteemed composition by telling a story of how it *had to be* exactly as it was is something of a mystery in any case—a mystery faintly suggestive of some character defect in the storyteller."[17] And Kevin Korsyn has recently suggested what this "character defect" might be:

> One source of ideological mystification is our tendency to use art to recuperate stable and reassuring ideas of selfhood. . . . In Romantic discourse, the work of art acquired something like a soul. It was not merely coherent or unified; it was alive, it had the unity of a mind or consciousness. The encounter with a work of art was conceived more as one between two subjects than as the experience of an object. . . . This "cryptosubjectivity" (as Eagleton calls it) explains our investment in the idea of musical unity: it is often our own unity that is at stake. The organic work of art has become a substitute for the soul.[18]

In insisting on analysis that compulsively demonstrates unity we thus hedge against the arbitrary that is seen as threatening the integrity of our own selves.

This last turn suggests that the Beethovenian prepossession is an unhealthy one. On the one hand we identify in a positive way with a trajectory that actually seems to empower us; but on the other, we have become soulless creatures imposing that trajectory on everything we hear in order to preserve our own now dislocated integrity. It seems that in treating Beethoven as a demigod figure, a force of nature, we value his music as the expression of musical necessity and proceed to use the model of his music as a way to reassure ourselves of our own value, our own necessity. Are the values of self instantiated by the heroic style doomed to play out in this way? Can we subscribe to Beethoven's hero without limiting ourselves to Beethoven Hero?

The values of self have ever been double-edged, and they are implicated in what may well be the central dilemma of human existence and co-existence. Integrity and completion undoubtedly contribute to a healthy self-image. But the element of impermeability implied by these attributes is something else again—a self-concept that fosters self-versus-other is worrying. Historically, the Germanic imperative of the *Aufheben* of the other through the self has had dire consequences. In musical thought, the compulsory ascription of necessity closes the work off, makes of it a fully determined entity, and implies that it has one central meaning as the fully determined product of a causal world. It would seem that anything we identify so deeply with, that implicates our sense of self, must be rendered impermeable—and demonstrating how it qualifies as a product of necessity apparently guarantees such impermeability. Music—the "universal language"—ends up as yet another token of tribal insecurity, part of a sense of identity that must be defended against the encroachments of other tribes, other identities.

The glorious scenario of self merging with Worldself instantiated by the heroic style has never been viable as a way of being in the world. To cast the world in the image of the self is not just a matter of inverting the terms of casting the self in the image of the world: casting the self in the image of the world is a way of constructing the self, whereas casting the world in the image of the self is a way of constructing the other. This is how the feeling of glorious consummation so singularly afforded by Beethoven's heroic style can lead to a collective self impermeable to any other musical impulse. Staying within the terms of our metaphor of the two heroic types, we might say that an internal identification with the human hero (tantamount to a discovery of the hero within us) is not the same as an externalized fetishization of this impulse into the worshiped figure of the demigod. Thus I am not demanding that we must henceforth consider our prepossession by the Beethovenian paradigm to be thoroughly suspect. Instead we must be clear about why we have been prepossessed, why this music has been so important to us. This we have largely failed to do in this century, and I believe that this failure has facilitated the externalization of the heroic impulse, and the concomitant closings of the work, the canon, and musical history.

We may consider the ambivalent reception accorded to the work of Rudolph Réti in musical academia as a telling example of this collective failure to address overtly the ethical dimension of the music we value. The most direct way to gauge the reception of Réti's work is to compare it to that of Schenker's. Despite certain similarities in terms of latency and organically conceived unity, Réti's thematic process was ultimately seen as a far less satisfying and powerful tool than Schenkerian voice-leading analysis. The latter's contrapuntal metalanguage allows him to account for more notes and to make clearer distinctions as to their hierarchical arrangements, whereas the common objection to Réti is that he does not do these things. David Epstein, for example, faults Réti for failing to develop criteria with which analysts may isolate important motivic relations.[19] We deride Réti because his theory is not generalizable, or because he perforce finds what he is looking for,[20] or because the context-free simplicity of his cells virtually guarantees their ubiquity. But strictly speaking, similar charges can be leveled at Schenker: he too finds what he is looking for, and it is simply not possible to formalize his theory (it is arguable whether or not he would even consider his work as a theory in that sense).

Thus these objections strike me as beside the point, as easy observations that hide the real discomfort with Réti. I would instead contend that the primary objection to Réti rests on his need to merge analysis with criticism, which was no doubt seen as a regression in an age that prided itself on overcoming the allegedly sloppy subjectivism of nineteenth-century metaphorical criticism (I say "allegedly sloppy" because many practicing theorists know of such criticism only as the bête noir so consistently tracked down and harassed in Schenker's writings). By being so explicit about the ethical forces that shape his theory, Réti blows everyone else's cover by letting carefully vetted notions of heroism that had been ushered out the back door back in through the front door. He thus makes explicit what Schenker worked hard to repress, what he in fact transferred from the listening experience to the concept of the artist as heroic genius.

Réti's work on thematic process is not so much about how music works as it is a generalization about human nature (specifically the ethical dimension of heroism) and about the ability of music to engage human nature by representing it allegorically. Works gain coherence from human drama; music is about us. In fact, Réti's theory treats musical works as if they were human analogues—built up of living cells, they ultimately evince a life force. On the other hand, the basis of Schenker's work is ostensibly a generalization about Music itself; for Schenker, works gain coherence from the *Ursatz*. Music is about itself, and it is about musical Genius.[21]

Schenker's view has come to be more acceptable than Réti's, for as we pull away from these works historically, our engagement with them is less a matter of their mattering to us and more a matter of their belonging to us, a matter of cultural acquisition, of the guarantee that what we are troubling ourselves with are in fact bona fide masterworks. We collect rather than connect. It is evidently uncomfortable to think that these works could be about us in any significant way; the way to deal with them is to locate their magic in the figure of the artistic genius and then to be able to say why they are works of genius. We thereby gain an association with genius while shedding the responsibility of leaving ourselves emotionally open to our favorite musics. We gain accreditation and lose connection. Réti—no matter how naive and simplistic his evidentiary contrivances, or even his view of human nature—was at least not in the business of kidding himself about what was important to him in Beethoven. The contrary fortunes of Réti and Schenker in this country indicate the extent to which we have shifted from internally identifying with Beethoven's hero to externally identifying with Beethoven Hero.

Making the ethical values of music covert has had a deleterious effect on our ability to keep musical works open and to keep ourselves open in our interactions with these works. Thus we have taken something akin to a religious experience and transformed it into the proselytizing dogma of an established church. We have traded personal connection for professional connections. Doing so, we have let the closure of Beethoven's heroic style close much more than a single movement or an entire symphony: it has gone on to close the musical work and to close music history. Such closure is a powerful force; as a means of getting our minds around things, it allows us to ward off the fear of the unknown. Closure enables us to handle works of art as if they were monads, to collect them, arrange them into canons, to lock them up and keep the key, and then to sell the use of that key to others. Our involvement with music becomes debased, reduced to a form of academic commerce.

Allowing music to speak to us in the first place at the level of the self has thus proved a dangerous business, for it has arguably led to a privileging of one particular way of taking in music, a posture so defensive that it registers almost as a survival tactic—as if to question that one way of hearing music would be to question one's personal integrity. And allowing ourselves to speak about music as if it engaged us at the level of self is also dangerous business, if the fate of Réti is any indication. But neither of these problems—the one a matter of psychological projection, the other of professional repression—should discourage us from doing so. It would be better to recognize that music does indeed play to one's sense of self (that is one of its glories) and that it fosters an identification between individual and universal by being simultaneously public and personal. But does this mean that one of its most significant self-scenarios, and arguably its most flattering one, must of necessity be the measure of all such encounters between music and self? Has the musical process of the heroic style indeed assumed the role of a Kantian transcendental category; has it become an a priori condition of hearing music?

All this begs the question of an alternative perspective. I have argued in the preceding that it is not possible to attain to a true alternative from within the terms of the reigning standpoint; attempts to do so simply appeal to a space that represents the complementary opposite to the heroic-style paradigm. The Beethovenian paradigm still controls the shape of both spaces, and the resulting duality provides but a crude taxonomy. Instead we need to do the seemingly impossible: any real move beyond our situatedness in the Beethovenian paradigm requires that we transcend ourselves, that we somehow rise above the very foundations of our discourse. Making such an effort gains a special poignancy, because the heroic style continues to tell us things we want, and probably need, to hear. And yet, one of the things it has been heard to relate is the effort of overcoming oneself. Thus making the struggle to hear beyond the heroic style may even seem . . . heroic.

EPILOGUE AND PROLEGOMENA

> Wir Deutschen sind Hegelianer, auch wenn es nie einen Hegel gegeben hätte, insofern wir (im Gegensatz zu allen Lateinern) dem Werden, der Entwicklung instinktiv einen tieferen Sinn und reicheren Wert zumessen als dem, was "ist."

> (Even if there had never been a Hegel, we Germans would be Hegelians, inasmuch as we [in contradistinction to the Latin races] instinctively accord a deeper sense and greater worth to that which becomes and evolves rather than to that which "is.")

> (*Nietzsche*, Fröhliche Wissenschaft §357)

By indicating a need to transcend the hegemony of Beethoven's heroic style, we complete a motion; we have moved from understanding a powerful paradigm in the reception of Beethoven's music to critiquing that paradigm in its present, covert, form. As the heading to this section implies, what follows is situated in the space "after the end" and "before the beginning." Where are we left by this journey, and where might we go from here? As a response to these questions I wish merely to initiate a tentative exploration, one motivated not only by what we have to unlearn but also by what we may yet have to learn from Beethoven and from music.

I would like to return to the notion of presence and suggest that as the fundamental metaphor applied to Beethoven's music, it can provide a point of departure for attenuating our urge to make teleological process the exclusive and defining agenda of music. The presence felt in Beethoven's heroic style has always been assumed to involve the growth or destiny of a thematic subject. Presence has come to mean this type of process, an equation that is particularly compelling, for the musical theme that seems to develop is a strong attractor for one's sense of self. But presence, in the way I wish to think of it, is not equivalent to process. It is prior to our sense of process, and it remains after one has taken the measure of process. The story of thematic destiny may well be the most convenient analogue for our feeling that there is an immanent presence, human and engaging, in Beethoven's music and, indeed, in all music. But have we simply talked ourselves into the idea that our engagement with music is due primarily to an unending fascination with its narrative flow? To ask this is to confront our most fundamental assumptions about the musical experience as we deal with it in academic music theory and criticism, assumptions about our epistemological interactions with music.

I hope to have shown that the Beethoven model has helped generate the most influential recent tonal theories, thus shaping the way we construct music. But despite the fact that our preoccupation with temporal process, translated into the values of analytical method, has given us so much to do as musical thinkers, there has always been something naggingly unsatisfactory about accounts of music that read like unfolding dramas, that nudge the listener into a processual texture of implications, expectations, and realizations. Such accounts are controlled by the paradigm of the heroic style: the engaging pull of this style compels us to process all music in a linear fashion, to expect implications to be realized, balances to be disturbed and then restored, closure to be unarguable, endings to be culminations. (And when our expectations along these lines are thwarted, we either denigrate such music or rehabilitate it as the underprivileged alternative.)

Do we really hear music this way? Do we take in music first and foremost as a process, listening cumulatively to each successive stage? In this view of hearing, the model listener would become an expert tracker of the musical process, a kind of tallying contraption that actually gets better with each hearing, like an Artificial Intelligence machine that learns. Among other things, such a perspective asks us to believe that we connect hidden motivic relationships at the far ends of a long work. Now it will not do to doubt the sincerity of those who claim to hear these things: of course one can learn to hear this way; one can learn to hear almost anything, with the appropriate training. But to claim that the fundamental reality of the listening experience has to do with holding musical events in one's mind specifically in order to make connections with later events is at bottom a behaviorist conceit, tantamount to claiming that listening to music is an act of processing. Thus the assumption that music is a cumulative process leads to the assumption of such processing on the part of the listener.

Is the musical experience primarily one of keeping intellectual tabs on a piece of music? This type of hearing certainly exudes a strong force on the "trained listener"—for how often does one make the effort to know where one is in a piece, and characterize that knowledge by the ability to say things like "we are now in the bridge to the second theme group"; and how often does one feel inadequate if one does not know this sort of thing?[22] Such knowledge is like knowing what mile marker you have just passed on the highway, where you are on the map. As a way of marking the experience it can be very fulfilling, indeed, an important part of the journey—but does the ability to place yourself on the map, knowing how far you have come, how far you have left to go, does this type of knowledge take precedence over an awareness of your actual surroundings, of where you in fact are?

I fear that our behaviorist adherence to the process model acts as a way of disengaging, of putting oneself outside the experience in order to keep track of it. Such tracking becomes a strategy of control, a way to stay on top of the piece, as if that were what music invites us to do. Does music invite us to control it? If this were the case, why wouldn't we tire of the experience once we have it under control? The standard answer to this would probably be that we never control it; we never fully know the music but are always and only approaching such knowledge. This is usually expressed with the creaky claim that we hear something new each time we listen. And again listening is characterized as a process, both in the sense of processing information and in the sense of mastering the music through a slow process of many hearings and close study. But is it simply such gradual mastery that keeps us coming back?

Why *do* we keep listening to our favorite musics? This is a very simple question that has never been answered adequately by the process model of the musical experience.[23] Do we really return to experience the music we value in the hope and expectation of hearing something new each time? On the contrary, I believe we return because we hear nearly the same thing each time, because the music becomes for us a magical presence we are eager to experience again. That we are enabled to enjoy an experience repeatedly precisely because it remains basically the same may seem a paradoxical argument, and anti-intellectual in the extreme. But the musical experience is no ordinary experience; I would go so far to suggest that it is closer to the sense of uncanny presence felt by Hoffmann than it is to the tracking of a coherent process, however compelling that process may be.

Of what does this presence consist? Sustained engagement is obviously an important part of such a listening experience, registering as a sense of involvement that persists, in the case of the heroic style, even when we start to hear Beethoven's voice assume a narrator's distance from the musical process. As noted in chapter 2, being engaged by the present moment translates into being faced with a presence. This is the source of the music's authority: the presence in Beethoven's music is simultaneously the uncanny effect of an actual presence and the engaging effect of being acutely alive to the present moment—at bottom these are the same. Music performs this merger of subjective presence and objective presence like nothing else. Thus our expectation of keeping cumulative track of the musical process and then reporting on it is epiphenomenal to the idea of our involvement in the present moment. This is not to deny that any present moment in music takes much of its meaning from what happened earlier and from a sense of what will happen next. But the primary experience is one of presence.

This is why we can listen to the music we value so often: it always brings us to the same place, always invokes the same uncanny presence. Thus it functions like the unveiling of a Grail whose magic is never attenuated, no matter how much one analyzes its details. The musical experience seems to become timeless, because it involves a repeatable sense of place, of presence. In other words, the thrill of listening to music may be more a matter of simply being in the world of the piece, being in the presence of the piece. This is comparable to the pleasure of watching a favorite movie repeatedly. It is certainly true that we might pick up new details of the unfolding of the plot with each viewing, but what really keeps us there is the world the movie creates: we like being there.

Yet from this view of music as a seemingly timeless place that can be revisited again and again with similar effect we should not conclude that the sense of presence I have been arguing for is an essential, unchanging part of a piece of music, independent of the listener. It should go without saying that such presence depends on our presence, and is not the same for everyone: it is profoundly individual yet not hermetically so, otherwise we would not be able to communicate with one another about it. Its integrity as an experience that appears to stay nearly the same, time after time, is due to the integrity of our own selves. And its communicability is contingent upon the fact that as citizens of the same era and tradition, we are not so different from one another as we might imagine. This is how music can tell us about ourselves without convincing us to make ourselves impermeable, and how music can tell us about each other, can provide an opportunity to connect with each other. We have all felt its presence.

I think we have been in the business of telling ourselves that process tracking is the main reason we are engaged by music—it is an all too available scenario, and its ready attachment to one particularly compelling set of values of the self gives it a formidable pedigree. There can be no doubt that process is indeed important as a means of coherence and significance, to the degree that what we call musical syntax is impossible to separate from musical meaning and arguably creates the possibility of such meaning. But I am suggesting that such process is not the exclusive attraction of music, not its ontological bottom line. If it were, then any music's presence would depend on its use of a syntax comparable to that of functional tonality. Of course the presence of Beethoven's heroic-style music is more likely to seize us and carry us along, because of its emphasis on the potential drama of tonal syntax; this music makes the processual sense of presence a primary issue. That is why the heroic style—the master trope of temporal culmination—quickly became the embodiment of all Western art music, encouraging us to think of all musical presence in terms of a left-to-right cumulative process: like Goethe's telling of the Faust legend, Beethoven's music allows us to believe that salvation is in the striving—and only in the striving.

But maybe we hear even the heroic style more spatially than we would be inclined to admit. Perhaps our experience of this music is just as much one of memorable moments, of "places," as it is one of temporal process. As we have seen, crux points often narrate the form in the heroic style, telling us our place by means of monumentality (e.g., the *Eroica* coda) or a feeling of uncanny incursion (e.g., the *Eroica* horn call). Such moments act as emblematic concentrations of the music's self-aware presence; they stand both within and without the temporal flow. The modeling of self-consciousness we thus detect in the heroic style can offer a view of the musical experience that is not strictly dependent on process and teleological trajectory: the primary experience is of an authoritative presence that becomes an internal voice. Or, in Eliot Handelman's persuasive phrase, music acts as a "secondary consciousness."[24] This transformation of external into internal is brought about by a sense of engaged connection with the present moment: one identifies with the authoritative narrator; one feels oneself both enacting and being enacted; one is empowered. This type of involvement can serve as a general model of our interaction with music. As J. K. Randall puts it, "A listener *undergoes*, or *becomes*, or simply *is*, the music, the utterance: is *within, happening*—not without, observing."[25]

The view of musical presence that I have provisionally suggested and so tentatively sketched carries imposing consequences for the way we conceptualize the musical experience. Rethinking music through the notion of presence and consciousness allows us to disturb the processual, cumulative standpoint to which we have grown so accustomed.[26] If we can thus attenuate the valuation of process, we will be less inclined to read a composer like Schubert as the negative half of a binary opposition, as "process-minus," or Beethoven simply as "process-plus." Instead we will ask why we value the presence of any given music and how we are present in the experience of that music. This is more difficult to do than it may seem, for the attempt to thwart current academic discourse is not to be construed as a refusal to think, in favor of some "be here now" haziness, a "dumbing down" in order to encourage emotional groping—it is rather the challenging business of talking about why music matters to us as something more than the occasion for a specialized branch of academic study. Indeed, this is the most difficult thing to do: although we all understand that music is vitally important to us, we do not yet possess a discourse equal to that understanding.

From the beginning, Beethoven was felt to bring "the human element . . . to the fore as the primary argument of musical art."[27] These words mark a pervasive conviction; they form the cornerstone of Beethoven's place as the principal mythmaker of modern musical thought. Turning away from the processual in favor of a more fundamental sense of presence does nothing to alter Beethoven's stature in this regard. Because his music has always been heard to speak directly to the human condition, we have always heeded Beethoven's voice: in effect, Beethoven made Music's presence felt. Our tendency, in turn, to make his music the very embodiment of Music is a measure of what we want music to be, and what it consequently is for us. Unbelievably enough, it can yet be more.

I began by retelling the story of Beethoven's hero; I end here, having attempted to tell the story of Beethoven Hero. In this story, a demigod granted us the power of closure. We have enjoyed that power, fashioning the musical work (and, with it, the Western musical canon) as a closed world, an enchanted island. And we ourselves have eagerly made a home on that island, lured there by the Siren song of self sung by Beethoven's heroic style, kept there by the continuing pull of a now covert moral imperative, in which duty and inclination seem somehow to merge.

But it is time to dissolve the terms of this our happy thralldom, to forsake the comforts of our insular domain, place our sails in the way of new winds, and face the dangerous promise of an open sea. We must look away from the Work as a world and toward the World in the work. Only then may we acknowledge that we interact with music in ways that speak of so much more than the singular experience of the heroic style, however appealing its solipsistic culmination and completion of self, ways that speak of human identities as broadly conceived as the world is wide. And this is how we may best continue to honor Beethoven Hero, by staying in touch with the hero within ourselves and others, the hero whose presence is music.

NOTES

INTRODUCTION

1. This list grows somewhat if we include earlier or later works that partake to some degree of the heroic style, such as the *Pathétique* Sonata, Op. 13, the late sonatas Opp. 106 and 111, and the Ninth Symphony.

2. Hans Heinrich Eggebrecht, *Zur Geschichte der Beethoven-Rezeption* (Mainz: Akademie der Wissenschaften und der Literatur, 1972), 8. Busoni's words originally appeared in his "Was gab uns Beethoven?" *Die Musik* 15, no. 1 (October 1922): 20.

3. Eggebrecht, *Zur Geschichte der Beethoven-Rezeption*, 38.

4. Cited in ibid., 61. The passage is from Nietzsche's *Unzeitgemäße Betrachtungen, Viertes Stück: Richard Wagner in Bayreuth*, in *Friedrich Nietzsche Gesammelte Werke*, vol. 7 (Munich: Musarion, 1922), 312.

5. From a discussion of Beethoven intended at one time for inclusion in his work *William Shakespeare*. See *Victor Hugo Oeuvres Complètes*, édition chronologique, vol. 12, ed. Jean Massin (Paris: Le club Français du Livre, 1969), 408.

6. Milan Kundera, *The Unbearable Lightness of Being* (New York: Harper-Collins, 1984), 33. My thanks to Kristin Knittel for bringing this passage to my attention.

7. From his essay "Beethoven's 'heroische Symphonie.'" Richard Wagner, *Gesammelte Schriften und Dichtungen* (Leipzig: E. W. Fritzsch, 1871–83), vol. 5, 219. The translation is mine, as are all that follow unless otherwise noted.

8. Richard Wagner, *Gesammelte Schriften und Dichtungen*, vol. 1, 182.

9. Eggebrecht, *Zur Geschichte der Beethoven-Rezeption*, 41.

10. The letter is dated 19 October 1815. Cited in ibid., 29.

11. On the history of the phrase *élan terrible* as used in connection with Beethoven's music see Ulrich Schmitt, *Revolution im Konzertsaal: Zur Beethoven-Rezeption im 19. Jahrhundert* (Mainz: Schott, 1990), 192ff.

12. The most thorough and up-to-date investigation of these aspects of the heroic style is Michael Broyles, *Beethoven: The Emergence and Evolution of Beethoven's Heroic Style* (New York: Excelsior, 1987).

13. Maynard Solomon's *Beethoven* (New York: Schirmer Books, 1977) remains the most influential treatment of these themes.

14. For such a reception history of the *Eroica* (though heavily interpreted) see Martin Geck and Peter Schleuning, *"Geschrieben auf Bonaparte": Beethoven's "Eroica": Revolution, Reaktion, Rezeption* (Reinbek bei Hamburg: Rowohlt, 1989). For a more recent study, one that impressively combines a reception history of the *Eroica* with a usefully conceptualized history of Beethoven criticism, see Thomas Sipe, "Interpreting Beethoven: History, Aesthetics, and Critical Reception" (Ph.D. dissertation, University of Pennsylvania, 1992). Other important reception studies include Leo Schrade's classic study, *Beethoven in France: The Growth of an Idea* (New Haven: Yale University Press, 1942); Robin Wallace,

Beethoven's Critics: Aesthetic Dilemmas and Resolutions during the Composer's Lifetime (Cambridge: Cambridge University Press, 1986); Alessandra Comini, *The Changing Image of Beethoven: A Study in Mythmaking* (New York: Rizzoli, 1987); Kristin M. Knittel, "From Chaos to History: The Reception of Beethoven's Late Quartets" (Ph.D. dissertation, Princeton University, 1992); and Ulrich Schmitt, *Revolution im Konzertsaal*. Schmitt's book is particularly striking in its mélange of political and sociotechnological perspectives on Beethoven's impact as a "revolutionary" composer.

CHAPTER ONE
BEETHOVEN'S HERO

1. Thomas Sipe offers a detailed and rewarding examination of the *Eroica* interpretations of A. B. Marx, Romain Rolland, and Peter Schleuning in his "Interpreting Beethoven: History, Aesthetics, and Critical Reception" (Ph.D. dissertation, University of Pennsylvania, 1992), 251–315.

2. Wilhelm von Lenz, *Beethoven: Eine Kunst-Studie. Dritter Theil, Zweite Abtheilung: Kritischer Katalog sämmtlicher Werke Beethovens mit Analysen derselben, Zweiter Theil, Erste Hälfte* (Op. 21 to Op. 55) (Hamburg: Hoffmann and Campe, 1860), 300.

3. The force of James Webster's recent reevaluation of the instrumental music of Haydn depends on this perception. See Webster, *Haydn's "Farewell" Symphony and the Idea of Classical Style* (Cambridge: Cambridge University Press, 1991).

4. A. B. Marx, *Ludwig van Beethoven: Leben und Schaffen*, 3d ed. (Berlin, 1875), vol. 1, 245–61; and Aléxandre Oulibicheff, *Beethoven, ses critiques, ses glossateurs* (Leipzig: F. A. Brockhaus, 1857), 173–80. The first edition of Marx's biography appeared in 1859.

5. For more on this type of heroic concept and how it informs the criticism of A. B. Marx, see my "Criticism, Faith, and the *Idee*: A. B. Marx's Early Reception of Beethoven," *19th-Century Music* 13 (Spring 1990): 191f.

6. Marx, *Ludwig van Beethoven*, 247–48.

7. Ibid., 247; Oulibicheff, *Beethoven*, 175.

8. I discuss this aspect of Marx's program in "Aesthetics, Theory and History in the Works of A. B. Marx" (Ph.D. dissertation, Brandeis University, 1988), chap. 5.

9. See Alfred Heuss, *Beethoven: Eine Charakteristik* (Leipzig, 1921), 38.

10. Ibid., 41.

11. Paul Bekker, *Beethoven* (Berlin: Schuster and Loeffler, 1911), 171.

12. Except for the Finale, which Schering associates with the Prometheus legend. Arnold Schering, "Die *Eroica*, eine Homer-Symphonie Beethovens?" *Neues Beethoven Jahrbuch* 5 (1933): 163ff. Schering takes his cue from Berlioz, who explicitly associated the symphony as a whole with the work of Homer: "Beethoven ... read Homer habitually, and in his magnificent musical epic [*épopée*], which is said to be—rightly or wrongly—inspired by a modern hero, the memories of the ancient *Iliad* play an admirably beautiful but no less evident role." Berlioz, *À Travers Chants* (Paris: Gründ, 1971), 50.

13. Ibid., 166.

14. Romain Rolland, *Beethoven the Creator. The Great Creative Epochs: I (From the "Eroica" to the "Appassionata")*, trans. Ernest Newman (New York: Garden City Publishing, 1937), 81–83.

15. David Epstein, *Beyond Orpheus: Studies in Musical Structure* (Cambridge, Mass.: MIT Press, 1979), 129ff.

16. A. B. Marx, for example, was a leading authority on musical form. Within the pedagogical confines of his *Lehre von der musikalischen Komposition* (1837–47), Marx investigated Beethoven's use of sonata form at great length.

17. As, e.g., in Heinrich Schenker, *Harmony*, ed. Oswald Jonas and trans. Elizabeth Mann Borgese (Chicago: University of Chicago Press, 1954), 12f.

18. This effect will be explored further in chapter 2.

19. There are of course precedents in Haydn and Mozart for introducing new thematic material within the development section. James Webster compares the new theme of the *Eroica* with one of the most striking of these instances in his study "The D-Major Interlude in Haydn's 'Farewell Symphony,'" in *Studies in Musical Sources and Style: Essays in Honor of Jan LaRue*, ed. Eugene K. Wolf and Edward H. Roesner (Madison, Wis.: A-R, 1991), 380. For Webster, Haydn's use of a new theme is procedurally very different from Beethoven's: the D-major interlude is inexplicable within the bounds of Haydn's first movement alone and forms part of the through-composed strategy of the entire symphony.

20. See August Halm, "Über den Wert musikalischer Analysen, I: Der Fremdkörper im ersten Satz der *Eroica*," *Die Musik* 21, no. 2 (1929): 481–84; and Heinrich Schenker, "Beethovens Dritte Sinfonie, in ihrem wahren Inhalt zum erstenmal dargestellt," *Das Meisterwerk in der Musik*, vol. 3 (Munich, 1930), 29–101. For a more recent treatment of the new theme in this spirit see Robert B. Meikle, "Thematic Transformation in the First Movement of Beethoven's *Eroica* Symphony," *Music Review* 32, no. 3 (August 1971): 205–18.

21. Such is not the case with Halm, however. After analyzing the new theme and showing its relation to the first theme, Halm concludes that such an analysis does little for his continuing sense that the new theme is a "foreign body." Halm, "Über den Wert musikalischer Analysen," 483.

22. Marx, *Ludwig van Beethoven*, 254–55.

23. Martin Geck and Peter Schleuning, *"Geschrieben auf Bonaparte": Beethoven's "Eroica": Revolution, Reaktion, Rezeption* (Reinbek bei Hamburg: Rowohlt, 1989), 118. Schleuning's interpretation originally appeared in "Beethoven in alter Deutung: Der 'neue Weg' mit der 'Sinfonia *Eroica*,'" *Archiv für Musikwissenschaft* 44, no. 3 (1987): 165–94.

24. Lenz clearly associates the hero with Beethoven in this instance. Lenz, *Beethoven*, 293.

25. Bekker, *Beethoven*, 171–72.

26. Schering, "Die *Eroica*," 169.

27. Marx, *Ludwig van Beethoven*, 253–54.

28. Schenker understands the surface diminution of the new theme as a summary of several aspects of the upper-voice motion from bars 242 to 279. This is a separate claim from his assertion of latent similarities between the

new theme and the first theme, similarities obvious only after reductive analysis. See Schenker, "Beethovens Dritte Sinfonie," 50.

29. Ibid., 44.

30. Thomas Sipe points out another aspect of the musical process that contributes to this sense of continuity: the bass line descent (D–C–B–A♯–A–G) in bars 248–75, which is then reversed by the ascent to A in 276, thus profiling the famously dissonant chords even more markedly. Sipe, "Interpreting Beethoven," 270f.

31. In his "Reconstructing a Musical Rhetoric (on Josquin's *Domine, ne in furore tuo*)," a paper delivered at the 1988 AMS-SMT meeting in Baltimore, Leslie David Blasius proposed the term "rhetoric" to denote a similar process of heightened continuity involving a disruption of normative syntax.

32. "Evil chord" is from Marx (see n. 33).

33. Here are some typical descriptions of this climax. Berlioz: " One cannot avoid starting with fright at this picture of indomitable fury. It is the voice of despair and almost of madness." Berlioz, *À Travers Chants*, 41. Wagner hears a "world crusher, a titan (who wrestles with the gods)." Wagner, "Beethoven's 'heroische Symphonie'" (1851), in *Gesammelte Schriften und Dichtungen* (Leipzig: E. W. Fritzsch, 1871–83), vol. 5, 220. In A. B. Marx's view, "At last, like two men fighting chest to chest, all the winds and all the strings . . . stand immovable—choir against choir—on an evil chord." Marx, *Ludwig van Beethoven*, 253. Oulibicheff: "The forces [of the charging army] shatter against a superior resistance, which Beethoven will not name. Is it God, is it the enemy—I know not." Oulibicheff, *Beethoven*, 177. Wilhelm von Lenz: "With thirty-two stabbing thrusts, Caesar is slain at the foot of Pompey's column." Lenz, *Beethoven*, 295. Finally, in Peter Schleuning's recent interpretation, an enraged Prometheus is on the point of destroying his own work. Geck and Schleuning, *"Geschrieben auf Bonaparte,"* 118.

34. The key area of the new theme in this movement is marked by Leonard Ratner as the "area of furthest remove." This observation reflects his general view that classical style developments often reach a point of furthest harmonic remove, which then acts as a structural fulcrum within the section. See Ratner, *Classic Music: Expression, Form, and Style* (New York: Schirmer Books, 1980), 226–28. My own characterization of the new theme as an antipode emphasizes its thematic and semantic aspects as well as its harmonic implications.

35. The term "syntactical climax" is from Leonard Meyer. See, e.g., his article "Exploiting Limits: Creation, Archetypes, and Style Change," *Daedalus* 109, no. 2 (Spring 1980): 189.

36. Drawing on the frequent characterization of the sonata-form second theme as a lyrical counterpart to the first theme, Hermann Kretzschmar makes a similar point, referring to the new theme of the *Eroica* as the essential second theme of the movement. See Kretzschmar, *Führer durch den Concertsaal: Sinfonie und Suite*, 3d ed. (Leipzig, 1898), vol. 1, 142. August Halm also refers to the new theme as the movement's second theme. Halm, "Über den Wert musikalischer Analysen," 484.

37. For Philip G. Downs, the immediate aftermath of the new theme is at the heart of his interpretation of the movement. In his reading the new theme

marks a psychological compromise, which is then rejected by the C-major entrance of the first theme, which itself is rejected in turn by the E♭-minor new theme. The whole business is an involved process of psychological adjustment that Downs characterizes as heroic. See Philip G. Downs, "Beethoven's 'New Way' and the *Eroica*," in *The Creative World of Beethoven*, ed. Paul Henry Lang (New York: Norton, 1970), 94f. and 102.

38. In his engaging and broadly conceived study of the first movement of the *Eroica*, Lewis Lockwood comments on the particular attraction of that movement for this type of analysis: "One could write a brief history of the idea of motivic interconnection from 'Eroica' commentaries alone, so pervasive is the concept in writings on the Symphony's first movement." Lockwood, "'Eroica' Perspectives: Strategy and Design in the First Movement," *Beethoven Studies*, vol. 3, ed. Alan Tyson (Cambridge: Cambridge University Press, 1982), 88.

39. Interestingly enough, another analyst, more strictly formalist than Schenker, also sees the new theme as an important turning point. Alfred Lorenz, who makes it his business to eschew "greuliche Musikführerweis" (172) reads the development section as a large bar form, with the new theme ushering in the crucial *Abgesang* and its synthesizing role. Alfred Lorenz, "Worauf beruht die bekannte Wirkung der Durchführung im I. Eroicasatze," in *Neues Beethoven-Jahrbuch*, ed. Adolf Sandberger, vol. 1 (1924), 159–83.

40. Schering, "Die *Eroica*," 170.

41. Bekker, *Beethoven*, 172.

42. This characterization does not form part of Marx's programmatic treatment of the movement but is offered elsewhere in his biography of Beethoven as a reaction to Lenz's description of the horn call as "hovering, lost, *in gurgite vasto*." See Marx, *Ludwig van Beethoven*, 281.

43. Cf. Rolland: "Suddenly the summons of destiny is heard pianissimo against this curtain of shifting purple haze." *Beethoven the Creator*, 85.

44. Lenz, *Beethoven*, 297.

45. Heinrich Schenker, *Harmony*, 162–63.

46. But cf. Donald Francis Tovey's uncharacteristically glib reading of this passage. For him one of the horn players simply cannot stand the suspense any longer and must out with it. Tovey, *Essays in Musical Analysis*, vol. 1: *Symphonies* (London: Oxford University Press, 1935), 31. Downs, too, hears the horn call as "a stroke of humor," one "in which the formality of the recapitulation of the old version of the theme forces the new version to give way to it, and the new version has the strength to stand back and await its due place. . . . Self-assurance makes humor a possibility." Downs, "Beethoven's 'New Way,'" 98.

47. Both Bekker and Kretzschmar link this climax specifically to the one at bars 276ff. After the reactive new theme the struggle begins again, reaches a high point at 362, and is eventually followed by "deathly stillness" (Kretzschmar) or "dreamlike meditation" (Bekker). Kretzschmar, *Führer durch den Concertsaal*, 143; Bekker, *Beethoven*, 172.

48. A hypermetric reading of the section containing the horn call reveals that it is not just the quiet scoring that mitigates against the arrival of the recapitulation at bar 396. The section from 366 on can be heard as two large-scale

phrases of 4×4 bars each; the first extends from 366 to 381, and the second extends from 382 to the onset of the recapitulation. The division between these two hyperphrases is clearly marked at 382 by the onset of the tremoli. It does not seem unreasonable to hear 366–81 as a downbeat and 382–97 as a reactive upbeat that then leads to the recapitulation. Thus the arrival of the recapitulated theme is clearly forecast for bar 398; starting the recapitulation at bar 396, where the horn call now takes place, would disrupt the expectation engendered by this hypermetric symmetry.

49. Gregory Nagy, *The Best of the Achaeans: Concepts of the Hero in Archaic Greek Poetry* (Baltimore: Johns Hopkins University Press, 1979), 146.

50. See p. xv of the introduction on Wagner's characterization of the *Eroica* Symphony as an "unerhörte Tat."

51. Cf. Geck and Schleuning, *"Geschrieben auf Bonaparte,"* 122

52. Exceptions include the readings of Schering and Schleuning.

53. Marx, *Ludwig van Beethoven*, 256.

54. Lenz, *Beethoven*, 296.

55. Cf. Walter Riezler's description of this passage: "Now at last, after six hundred and thirty bars, the principal motive seems to be fully deployed—and not merely in its capacity as the mainspring of the movement. It makes a last effort, more determined even than at the opening of the recapitulation, to expand into a true symphonic "theme." Riezler, *Beethoven*, trans. G.D.H. Pidcock (New York: Dutton, 1938), 280.

56. My thanks to Robert Morgan, who, in reacting to an earlier version of this chapter, urged me to sharpen the distinction between this passage in the coda and the nature of a theme in the classical style.

57. Schleuning mentions the gradually developing emphasis throughout the movement on the fifth scale degree of the theme, incorporating it into his Prometheus program. Geck and Schleuning, *"Geschrieben auf Bonaparte,"* 116–24.

58. This aspect of the movement's design is revealed and developed by Lewis Lockwood in his " 'Eroica' Perspectives."

59. Homer, *The Iliad of Homer*, trans. Richmond Lattimore (Chicago: University of Chicago Press, 1951), 209.

60. Oulibicheff, *Beethoven*, 178.

61. Marx, *Ludwig van Beethoven*, 284.

62. Joseph Kerman, "Notes on Beethoven's Codas," *Beethoven Studies*, vol. 3, 141–59; and Charles Rosen, *Sonata Forms*, rev. ed. (New York: Norton, 1988), 324–52.

63. Rosen, *Sonata Forms*, 290–93. Rosen's argument is worded more strongly; in his view, Beethoven's approach to the F-major passage actually transforms the function of that key from a dominant to a subdominant. Tovey has also pointed out that this F major is not to be thought of as an applied dominant; see his *Beethoven* (London: Oxford University Press, 1965), 49. Lorenz interprets the use of F and Db in a strictly functionalist manner: F = V/V (D: D) and Db = IV/IV (S: S). These keys are said to surround the tonic Eb cadentially through their dominant and subdominant functions. Lorenz, "Worauf beruht die bekannte Wirkung," 174.

64. Heuss worries the ambiguity of C♯ and D♭ in similar terms: "But what kind of tone is the C♯; what is its name, what does it reveal, where is it going? Is it a D♭, headed to the subdominant? Does this hero thus harbor elements within himself that will lead him into the abyss, perhaps to his doom? Or is it a C♯, a tone from an extremely remote key? Might it then express the idea that this hero will be capable of grasping and putting into action the boldest and most extreme designs? What is this tone, with its demonic ambiguity, this tone whose further progress, whether up or down, no one could predict? What devilish indefinability! This is indeed a man of whom one never knows just what he really will do." Heuss, *Beethoven*, 38.

65. Marx, *Ludwig van Beethoven*, 252–53.

66. Ratner identifies a similar strategy in the general harmonic process of codas in the classical style: "Their opening digressions create a harmonic 'whiplash' that prepares the final tonic with increased force, a supreme effect of periodicity." *Classic Music*, 231.

67. According to Carolyn Abbate, Marx's characterization of the *Eroica* in terms of an epic opens the possibility of diegetic narration, "in which a narrating voice retells or recounts events retrospectively, and at a critical distance." See Abbate, *Unsung Voices: Opera and Musical Narrative in the Nineteenth Century* (Princeton: Princeton University Press, 1991), 23.

68. For a comprehensive critique of Schering's hermeneutics, see Arno Forchert, "Scherings Beethovendeutung und ihre methodischen Voraussetzungen," in *Beiträge zur musikalischen Hermeneutik*, ed. Carl Dahlhaus, *Studien zur Musikgeschichte des 19. Jahrhunderts*, vol. 43 (Regensburg: Gustav Bosse, 1975), 41–52.

69. For a more detailed argument supporting this view of Marx's *Idee*, see my "Criticism, Faith, and the *Idee*." On the importance of the *Eroica* as an *Idee*-bearing work, cf. Martin Geck: "The *Eroica* is the first musical work found worthy of presentation to a broader, and not just musically initiated, public as an important contribution to the cultural and ideal formation of the present age. With this work, music is freed from the ghetto of a specialist's art and stands at the side of other arts and sciences, such as literature. Beethoven achieved his goal of being considered a tone poet [*Tondichter*] rather than a mere composer [*Tonsetzer*]; one would now be able to discuss his music like one might discuss a drama by Goethe." Geck and Schleuning, *"Geschrieben auf Bonaparte,"* 232.

70. "Many commentators have speculated as to who the hero of the symphony may be, for heroism there certainly is. But it is not the heroism of the military hero, for the man who has the strength to overcome himself is the rarest kind of hero. Beethoven's wish to benefit humanity is realized. The new way which was revealed was one in which Beethoven was able for perhaps the only time in music, to show the listener an analogue of his own potentiality for perfection. *A higher revelation than all wisdom and philosophy.*" Downs, "Beethoven's 'New Way,'" 102.

71. Cf. my essay "How Music Matters: Poetic Content Revisited," in *Rethinking Music*, ed. Nicholas Cook and Mark Everist (Oxford University Press, forthcoming).

72. My thanks to Roger Parker for encouraging me to address this aspect of the symphony's programmatic reception.

73. See p. xv of the introduction.

74. Represented, for example, by Arnold Schmitz's attempt to distance Beethoven from the heavily romanticized aspects of his reception in *Das romantische Beethoven-Bild* (Berlin: Dümmler, 1927). See also Hans Heinrich Eggebrecht, *Zur Geschichte der Beethoven-Rezeption* (Mainz: Akademie der Wissenschaften und der Literatur, 1972), 13–15.

75. The importance of an extramusical standpoint for the understanding of Beethoven's instrumental music is acknowledged in the work of Arnold Schering in the 1930s, Harry Goldschmidt in the 1960s and 1970s, and Owen Jander, Maynard Solomon, Peter Schleuning, and Christopher Reynolds in the 1980s. See, among others, Schering, *Beethoven und die Dichtung* (Berlin, 1936); Goldschmidt, *Beethoven-Studien I: Die Erscheinung Beethoven* (Leipzig, 1974); Jander, "Beethoven's 'Orpheus in Hades': The *Andante con moto* of the Fourth Piano Concerto," *19th-Century Music* 8 (Spring 1985): 195–212; Solomon, "Beethoven's Ninth Symphony: A Search for Order," *19th-Century Music* 10 (Summer 1986): 3–23; Schleuning, "Beethoven in alter Deutung"; and Reynolds, "The Representational Impulse in Late Beethoven, II: String Quartet in F Major, Op. 135," *Acta Musicologica* 40, no. 1 (1988): 180–94.

CHAPTER TWO
MUSICAL VALUES: PRESENCE AND ENGAGEMENT
IN THE HEROIC STYLE

1. In an important and strangely underacknowledged book on this subject, David Greene has epitomized the classical style as a musical language of paired phrases, arguing that this fact allows Beethoven to manipulate temporality in the ways he does. David B. Greene, *Temporal Processes in Beethoven's Music* (New York: Gordon and Breach, 1982).

2. Richard Wagner, "Beethovens 'heroische Symphonie,'" (1851), in *Gesammelte Schriften und Dichtungen* (Leipzig: E. W. Fritzsch, 1871–83), vol. 5, 220; and Philip G. Downs, "Beethoven's 'New Way' and the *Eroica*," in *The Creative World of Beethoven*, ed. Paul Henry Lang (New York: Norton, 1970).

3. "The trouble with *Leonora No. 3* is that, like all great instrumental music from Haydn onwards, it is about ten times as dramatic as anything that could possibly be put on the stage." Tovey, *Essays in Musical Analysis*, vol. 4: *Illustrative Music* (London: Oxford University Press, 1937), 31.

4. Such engagement accounts for the hermeneutic imperative expressed by A. B. Marx in reaction to Beethoven's music: the best way to understand the musical art work of another self is to know one's own self. This appeal represented a new direction in music criticism, for the primary arbiter of musical judgment was no longer a knowledge of musical *Satzlehre* or even the possession of taste but now the direct recourse to the totality of one's own spirit. See my "Criticism, Faith, and the *Idee*: A. B. Marx's Early Reception of Beethoven," *19th-Century Music* 13 (Spring 1990): 186.

5. This supports a point made in chapter 1: the music is not about any specific programs; rather, the specific programs are about the music.

6. Richard Wagner, *Beethoven* (Leipzig: E. W. Fritzsch, 1870), 29. The translation is an adjusted version of William Ashton Ellis, *Richard Wagner's Prose Works*, vol. 5: *Actors and Singers* (London: Routledge and Kegan Paul, 1896; reprint, New York: Broude Brothers, 1966), 87.

7. It goes without saying that these attitudes are intimately associated with the biographical assumptions surrounding each composer: Beethoven struggled with musical language; Mozart was preternaturally gifted and spoke the language effortlessly. While it can be shown that many assumptions about the music are cued to biographical issues such as these—and for a wonderfully effective example of this argument see Kristin Knittel, "From Chaos to History: The Reception of Beethoven's Late Quartets" (Ph.D. dissertation, Princeton University, 1992)—my interest here is on the impact of the music, for the reasons stated in the introduction.

8. E.T.A. Hoffmann, *E.T.A. Hoffmann's Musical Writings: "Kreisleriana," "The Poet and the Composer," Music Criticism*, ed. David Charlton (Cambridge: Cambridge University Press, 1989), 239.

9. Cf. Joseph Kerman: "What Thomas Mann described as 'the naked human voice' sounds with particular urgency in the Fifth Symphony." Kerman hears the repercussions and fermatas of this motto as releasing "primal, unmediated emotional energies." In his view, these features show up throughout the symphony as a kind of subartistic stammering. Kerman, "Taking the Fifth," in *Write All These Down: Essays on Music* (Berkeley and Los Angeles: University of California Press, 1994), 208.

10. These notes fall just below the instrument's break, are hard to play expressively, and tend to have a thin, metallic, reedy, and breathy sound—they cannot be made mellow. The effect is somewhat analogous to that of open strings on a string instrument. My thanks to Jeffrey West for these observations.

11. For the influential role of this very descent on Heinrich Schenker's theory of *Urlinie*, see chapter 3, section III.

12. Kerman, "Taking the Fifth," 215.

13. It is amusing to consider the levels of irony at work in a recent commercial manifestation of this opening motto, namely, the Beethoven doorbell, which renders a characteristically clipped and nasal electronic version of the motto when someone comes calling. Here the motto literally announces a presence at one's door, but that is all it does.

14. Tovey, *Essays in Musical Analysis*, vol. 1: *Symphonies* (London: Oxford University Press, 1935), 38.

15. Cf. the augmented-sixth arrival on the dominant in the early bars of Mozart's K. 550, another dramatically conceived piece in the minor mode.

16. In a sense, Beethoven's opening trumps that of Mozart, for Beethoven's rhythm is a kind of enhanced anapest (⌣⌣⌣– for ⌣⌣–). Both movements may be said to tap into the ancient power of the anapest rhythm, known to Greek tragedians as the most effective rhythm for expressing action in choruses.

17. Other examples include the first movements of Mozart's G-minor Symphony, K. 550; Beethoven's Piano Sonatas Op. 2, no. 1, and Op. 53; and Haydn's Piano Sonata in E minor, Hob. XVI:34.

18. We shall return to this equation presently, as well as in chapter 4, section II.

19. Charles Rosen, *The Classical Style: Haydn, Mozart, Beethoven* (New York: Norton, 1972), 387.

20. This useful term was brought to my attention by the composer Conrad Pope in a graduate seminar on music analysis at Brandeis University.

21. Arnold Schering, *Humor, Heldentum, Tragik bei Beethoven: Über einige Grundsymbole der Tonsprache Beethovens* (Strasbourg: Librairie Heitz, 1955), 45.

22. Tovey, *Essays in Musical Analysis*, vol. 5: *Vocal Music* (London: Oxford University Press, 1937), 115.

23. Robert Morgan's pioneering article on tonal rhythm discusses the importance of opening and closing accents and on larger sections of music as constituting one rhythmic event; among his examples are sections of Beethoven's Fifth and Eighth Symphonies. See Morgan, "The Theory and Analysis of Tonal Rhythm," *Musical Quarterly* 64, no. 4 (October 1978): 435–73.

24. See ibid., 464–71, for the dispute between Schenker, Imbrie, and Morgan himself on the ambiguous phrase structure of this section.

25. The trumpet call in the Third *Leonore* Overture marks another famous example of impasse followed by drastic change. In the case of the overture this may be understood as a truly narrating disjunction, for it is motivated externally and sounds literally as an external voice.

26. As is the case with the E-minor "new theme" in the *Eroica*, the F♯-minor episode in the Fifth Symphony development is an example of Leonard Ratner's "point of furthest remove." See Ratner, *Classic Music: Expression, Form, and Style* (New York: Schirmer Books, 1980), 226ff.

27. Heinrich Schenker elaborates on this voice-leading progression in *Beethoven V. Sinfonie* (Vienna: Universal Edition, 1925), 12.

28. The climactic treatment of A♭ and F before the recapitulation makes their appearance after the half cadence superfluous—here Beethoven reverses part of the exposition (as he does in the recapitulation of the first movement of the String Quartet Op. 59, no. 1).

29. Cf. Schering's reading of the Eighth Symphony, which invokes the idea of automata by relating this movement to Goethe's ballad *The Sorcerer's Apprentice*. Schering, *Humor, Heldentum, Tragik bei Beethoven*, 13–40.

30. Tovey, *Essays in Musical Analysis*, vol. 1, 64.

31. In "How Music Matters: Poetic Content Revisited," in *Rethinking Music*, ed. Nicholas Cook and Mark Everist (London: Oxford University Press, forthcoming), I discuss the use of the oboe throughout this symphony as a narrating "voice-over" that signals retrospection.

32. In fact, if one considers the role of the horn call, this could be construed as a triple recapitulation: the premature horn call, the first theme undercut, and the first theme triumphant.

33. See Lockwood, "'Eroica' Perspectives: Strategy and Design in the First

Movement," *Beethoven Studies*, vol. 3, ed. Alan Tyson (Cambridge: Cambridge University Press, 1982).

34. Ibid., 99.

35. Beethoven's use of these two upbeat chords explicitly turns an opening downbeat into a closing downbeat. This transformation will become important in our discussion later in this chapter (and in chapter 4) of the nature of completion in Beethoven's heroic-style sonata form.

36. Schenker's wonderfully charged participial adjectives, in "gemusster wie gewollter Weg," can be but weakly put across in English. Schenker, "Beethovens Dritte Sinfonie, in ihrem wahren Inhalt zum erstenmal dargestellt," *Das Meisterwerk in der Musik*, vol. 3 (Munich, 1930) 32.

37. An exception to the feeling of monumental closure is provided by the *Coriolan* Overture, where the absence of such closure represents the fate of its eponymous hero. The overture does not close, it expires.

38. Lawrence Kramer, *Music and Poetry: The Nineteenth Century and After* (Berkeley and Los Angeles: University of California Press, 1984), 235.

39. Ibid.

40. Tovey, *A Companion to Beethoven's Pianoforte Sonatas* (London: Associated Board of the Royal Schools of Music, 1931), 169.

41. The finale's transformation to major is accompanied by trombones and piccolo, two very marked instruments in this style, whose connotations invoke a complex extramusical symbology both sacred and secular.

42. Lewis Lockwood discusses this coda as having a two-part structure; one of its formal functions is thus to balance the two-part structure of the "Middle Section" of the movement (i.e., the two large sections of the development section, articulated by the return of the Scherzo in bar 153). Lockwood, "On the Coda of the Finale of Beethoven's Fifth Symphony," in *Divertimento für Hermann J. Abs* (Bonn: Beethoven-Haus, 1981), 45.

43. One recalls Fétis's suggestion that Beethoven should have used the finale of the Fifth Symphony in the *Eroica*, in order to conclude the latter work in a more appropriately heroic fashion.

44. See Peter Schleuning's interpretation, in Martin Geck and Peter Schleuning, *"Geschrieben auf Bonaparte": Beethoven's "Eroica": Revolution, Reaktion, Rezeption* (Reinbek bei Hamburg: Rowohlt, 1989).

45. For Carl Dahlhaus, one of the signal traits of Beethoven's "new way" is the radical nature of his thematic material: taking the place of an exposition of a theme is a process in which a thematic protoform moves directly to elaboration, and what passes for the theme is involved from the outset in a developmental process, "either as anticipation of thematic working to come, or as consequence of thematic working already past." The theme exists through such transformations; it has no existence as a substantive structure. Thus Dahlhaus prefers to speak not of a theme but of a thematic configuration. Dahlhaus, *Ludwig van Beethoven: Approaches to His Music*, trans. Mary Whittall (Oxford: Clarendon Press, 1991), 170f.

46. Tovey's view is worth quoting at length: "The simple truth is that Beethoven could not do without just such purely rhythmic figures at this stage of

his art. It was absolutely necessary that every inner part in his texture should assert its own life; but at the same time it was equally necessary that it should not cause constant or rapid changes of harmony by doing so. Figures that can identify a theme while remaining on one note are the natural response to these requirements. . . . It is astonishing how many of Beethoven's themes can be recognized by their bare rhythm without quoting any melody at all." Tovey, *Essays in Musical Analysis*, vol. 1, 39.

47. Yet compare these moments to the situation in much of the "Pastoral" Symphony, where motivic repetitions seem to *unwind* the spring, to relax the forward motion. I shall discuss this curious phenomenon briefly in chapter 5, section II.

48. Theodor Adorno, "On the Problem of Musical Analysis" (introduced and trans. Max Paddison), *Music Analysis* 1, no. 2 (1982): 183.

49. Thus inspired invention (*inventio*), as considered in musico-aesthetic theory, shifts from the creation of a theme to the creation/realization of an overall formal process. In chapter 3 I shall examine one way in which this shift is felt in nineteenth-century form theory.

50. As Greene puts it, in a discussion of Beethoven's "Archduke" Trio, "Only a heroic will can give the outer world a shape congruent with its own." Greene, *Temporal Processes in Beethoven's Music*, 100.

51. As we shall see in chapter 3, the force of this assumption remains largely unabated, and it stems directly from the perception of presence and inner necessity in the works of Beethoven's heroic style. And in chapter 4, I shall associate this process with the various ways of modeling the self that become manifest in the age of Goethe.

52. A refreshing antidote to this view is supplied by Leonard Meyer: "Beethoven overturned no fundamental syntactic rules. Rather, he was an incomparable strategist who exploited limits—the rules, forms, and conventions that he inherited from predecessors such as Haydn and Mozart, Handel and Bach—in richly inventive and strikingly original ways." Meyer, "Exploiting Limits: Creation, Archetypes, and Style Change," *Daedalus* 109, no. 2 (Spring 1980): 178.

53. James Webster, *Haydn's "Farewell" Symphony and the Idea of Classical Style* (Cambridge, 1991).

54. A similar case could be made by comparing the return of the Minuet in the finale of Haydn's Symphony no. 46 with the much more widely celebrated and discussed return of the Scherzo in the finale of Beethoven's Fifth Symphony.

55. Cf. Charles Rosen's illuminating view of Haydn as an artist of the pastoral. Rosen, *The Classical Style*, 162f.

56. This is not to say that Haydn's music was not conceived in primarily ethical terms. As Webster has shown, the high-Viennese classical style of Haydn (and Mozart) is generally marked by "deep ethical concerns" (Webster, *Haydn's "Farewell" Symphony*, 373). But I am talking about the predominant and undeniable effect of these respective musics on two centuries of listeners.

CHAPTER THREE
INSTITUTIONAL VALUES:
BEETHOVEN AND THE THEORISTS

1. For two excellent examples of this type of literary criticism, see Friedrich Schlegel's "Über Goethes Meister," which first appeared in the *Athenäum: Eine Zeitschrift von August Wilhelm Schlegel und Friedrich Schlegel*, vol. 1, part 2 (Berlin: Friedrich Vierweg, 1798), 147–78; and August Schlegel's 1797 essay "Shakespeare's *Romeo and Juliet*." The latter has been reprinted in August Wilhelm Schlegel, *Kritische Schriften*, ed. Emil Staiger (Zurich: Artemis, 1962), 92–113.

2. I spend some time comparing this aspect of these two theorists in "Method and Motivation in Hugo Riemann's History of Harmonic Theory," *Music Theory Spectrum* 14, no. 2 (Spring 1992): 1–14.

3. Jacques Handschin has linked Riemann's conceptualization of tonality to the harmonic practice of classic and romantic music of the German tradition. See Handschin, *Der Toncharakter: Eine Einführung in die Tonpsychologie* (Zürich: Atlantis Verlag, 1948), 268.

4. For the purposes of the present discussion, I have decided to let Rudolph Réti, and not Schoenberg himself, be the representative theorist for this way of thinking. There are so many issues at stake in the musical thought of Schoenberg that his inclusion here would involve an unwieldy degree of qualification. Another factor in my decision is the recent publication of Schoenberg's so-called *Gedanke* manuscript and other fragments by Patricia Carpenter and Severine Neff; see *Schoenberg's Musical Idea: The Logic, Technique, and Art of Its Presentation*, ed. and trans. Patricia Carpenter and Severine Neff (New York: Columbia University Press, 1994), as well as *Coherence, Counterpoint, Instrumentation, Instruction in Form*, trans. Charlotte M. Cross and Severine Neff (Lincoln: University of Nebraska Press, 1994). Until the ongoing process of re-evaluation of Schoenberg's thought in terms of such new primary sources has settled to some degree, it seems ill advised to indulge in any broad interpretation of his analytical work.

5. Cf. Dahlhaus, *Nineteenth-Century Music*, trans. J. Bradford Robinson (Berkeley and Los Angeles: University of California Press, 1989), 11: "It is no coincidence that virtually all analytic methods of the nineteenth and twentieth centuries, from Adolf Bernhard Marx's to Hugo Riemann's, from Heinrich Schenker's to Rudolf Réti's, took their examples primarily from Beethoven."

6. This is often noted by Dahlhaus; see, e.g., ibid., 35.

7. For a later summation of this view, see Marx, *Ludwig van Beethoven: Leben und Schaffen*, 3d ed. (Berlin, 1875), vol. 1, 261–66 (the beginning of the chapter entitled "Die Sinfonia Eroica und die Idealmusik").

8. Marx, "Etwas über die Symphonie und Beethovens Leistung in diesem Fache," *Berliner Allgemeine musikalische Zeitung* 1 (1824): 174.

9. Ibid., 165ff., 173ff., and 181ff..

10. Marx's pedagogical system thus bears a striking resemblance to recent structuralist methods of language pedagogy, in which elements of morpho-

logy (declensions, conjugations, etc.) are introduced within the context of grammatical utterances.

11. For the most complete treatment of this aspect of Marx's work see Kurt-Erich Eicke, *Der Streit zwischen Adolph Bernhard Marx und Gottfried Wilhelm Fink um die Kompositionslehre*, Kölner Beiträge zur Musikforschung, ed. Karl Gustav Fellerer, vol. 42 (Regensburg: Gustav Bosse Verlag, 1966).

12. Marx, "Die Form in der Musik," in *Die Wissenschaften im neunzehnten Jahrhundert*, vol. 2, ed. Dr. J. A. Romberg (Leipzig: Romberg's Verlag, 1856), 40.

13. I argue this point in more detail in "The Role of Sonata Form in A. B. Marx's Theory of Form," *Journal of Music Theory* 33, no. 2 (Fall 1989): 264f.

14. Carl Dahlhaus and Lotte Thaler both make a direct comparison of Goethe's plant metamorphosis and Marx's *Formenlehre*. See Dahlhaus, "Ästhetische Prämissen der 'Sonatenform' bei Adolf Bernhard Marx," *Archiv für Musikwissenschaft* 41 (1984): 73–85; and Lotte Thaler, *Organische Form in der Musiktheorie des 19. und beginnenden 20. Jahrhunderts* (Munich: Musikverlag E. Katzbichler, 1984): 66–76.

15. Marx, *Die Lehre von der musikalischen Komposition, praktisch-theoretisch*, 2d ed. (Leipzig: Breitkopf and Härtel, 1841), vol. 1, 399.

16. Here, too, Marx's work bears similarities to the morphological thought of Goethe. For Goethe, individual plants are seen as specific manifestations of an underlying and prototypical growth process. Ernst Cassirer provides a richly informative discussion of Goethe's plant theory, with particular emphasis on the relationship of general to particular, in his *Freiheit und Form: Studien zur deutschen Geistesgeschichte* (Berlin: Bruno Cassirer, 1922), 321–56.

17. Johann Bernhard Logier, *System der Musik-Wissenschaft und der praktischen Composition* (Berlin: H.A.W. Logier, 1827), 330–43.

18. There are several reasons why I am not illustrating Marx's method with a piano sonata more overtly heroic, such as the *Waldstein* or the *Appassionata*. First is the simple fact that Marx's account of Op. 31, no. 1, is the most complete reading in his treatise of any of the piano sonatas. This example is not unrelated to issues that arise in the *Waldstein*, for it shares some idiosyncratic tonal features with that sonata. Also, the three Op. 31 sonatas represent pioneering works of Beethoven's "new way" (though the biographical import of this famous designation has recently been contested—see Hans-Werner Küthen, "Beethovens 'wirklich ganz neue Manier'—Eine Persiflage," in *Beiträge zu Beethovens Kammermusik*, ed. Sieghard Brandenburg and Helmut Loos [Munich: G. Henle Verlag, 1987], 216–24); thus some of the technical features of the heroic style are found here as well. But more important is the idea that the underlying values engaged by Marx in attempting to understand a work like Op. 31, no. 1 are those that work best with the heroic style. In other words, one does not need to point to the literal treatment of heroic-style pieces in Marx's work in order to show the influence of their values.

19. This claim shows that Marx is thinking more in terms of abstract key relations than actual practice: it is hard to imagine Beethoven using the minor mediant for a second-theme area in a major-key work. My thanks to Charles Rosen for pointing this out.

20. Robert Winter, "The Bifocal Close and the Evolution of the Classical Style," *Journal of the American Musicological Society* 42, no. 2 (Summer 1989): 275–337.

21. Marx's derivation of musical forms works in a similar fashion: each form is said to solve a problem of the previous form, and yet to create a new problem. The only form that creates no new problems and thus represents a kind of ultimate solution is sonata form. For a discussion of this aspect of Marx's *Formenlehre*, see my "The Role of Sonata Form in A. B. Marx's Theory of Form."

22. As found in Heinrich Christoph Koch, *Versuch einer Anleitung zur Komposition*, 3 vols. (Leipzig: Böhme, 1782–93).

23. Hugo Riemann, "Gang," in *Hugo Riemanns Musik Lexicon*, 11th ed. (Berlin: Max Hesses Verlag, 1929). Elsewhere he refers to it as a *Notlüge* ("white lie"), as cited in Lotte Thaler, *Organische Form*, 101.

24. Thaler, *Organische Form*, 100.

25. This is spelled out by Ivan Waldbauer in his excellent study "Riemann's Periodization Revisited and Revised," *Journal of Music Theory* 33, no. 2 (Fall 1989): 338. Example 3 is an adaptation of Waldbauer's example 1, 339.

26. The connection between the two prototypes is never made completely clear theoretically. Ibid., 338.

27. This process is reflected in the syntax of any complete cadence. An opening tonic is a syntactically free constituent; it can go to any other harmony. The final tonic is the only thing that can happen after V^7. (I'm speaking theoretically, of course. We all know that anything can happen after V^7, which leads to the supposition that there is no truly ungrammatical musical utterance, a supposition that is fruitfully pursued in Brian Hyer's "Tonal Intuitions in *Tristan und Isolde*" (Ph.D. dissertation, Yale University, 1989), 313ff.)

28. We might say that for Riemann the work is extensively open and intensively closed, while for Marx the work is intensively open and extensively closed.

29. The analysis of this movement is found in Hugo Riemann, *L. van Beethovens sämtliche Klavier-sonaten: Ästhetische und formal-technische Analyse mit historischen Notizen*, vol. 2: *Sonate XIV–XXVI*, 3d ed. (Berlin: Max Hesses Verlag, 1920), 318–40.

30. Riemann, ibid., 321. Riemann also finds this procedure in the opening of the *Waldstein* first movement and that of the *Appassionata* (in the latter case, the use of minor brings about some modifications).

31. This is similar to the effect that Rosen notes in the Fourth Piano Concerto. See chapter 2, 39f.

32. Hugo Riemann, *Geschichte der Musik seit Beethoven (1800–1900)* (Berlin: W. Spemann, 1901), 97f.

33. Riemann, *Die Elemente der musikalischen Aesthetik* (Berlin: W. Spemann, 1900), 2.

34. Ibid., 156.

35. At a more basic level, Riemann does indeed countenance the necessity of a temporal perception of music, the perception of a process of transformation. Characteristically, the possibility of such a perception resides in the listener,

whose willed engagement ensures that a series of discrete sounds should indeed suggest a developing temporal process. See Riemann, *Die Elemente der musikalischen Aesthetik*, 40.

36. This point has been made by H. C. Wolff in his article on Riemann in *Musik in Geschichte und Gegenwart*, vol. 11, ed. Friedrich Blume (Kassel: Bärenreiter, 1963), and by Ruth Solie in her review of William C. Mickelsen's *Hugo Riemann's Theory of Harmony*, *19th-Century Music* 2, no. 2 (1978): 181.

37. On the importance of paired phrases for the temporal drama of the classical style, see David B. Greene, *Temporal Processes in Beethoven's Music* (New York: Gordon and Breach, 1982).

38. The Bach analyses are found in Riemann, *Handbuch der Fugen-Komposition* (Berlin: Hesse, 1906).

39. Of course, the *Ursatz* is not strictly an abstraction, nor is it strictly a musical phenomenon. Its ambiguous theoretical status is a result of using musical notation as a metalanguage. See Allan Keiler, "On Some Properties of Schenker's Pitch Derivations," *Music Perception* 1 (1983–84): 200–228.

40. Heinrich Schenker, *Der Tonwille: Flugblätter zum Zeugnis unwandelbarer Gesetze der Tonkunst einer neuen Jugend dargebracht von Heinrich Schenker*, vol. 2 (Vienna: Tonwille-Flugblätterverlag, 1922), 4.

41. Cf. Schenker's terse formulation, "ohne Ziel kein Inhalt" ("no content without a goal"), in *Der Freie Satz*, vol. 3 of *Neue Musikalische Theorien und Phantasien*, 2d ed., ed. Oswald Jonas (Vienna: Universal Edition, 1956), 29. (The original edition was published in 1935.)

42. Heinrich Schenker, *Beethoven V. Sinfonie* (Vienna: Universal Edition, 1925). Schenker's analysis of the first movement is translated in Elliot Forbes, ed., *Beethoven: Symphony No. 5 in C Minor*, Norton Critical Score (New York: Norton, 1971).

43. Heinrich Schenker, *Beethovens Neunte Sinfonie* (Vienna: Universal Edition, 1912), 8.

44. One cannot isolate Schenker's analysis of the Fifth Symphony from the rest of the *Tonwille* analyses, for many of them evince this mix of views about motivic content. Yet the analysis of the first movement of the Fifth is striking and central, and its *Urlinie* segments are at times very close to the sounding surface, as I shall argue presently. A recent study co-authored by Allen Cadwallader and William Pastille explores the development of motivic abstraction in the *Tonwille* analyses but does not attempt to engage specifically the issue of a descending *Urlinie*. See Allen Cadwallader and William Pastille, "Schenker's High-Level Motives," *Journal of Music Theory* 36, no. 1 (Spring 1992): 117–48. Other recent articles that deal in interesting ways both with the *Tonwille* analyses and with the use of motives in Schenkerian thought include Richard Cohn, "The Autonomy of Motives in Schenkerian Accounts of Tonal Music," *Music Theory Spectrum* 14, no. 2 (Fall 1992): 150–70; and Joseph Lubben, "Schenker the Progressive: Analytic Practice in *Der Tonwille*," ibid., vol. 15, no. 1 (Spring 1993): 59–75.

45. Schenker, *Beethoven V. Sinfonie*, 6.

46. Ibid., 9.

47. See, e.g., E.T.A. Hoffmann in 1810: "This has an ominous, eerie effect"

("Das wirkt wieder ahnungsvoll und schauerlich"). *E.T.A. Hoffmann's Musical Writings*, ed. David Charlton (Cambridge, 1989), 243.

48. For an influential discussion of Schenker's recognition of intrawork motivic coherence involving different structural levels, see Charles Burkhart, "Schenker's 'Motivic Parallelisms,'" *Journal of Music Theory* 22, no. 2 (Fall 1978), 145–76.

49. I am grateful to Joseph Dubiel and Stephen Peles for initiating this train of thought by underlining the problematic nature of Schenker's *Stufe* designation for the opening motive.

50. See Pastille and Cadwallader, "Schenker's High-Level Motives," 120ff.

51. Heinrich Schenker, *Die letzten Sonaten: Sonate A Dur Op. 101*, ed. Oswald Jonas (1920; reprint, Vienna: Universal Edition, 1972), 8.

52. The idea of the *Knotenpunkt* is a possible exception to this, as a generalizable aspect of the fundamental line; see, e.g., Schenker, *Die letzten Sonaten: Sonate A Dur Op. 101*, 36. See also Cadwallader and Pastille, "Schenker's High-Level Motives," 123.

53. The carets are first used in *Der Tonwille*, vol. 3 (1922), as part of Schenker's analysis of Haydn's late E♭-Major Piano Sonata.

54. "Ich habe die Urlinie erschaut, nicht errechnet!" ("I did not calculate the *Urlinie*, I beheld it!"), in Heinrich Schenker, "Fortsetzung der Urlinie-Betrachtungen," in *Das Meisterwerk in der Musik: Ein Jahrbuch*, vol. 2 (Munich: Drei Masken Verlag, 1926), 41.

55. Schenker, *Die letzten Sonaten: Sonate A Dur Op. 101*, 10.

56. Ibid., 8.

57. See chapter 2, 31.

58. Heinrich Schenker, "Fortsetzung der Urlinie-Betrachtungen," in *Das Meisterwerk in der Musik*, vol. 1 (Munich: Drei Masken Verlag, 1925), 198.

59. This presence was later attributed to the *Ursatz*. See Schenker, *Der Freie Satz*, 49–50.

60. It is interesting that Schenker himself did not use the word *structure*; the notion of structure as a metaphor for form is more in line with the positivist Anglo-American tradition that took up Schenker in the United States. On the topic of "structure" and Schenker, see Bryce Rytting's "Structure as a Technical Term in Schenkerian Analysis" (Ph.D. dissertation, Princeton University, forthcoming). Rytting argues that the Mannes School brought the notion of structure to Schenkerian discourse.

61. Rudolph Réti, *Thematic Patterns in Sonatas of Beethoven*, ed. Deryck Cooke (London: Faber and Faber, 1967), 17.

62. Ibid.

63. Carl Dahlhaus, "Textgeschichte und Rezeptionsgeschichte," in *Rezeptionsästhetik und Rezeptionsgeschichte in der Musikwissenschaft*, ed. Hermann Danuser and Friedhelm Krummacher (Laaber: Laaber-Verlag, 1991), 108.

64. Dahlhaus, *Ludwig van Beethoven: Approaches to His Music*, trans. Mary Whittall (Oxford: Clarendon Press, 1991), 89.

65. The following three examples are found in Réti's *Thematic Patterns in Sonatas of Beethoven*, 102–4.

66. For a more systematic treatment of such motivic transformations, see

Michael Schiano's theory of background motivic structure, as developed in "Arnold Schoenberg's *Grundgestalt* and its Influence" (Ph.D. dissertation, Brandeis University, 1992), especially chapter 4.

67. Réti, *Thematic Patterns in Sonatas of Beethoven*, 123.

68. This dichotomy is taken over from Schoenberg's *Fundamentals of Musical Composition*. See Ian Bent, "Analysis," in *The New Grove Dictionary of Music and Musicians*, ed. Stanley Sadie (London: Macmillan, 1980).

69. Réti, *Thematic Patterns in Sonatas of Beethoven*, 127.

70. Ibid.

71. James Webster's illuminating treatment of "Sandberger's tale" emphasizes the privileged role "thematische Arbeit" has played in this century as the distinctive feature of the classical style. Webster, *Haydn's "Farewell" Symphony and the Idea of Classical Style: Through-Composition and Cyclic Integration in His Instrumental Music* (Cambridge: Cambridge University Press, 1991), 341ff.

72. Réti, *Thematic Patterns in Sonatas of Beethoven*, 126.

73. Ibid., 143 and 141.

74. Réti, *The Thematic Process in Music* (1951; reprint, Westport, Conn.: Greenwood Press, 1978), 3.

75. Réti, *The Thematic Process in Music*, 171.

76. Ibid., 173.

77. Ibid., 183. Cf. as well Lawrence Kramer's reading of this coda in *Music and Poetry: The Nineteenth Century and After* (Berkeley and Los Angeles: University of California Press, 1984), 235.

78. Réti, *The Thematic Process in Music*, 185.

79. Ibid.

80. Ibid., 188.

81. Examples 17 and 18 are found in *The Thematic Process in Music*, 188–89.

82. Ibid., 189.

83. Ibid., 191. Réti thus recapitulates the romantic notion of art as *natura naturans*, as expressive of nature as a creative force. This view was an important aspect of the turn from mimetic to expressive conceptions of art in the late eighteenth century. (See M. H. Abrams's classic account of this turn in *The Mirror and the Lamp: Romantic Theory and the Critical Tradition* (Oxford: Oxford University Press, 1953), especially chapter 8.

84. Réti, *The Thematic Process in Music*, 192.

85. In chapter 5 I shall argue that it is this aspect of Réti's work—his making explicit the tacit, and to a large degree repressed, ethical basis of theorizing about music's materiality—that has contributed to the negative reception of his theory in recent years.

86. Réti, *The Thematic Process in Music*, 136. The hero here described sounds more like the hero of a *Bildungsroman* than of a drama.

87. The process of establishing new theories of music through the music of Beethoven has not abated. The latest and most systematic theory of musical semiosis appears in Robert S. Hatten's outstanding *Musical Meaning in Beethoven: Markedness, Correlation, Interpretation* (Bloomington: Indiana University

Press, 1994). Hatten's theory grounds the hermeneutic impulse perennially associated with Beethoven in a rigorously applied structuralist method.

88. Gary Taylor, *Reinventing Shakespeare: A Cultural History, from the Restoration to the Present* (Oxford: Oxford University Press, 1989).

CHAPTER FOUR
CULTURAL VALUES: BEETHOVEN, THE *GOETHEZEIT*,
AND THE HEROIC CONCEPT OF SELF

1. The concept of the "Age of Goethe" is treated with irony by Nicholas Boyle in his recent and voluminous study of Goethe: " 'The Age of Goethe' is simply the series of literary and intellectual temptations which, as it happens, Goethe resisted. That series may have its own logic, but it is not that logic which entitles it to bear the name of Goethe." See Nicholas Boyle, *Goethe: The Poet and the Age*, vol. 1: *The Poetry of Desire* (Oxford: Clarendon Press, 1991), 7. I prefer to leave to Boyle and others the question of the extent to which Goethe truly represents, and therefore qualifies as eponymous hero of, his age. Although Goethe does indeed figure heavily in my own interpretation of the age, I use the term *Goethezeit* largely for convenience, in order to contain within one resonant designation that broad expanse of German cultural history whose often disparate trends and preoccupations I believe to be relevant to the values of Beethoven's music.

2. From his essay "On Biography." Cited in Hayden White, *Metahistory: The Historical Imagination in Nineteenth-Century Europe* (Baltimore: Johns Hopkins University Press, 1973), 147.

3. Novalis, *Die Christenheit oder Europa: Ein Fragment* (1799) (Stuttgart: Philipp Reclam, 1966).

4. Including J. J. Winckelmann, Friedrich and Dorothea Schlegel, Zacharias Werner, and Clemens Brentano.

5. See, e.g., *Jenseits von Gut und Böse*, sec. 1, par. 11, in Friedrich Nietzsche, *Gesammelte Werke*, vol. 15 (Munich: Musarion, 1925), 17.

6. René Wellek, *A History of Modern Criticism, 1750–1950*, vol. 2: *The Romantic Age* (Cambridge: Cambridge University Press, 1981), 232.

7. "Gerettet ist der edle Glied / der Geisterwelt vom Bösen: / wer immer strebend sich bemüht, / den können wir erlösen" ("Saved is the noble member / of the spirit world from evil: / he who, ever striving, toils, / him we can redeem"). Goethe, *Faust*, part 2, lines 11, 934–37.

8. "Wie von unsichtbaren Geistern gepeitscht, gehen die Sonnenpferde der Zeit mit unsers Schicksals leichtem Wagen durch; und uns bleibt nichts, als mutig gefasst, die Zügel festzuhalten, und bald rechts bald links, vom Steine hier, vom Sturze da, die Räder wegzulenken. Wohin es geht, wer weiss es? Erinnert er sich doch kaum, woher er kam!" Goethe, *Egmont*, act 2. The translation in the text is from Goethe, *Egmont: A Tragedy in Five Acts*, trans. Charles E. Passage (New York: Frederick Ungar, 1980), 49.

9. From the American Declaration of Independence: "We hold these truths to be self-evident, that all men are created equal, that they are endowed by

their Creator with certain unalienable Rights, that among these are Life, Liberty and the pursuit of Happiness."

10. This dilemma is wonderfully explored by James M. Redfield in *Nature and Culture in the Iliad: The Tragedy of Hector* (Chicago: University of Chicago Press, 1975), 101.

11. In his essay on the *Leonore* Overtures, Tovey makes a similar point: "If there is one thing certain about art and life, it is that the heroic acts or sufferings of the individual are as big as the mind can hold, and that the horrors and heroisms of a besieged city are not emotionally cumulative." Tovey, *Essays in Musical Analysis*, vol. 5: *Vocal Music* (London: Oxford University Press, 1937), 31.

12. "Der Sinn erweitert aber lähmt; die Tat belebt aber beschränkt." Book 8, chapter 5.

13. Georg Wilhelm Friedrich Hegel, *Phänomenologie des Geistes*, in *Gesammelte Werke*, vol. 9 (Hamburg: Felix Meiner, 1980), 33f.

14. Ibid., 35.

15. Ibid., 434.

16. This translation is by Max Knight and Joseph Fabry; it can be found in *Who is Goethe?* ed. Katharina Mommsen, trans. Leslie and Jeanne Willson et al. (Boston: Suhrkamp/Insel Publishers Boston, 1983), 119.

17. These views show the depth of our attachment to the concept of theme as a narrative strategy, for they are ways of reconceiving the notion of theme so as to make it compatible with process—the primacy of theme cannot be abandoned by these theorists, hence the definition of theme must change.

18. See Rosen's wonderful précis of eighteenth-century comedy in *The Classical Style: Haydn, Mozart, Beethoven* (New York: Norton, 1972), 312ff.

19. David B. Greene, *Temporal Processes in Beethoven's Music* (New York: Gordon and Breach, 1982), 18–19.

20. Cf. Carl Dahlhaus's view on the conflict between harmonic and thematic views, and his synthesis thereof, in *Ludwig van Beethoven: Approaches to His Music*, trans. Mary Whittall (Oxford: Clarendon Press, 1991), 97ff.

21. Such is the twentieth-century view of August Halm and Theodor Adorno, who both stress that Beethoven's themes often sacrifice thematic character so that they may better serve the whole, whether that whole is conceptualized as an idea (Halm) or as a process of Becoming (Adorno). See Adorno, "On the Problem of Musical Analysis" (introduced and trans. Max Paddison), *Music Analysis* 1, no. 2 (1982): 179; and August Halm, *Von Zwei Kulturen der Musik* (Stuttgart: Ernst Klett, 1947), 33, 77.

22. But Adorno likens this to the work of Kant, in which the objectively given world of experience is questioned and then re-created by the Subject and its forms. Adorno, "On the Problem of Musical Analysis," 175.

23. Peter L. Thorslev, Jr., *The Byronic Hero: Types and Prototypes* (Minneapolis: University of Minnesota Press, 1962), 88f.

24. Cf. Rose Rosengard Subotnik: "Whereas once the general was considered logically and even morally prior to the individual, the impression made

by Beethoven's music, especially the second-period music, helped sustain, indeed even create, the romantic dream that the individual could become the new locus of the universal." Subotnik, *Developing Variations: Style and Ideology in Western Music* (Minneapolis: University of Minnesota Press, 1991), 180.

25. Thus the urge to interpret the hero in Beethoven's heroic style as self-overcoming. See, e.g., Philip G. Downs, "Beethoven's 'New Way' and the *Eroica*," in *The Creative World of Beethoven*, ed. Paul Henry Lang (New York: Norton, 1970).

26. Cf. Greene, who argues convincingly that the Beethovenian coda can transform a "past-orientation" into a "future-orientation." Greene, *Temporal Processes in Beethoven's Music*, 72.

27. This aspect of the *Bildungsroman* was brought to an extreme in Thomas Mann's *Magic Mountain*, in that he consciously designed his novel to be reread rather than read. The novel could pass for a twentieth-century parody of Hegel's targeted state of absolute knowledge: time appears to stand still as Western culture itself takes the cure, breathing the air of a magic mountain of world-weary ideation, its own paralyzing legacy.

28. For Dickens, of course, such references also served to keep interest alive long enough to compel one to buy the next issue of the serial.

29. Yet this view is still influential in Germany, if Dahlhaus is any indication; see Dahlhaus, *Ludwig van Beethoven*, 109ff.

30. Michael Broyles has comprehensively cataloged the elements of French Revolutionary music that bear upon Beethoven's heroic style; they include an overall tone of grandeur, a militaristic quality, an emphasis on vocal melody, and an emphasis on massive sonorities. Also important are various thematic similarities, including the rhythmic motive of Opp. 67 and 57, which Broyles finds in Cherubini and Méhul. See Broyles, *Beethoven: The Emergence and Evolution of the Heroic Style* (New York: Excelsior, 1987), especially 120ff.

31. Robert Hatten traces another, and very illuminating, connection between Beethoven and Goethe having to do with the topos of abnegation. See Robert S. Hatten, *Musical Meaning in Beethoven: Markedness, Correlation, and Interpretation* (Bloomington: Indiana University Press, 1994), esp. 281–86.

32. On Moritz's view of the active force in connection with Egmont, see Nicholas Boyle, *Goethe*, vol. 1, 517ff.

33. Ibid., 517.

34. Incidentally, this scene also forms the starting point for Arnold Schering's interpretation of Beethoven's overture as a study of Egmont's conflicting inner and outer personae. See Schering, *Humor, Heldentum, Tragik bei Beethoven: Über einige Grundsymbole der Tonsprache Beethovens* (Strasbourg: Librairie Heitz, 1955), 44.

35. As the play's first reviewer (in the *Allgemeine Literaturzeitung* of September 1788), Schiller referred to the ending as Goethe's "salto mortale" (somersault) into a world of opera.

36. This sort of plight relates *Egmont* to another of the poet's so-called Weimar plays, *Torquato Tasso*. In *Tasso*, the main character is a self-involved artist who becomes shipwrecked on the shoals of a basically political society.

37. In the case of Klärchen, the stage direction uses the verb *Bezeichnen* (mark, denote, designate) to describe what the music does to her death.

38. Trans. Charles E. Passage in *Egmont: A Tragedy in Five Acts*, 102.

39. Such an ending would thus prefigure the ending of Rilke's *Cornet*, where the sight of death-dealing swords becomes an aesthetic epiphany. (*Die Weise von Liebe und Tod des Cornets Christoph Rilke*, 1906)

40. Depending on one's point of view, either Goethe's bad faith about his ending prompted him to appropriate the overdetermined closure of music, or his supreme faith in the sense of his ending called for the only medium felt to be equal to such consummate finality.

41. Dahlhaus, *Ludwig van Beethoven*, 14.

42. Ernst Oster, "The Dramatic Character of the *Egmont* Overture," *Musicology* 2, no. 3 (1949), 269–85; reprinted in David Beach, ed., *Aspects of Schenkerian Theory* (New Haven: Yale University Press, 1983), 209–22.

43. Martha Calhoun, "Music as Subversive Text: Beethoven, Goethe and the Overture to *Egmont*," *Mosaic* 20, no. 1 (Winter 1987), 43–56.

44. In support of her reading, Calhoun cites Beethoven's note to the sketch: "The main point is that the Dutch at last defeat the Spaniards." Ibid., 50.

45. Edward T. Cone, *Musical Form and Musical Performance* (New York: Norton, 1968), 16.

46. Oster, "The Dramatic Character of the *Egmont* Overture," in Beach, *Aspects of Schenkerian Theory*, 221.

47. Hegel, *Phänomenologie des Geistes*, 103.

48. See Carolyn Abbate, *Unsung Voices: Opera and Musical Narrative in the Nineteenth Century* (Princeton: Princeton University Press, 1991), especially chapters 1 and 2.

49. Ibid., 29. In a rich meditation on narrativity and voice in Beethoven's String Quartet Op. 130, Richard Kramer explores aspects of mimesis and diegesis in late-period Beethoven. Richard Kramer, "Between Cavatina and Ouverture: Opus 130 and the Voices of Narrative," *Beethoven Forum* 1 (Lincoln: University of Nebraska Press, 1992), 165–89.

50. Rosen, *The Classical Style*, 460.

51. Cf. Charles Rosen's view of Mozart and musical convention: whereas Haydn and Beethoven treat conventions in idiosyncratic ways, "Mozart displays the conventions nakedly: his radical ideas co-exist side by side with the most commonplace ones, the latter transformed only by his exquisite workmanship." Rosen, "Radical, Conventional Mozart," *New York Review of Books* 38, no. 21 (19 December 1991): 53.

52. For a more developed version of this view of Mozart's opera, see my essay "Mozart's *felix culpa*: *Così fan tutte* and the Irony of Beauty," *Musical Quarterly* 78, no. 1 (Spring 1994): 77–98.

53. As in Rey M. Longyear, "Beethoven and Romantic Irony," in *The Creative World of Beethoven*, ed. Paul Henry Lang (New York: Norton, 1970), 145–62.

54. For a discussion of irony in Beethoven within the context of a semiotic theory of musical expression see Hatten, *Musical Meaning in Beethoven*, esp. 172–88.

CHAPTER FIVE
BEETHOVEN HERO

1. For a more detailed view of Marx's early criticism of Beethoven, see my "Criticism, Faith, and the *Idee*: A. B. Marx's Early Reception of Beethoven." *19th-Century Music* 13, no. 3 (Spring 1990): 191.

2. Wagner, *Gesammelte Schriften und Dichtungen* (Leipzig: E. W. Fritzsch, 1871–83), vol. 1, 180.

3. See chapter 1, 25.

4. Dahlhaus, *Ludwig van Beethoven: Approaches to His Music*, trans. Mary Whittall (Oxford: Clarendon Press, 1991), chapter 9; and Ludwig Finscher, "Beethovens Klaviersonate Opus 31, 3. Versuch einer Interpretation," in *Festschrift für Walter Wiora* (Kassel: Bärenreiter, 1967), 385–96.

5. On Schering's problematic attempt to reconcile aesthetics and history see Arno Forchert, "Scherings Beethovendeutung und ihre methodischen Voraussetzungen," in *Beiträge zur musikalischen Hermeneutik*, ed. Carl Dahlhaus (Regensburg: Gustav Bosse, 1975), 52.

6. Rudolph Réti, *The Thematic Process in Music* (1951; reprint, Westport, Conn.: Greenwood Press, 1978), 191.

7. This idea has been daringly essayed in the work of Eliot Handelman, who conceptualizes music as a secondary, and invasive, consciousness. See his "Music as Secondary Consciousness: An Implementation" (Ph.D. dissertation, Princeton University, 1991).

8. James Webster, *Haydn's "Farewell" Symphony and the Idea of Classical Style* (Cambridge: Cambridge University Press, 1991), 373.

9. Joseph Kerman, *Write All These Down: Essays on Music* (Berkeley and Los Angeles: University of California Press, 1994), 234.

10. Susan McClary discusses Schubert in terms of such "counternarratives" in "Constructions of Subjectivity in Schubert's Music," in *Queering the Pitch: The New Gay and Lesbian Musicology* (New York: Routledge, 1994), 205–33.

11. We have yet to determine the degree to which the formation of the Beethoven mythology was influenced by the literary apotheosis of Beethoven undertaken by such writers as Hoffmann, Bettina von Arnim, Ludwig Tieck (e.g., *Phantasus*), and Clemens Brentano (e.g., his poem "Nachklänge Beethovenscher Musik").

12. Wagner, *Beethoven* (Leipzig: E. W. Fritzsch, 1870), 26.

13. The importance of the *Kompositionslehre* for spiritual *Bildung* is a central argument in Marx's polemical assessment of the state of music pedagogy in nineteenth-century Germany. See his *Die alte Musiklehre im Streit mit unserer Zeit* (Leipzig: Breitkopf and Härtel, 1841), especially the preface, introduction, and first chapter.

14. Heinrich Schenker, "Beethovens Dritte Sinfonie, in ihrem wahren Inhalt zum erstenmal dargestellt," in *Das Meisterwerk in der Musik*, vol. 3 (Munich: Drei Masken Verlag, 1930), 32.

15. One might also draw parallels between Achilles and our biographical view of Beethoven. Achilles is a disdainful and sullen brooder; he sees his life

as fated for posthumous glory; he is (fatally) attached to a younger man who is not his son.

16. Gregory Nagy, *The Best of the Achaeans: Concepts of the Hero in Archaic Greek Poetry* (Baltimore: Johns Hopkins University Press, 1979), 69ff.

17. Joseph Dubiel, "'When You Are a Beethoven': Kinds of Rules in Schenker's *Counterpoint*," *Journal of Music Theory* 34, no. 2 (Fall 1990): 307. Dubiel continues: "Wouldn't it be enough to say that the piece *is* as it is, and that hearing it well means realizing how everything about it contributes in a variety of ways to a very full sense of *how* it is . . . ? What of value would be lost under this less grandiose explanatory program? The sense of the composer as inspired somnambulist, perhaps? But what is the value of that?" And later: "[We should work toward] the richest possible description of exactly *what* this composition, under this hearing, is."

18. Kevin Korsyn, "Brahms Research and Aesthetic Ideology," *Music Analysis* 12, no. 1 (March 1993): 91–92. Korsyn is drawing in part on the work of Terry Eagleton, *The Ideology of the Aesthetic* (Oxford: Basil Blackwell, 1990).

19. David Epstein, *Beyond Orpheus: Studies in Musical Structure* (Cambridge, Mass.: MIT Press, 1979), 10. A fascinating recent exception to this general state of affairs is found in Michael Schiano, "Arnold Schoenberg's *Grundgestalt* and Its Influence" (Ph.D. dissertation, Brandeis University, 1992). In developing his own theory of background motivic relationships, Schiano provides a more formal approach to Réti's work, concluding that Réti's imprecise use of language often misrepresents and ultimately undermines the importance of his musical discoveries.

20. Cf. Leonard Meyer, *Explaining Music: Essays and Explorations* (Berkeley and Los Angeles: University of California Press, 1973), 64.

21. That Schenker's theory of music is actually a theory of genius in music (musical mastery) is well argued by Nicholas Cook in "Schenker's Theory of Music as Ethics," *Journal of Musicology* 7, no. 4 (Fall 1989): 415–39.

22. For E.T.A. Hoffmann, only the half-trained amateur needs to make such things explicit, using them as a kind of scaffolding to assist in hearing the musical work. Neither the fully trained musician nor the untrained music lover has the same trouble understanding the music: the former has long since discarded the scaffolding and the latter simply does without it. See Hoffmann, "On a Remark of Sacchini's," in *E.T.A. Hoffmann's Musical Writings: "Kreisleriana," "The Poet and the Composer," Music Criticism*, ed. David Charlton (Cambridge: Cambridge University Press, 1989, 153). I thank Charles Rosen for reminding me of this passage in Hoffmann.

23. Edward T. Cone has bravely addressed this question by constructing a readerly analogy concerning a progression of different readings of a detective story. The result is a perceptual scenario in which the listener comes around full circle to the first blush of the initial hearing but with the knowledge of where the music will go—knowledge that contributes to the enjoyment of the play of the music's narrative. Thus Cone arrives at a solution that is almost mythical in its evocation of initial innocence and the return to grace through knowledge. But even so, his differentiated stages of hearing ultimately imply that plot construction—process and its construction—remains the chief attrac-

tion, that the main order of business in the listening experience is to keep abreast of expectations and realizations. See Cone, "Three Ways of Reading a Detective Story or a Brahms Intermezzo," reprinted in *Music—A View from Delft: Selected Essays* (Chicago: University of Chicago Press, 1989).

24. See n. 7.

25. J. K. Randall, liner notes to "Lyric Variations for Violin and Computer," *Open Space 5*, compact disc recording (Red Hook, N. Y.: Open Space, 1993).

26. I have clearly left unquestioned the metaphor itself of presence. But help is on the way: a brilliantly engaging treatment of this subject can be found in Stan Link, "Essay towards Musical Negation" (Ph.D. dissertation, Princeton University, 1995), especially chapter 2.

27. See the introduction, n. 2.

BIBLIOGRAPHY

Abbate, Carolyn. *Unsung Voices: Opera and Musical Narrative in the Nineteenth Century*. Princeton: Princeton University Press, 1991.

Abrams, M. H. *The Mirror and the Lamp: Romantic Theory and the Critical Tradition*. Oxford: Oxford University Press, 1953.

———. *Natural Supernaturalism: Tradition and Revolution in Romantic Literature*. New York: Norton, 1971.

Adorno, Theodor W. "On the Problem of Musical Analysis." Introduced and trans. Max Paddison. *Music Analysis* 1, no. 2 (1982): 169–87.

———. "Schubert." In *Musikalische Schriften*, vol. 4: *Moments musicaux, Impromptus*, 18–33. Frankfurt: Suhrkamp, 1982.

Agawu, V. Kofi. *Playing with Signs: A Semiotic Interpretation of Classic Music*. Princeton: Princeton University Press, 1991.

Bekker, Paul. *Beethoven* . Berlin: Schuster and Loeffler, 1911.

Bent, Ian. "Analysis." In *The New Grove Dictionary of Music and Musicians*, ed. Stanley Sadie. London: Macmillan, 1980.

Berlioz, Hector. *À Travers Chants*. Paris: Gründ, 1971.

Blackall, Eric A. *The Novels of the German Romantics*. Ithaca: Cornell University Press, 1983.

Boyle, Nicholas. *Goethe: The Poet and the Age*. Vol. 1: *The Poetry of Desire*. Oxford: Clarendon Press, 1991.

Broyles, Michael. *Beethoven: The Emergence and Evolution of the Heroic Style*. New York: Excelsior, 1987.

Burkhart, Charles. "Schenker's 'Motivic Parallelisms.'" *Journal of Music Theory* 22, no. 2 (Fall 1978): 145–76.

Burnham, Scott. "Aesthetics, Theory and History in the Works of A. B. Marx." Ph.D. dissertation, Brandeis University, 1988.

———. "Criticism, Faith, and the *Idee*: A. B. Marx's Early Reception of Beethoven." *19th-Century Music* 13, no. 3 (Spring 1990): 183–92.

———. "How Music Matters: Poetic Content Revisited." In *Rethinking Music*, ed. Nicholas Cook and Mark Everist. Oxford University Press, forthcoming.

———. "Method and Motivation in Hugo Riemann's History of Harmonic Theory." *Music Theory Spectrum* 14, no. 1 (Spring 1992): 1–14.

———. "The Role of Sonata Form in A. B. Marx's Theory of Form." *Journal of Music Theory* 33, no. 2 (Fall 1989): 247–71.

Cadwallader, Allen, and William Pastille. "Schenker's High-Level Motives." *Journal of Music Theory* 36, no. 1 (Spring 1992): 117–48.

Calhoun, Martha. "Music as Subversive Text: Beethoven, Goethe, and the Overture to *Egmont*." *Mosaic* 20, no. 1 (Winter 1987): 43–56.

Cassirer, Ernst. *Freiheit und Form: Studien zur deutschen Geistesgeschichte*. Berlin: Bruno Cassirer, 1922.

Cohn, Richard. "The Autonomy of Motives in Schenkerian Accounts of Tonal Music." *Music Theory Spectrum* 14, no. 2 (Fall 1992): 150–70.

Comini, Alessandra. *The Changing Image of Beethoven: A Study in Mythmaking*. New York: Rizzoli, 1987.

Cone, Edward T. *Music—A View from Delft: Selected Essays*. Chicago: University of Chicago Press, 1989.

————. *Musical Form and Musical Performance*. New York: Norton, 1968.

Cook, Nicholas. "Schenker's Theory of Music as Ethics." *Journal of Musicology* 7, no. 4 (Fall 1989): 415–39.

Dahlhaus, Carl. "Ästhetische Prämissen der 'Sonatenform' bei Adolf Bernhard Marx." *Archiv für Musikwissenschaft* 41 (1984): 73–85.

————. *The Idea of Absolute Music*. Trans. Roger Lustig. Chicago: University of Chicago Press, 1989.

————. *Ludwig van Beethoven: Approaches to His Music*. Trans. Mary Whittall. Oxford: Clarendon Press, 1991.

————. *Nineteenth-Century Music*. Trans. J. Bradford Robinson. Berkeley and Los Angeles: University of California Press, 1989.

————. "Textgeschichte und Rezeptionsgeschichte." In *Rezeptionsästhetik und Rezeptionsgeschichte in der Musikwissenschaft*, ed. Hermann Danuser and Friedhelm Krummacher, 105–14. Laaber: Laaber-Verlag, 1991.

Downs, Philip G. "Beethoven's 'New Way' and the *Eroica*." In *The Creative World of Beethoven*, ed. Paul Henry Lang, 83–102. New York: Norton, 1970.

Dubiel, Joseph. "'When You Are a Beethoven': Kinds of Rules in Schenker's *Counterpoint*." *Journal of Music Theory* 34, no. 2 (Fall 1990): 291–340.

Eggebrecht, Hans Heinrich. *Zur Geschichte der Beethoven-Rezeption: Beethoven 1970*. Mainz: Verlag der Akademie der Wissenschaften und der Literatur, 1972.

Eicke, Kurt-Erich. *Der Streit zwischen Adolph Bernhard Marx und Gottfried Wilhelm Fink um die Kompositionslehre*. Ed. Karl Gustav Fellerer. Kölner Beiträge zur Musikforschung, vol. 42. Regensburg: Gustav Bosse Verlag, 1966.

Epstein, David. *Beyond Orpheus: Studies in Musical Structure*. Cambridge, Mass.: MIT Press, 1979.

Finscher, Ludwig. "Beethovens Klaviersonate Opus 31, 3. Versuch einer Interpretation." In *Festschrift für Walter Wiora*, 385–96. Kassel: Bärenreiter, 1967.

Forchert, Arno. "Adolf Bernhard Marx und seine *Berliner Allgemeine musikalische Zeitung*." In *Studien zur Musikgeschichte Berlins im frühen 19. Jahrhundert*, ed. Carl Dahlhaus, 381–404. Studien zur Musikgeschichte des 19. Jahrhunderts, vol. 56. Regensburg: Gustav Bosse, 1980.

————. "Scherings Beethovendeutung und ihre methodischen Voraussetzungen." In *Beiträge zur musikalischen Hermeneutik*, ed. Carl Dahlhaus, 41–52. Studien zur Musikgeschichte des 19. Jahrhunderts, vol. 43. Regensburg: Gustav Bosse, 1975.

Geck, Martin, and Peter Schleuning. *"Geschrieben auf Bonaparte": Beethoven's "Eroica": Revolution, Reaktion, Rezeption*. Reinbek bei Hamburg: Rowohlt, 1989.

Goethe, Johann Wolfgang von. *Goethes Werke*. Hamburger Ausgabe in 14 Bänden. Hamburg: Christian Wegner, 1948–60.

Goldschmidt, Harry. *Beethoven-Studien I: Die Erscheinung Beethoven*. Leipzig: Deutscher Verlag für Musik, 1974.

Greene, David B. *Temporal Processes in Beethoven's Music*. New York: Gordon and Breach, 1982.

Grove, Sir George. *Beethoven and His Nine Symphonies*. London: Novello, 1896.

Halm, August. "Über den Wert musikalischer Analysen, I: Der Fremdkörper im ersten Satz der Eroica." *Die Musik* 12, no. 2 (1929): 481–84.

––––––. *Von Zwei Kulturen der Musik*. Stuttgart: Ernst Klett, 1947.

Handelman, Eliot. "Music as Secondary Consciousness: An Implementation." Ph.D. dissertation, Princeton University, 1991.

Handschin, Jacques. *Der Toncharakter: Eine Einführung in die Tonpsychologie*. Zürich: Atlantis Verlag, 1948.

Hatten, Robert S. *Musical Meaning in Beethoven: Markedness, Correlation, and Interpretation*. Bloomington: Indiana University Press, 1994.

Hegel, Georg Wilhelm Friedrich. *Phänomenologie des Geistes*. In *Gesammelte Werke*, vol. 9. Hamburg: Felix Meiner, 1980.

Heuss, Alfred. *Beethoven: Eine Charakteristik*. Leipzig: R. Voigtländers Verlag, 1921.

Hoffmann, E.T.A. *E.T.A. Hoffmann's Musical Writings: "Kreisleriana," "The Poet and the Composer," Music Criticism*. Ed. David Charlton. Cambridge: Cambridge University Press, 1989.

Hoffmannsthal, Hugo von. *Beethoven*. Vienna: Herbert Reichner, 1938.

Hölderlin, Friedrich. *"Hyperion" and Selected Poems*. Ed. Eric L. Santer. German Library, vol. 22. New York: Continuum, 1990.

Homer. *The Iliad of Homer*. Trans. Richmond Lattimore. Chicago: University of Chicago Press, 1951.

Hugo, Victor. *William Shakespeare*. In *Victor Hugo Oeuvres Complètes*, ed. Jean Massin, 127–448. Édition chronologique, vol. 12. Paris: Le club Français du Livre, 1969.

Jander, Owen. "Beethoven's 'Orpheus in Hades': The *Andante con moto* of the Fourth Piano Concerto." *19th-Century Music* 8 (Spring 1985): 195–212.

Jonas, Oswald. *Einführung in die Lehre Heinrich Schenkers: Das Wesen des musikalischen Kunstwerks*. Rev. ed. Vienna: Universal Edition, 1972.

Keiler, Allan. "On Some Properties of Schenker's Pitch Derivations." *Music Perception* 1 (1983–84): 200–228.

Kerman, Joseph. *The Beethoven Quartets*. New York: Norton, 1966.

––––––. "Notes on Beethoven's Codas." In *Beethoven Studies*, vol. 3, ed. Alan Tyson, 141–59. Cambridge: Cambridge University Press, 1982.

––––––. *Write All These Down: Essays on Music*. Berkeley and Los Angeles: University of California Press, 1994.

Koch, Heinrich Christoph. *Versuch einer Anleitung zur Komposition*. 3 vols. Leipzig: Böhme, 1782–93.

Korsyn, Kevin. "Brahms Research and Aesthetic Ideology." *Music Analysis* 12, no. 1 (March 1993): 89–103.

Knittel, Kristin M. "From Chaos to History: The Reception of Beethoven's Late Quartets." Ph.D. dissertation, Princeton University, 1992.

Kramer, Lawrence. *Music and Poetry: The Nineteenth Century and After*. Berkeley and Los Angeles: University of California Press, 1984.

Kramer, Richard. "Between Cavatina and Ouverture: Opus 130 and the Voices of Narrative." In *Beethoven Forum*, vol. 1, 165–89. Lincoln: University of Nebraska Press, 1992.

Kretzschmar, Hermann. *Führer durch den Concertsaal: Sinfonie und Suite*. 3d ed. Vol. 1. Leipzig: Breitkopf and Härtel, 1898.

Küthen, Hans-Werner. "Beethovens 'wirklich ganz neue Manier'—Eine Persiflage." In *Beiträge zu Beethovens Kammermusik*, ed. Sieghard Brandenburg and Helmut Loos, 216–24. Munich: G. Henle Verlag, 1987.

Lenz, Wilhelm von. *Beethoven: Eine Kunst-Studie*. Hamburg: Hoffmann and Campe, 1855–60.

Lockwood, Lewis. "'Eroica' Perspectives: Strategy and Design in the First Movement." In *Beethoven Studies*, vol. 3., ed. Alan Tyson, 85–105. Cambridge: Cambridge University Press, 1982.

———. "On the Coda of the Finale of Beethoven's Fifth Symphony." In *Divertimento für Hermann J. Abs*, ed. Martin Staehelin, 41–48. Bonn: Beethoven-Haus, 1981.

Longyear, Rey M. "Beethoven and Romantic Irony." In *The Creative World of Beethoven*, ed. Paul Henry Lang, 145–62. New York: Norton, 1970.

Lorenz, Alfred. "Worauf beruht die bekannte Wirkung der Durchführung im I. Eroicasatze." *Neues Beethoven-Jahrbuch*, ed. Adolf Sandberger, vol. 1 (1924): 159–83.

Lubben, Joseph. "Schenker the Progressive: Analytic Practice in *Der Tonwille*." *Music Theory Spectrum* 15, no. 1 (Spring 1993): 59–75.

Marx, Adolph Bernhard. *Die alte Musiklehre im Streit mit unserer Zeit*. Leipzig: Breitkopf and Härtel, 1841.

———. "Die Form in der Musik." In *Die Wissenschaften im neunzehnten Jahrhundert*, vol. 2, ed. Dr. J. A. Romberg, 21–48. Leipzig: Romberg's Verlag, 1856.

———. *Die Lehre von der musikalischen Komposition, praktisch-theoretisch*. 4 vols. 2d ed. Leipzig: Breitkopf and Härtel, 1841–51.

———. *Ludwig van Beethoven: Leben und Schaffen*. 3d ed. Berlin: Otto Janke, 1875.

———. *Die Musik des neunzehnten Jahrhunderts und ihre Pflege: Methode der Musik*. 2d ed. Leipzig: Breitkopf and Härtel, 1873.

Maus, Fred. "Music as Drama." *Music Theory Spectrum* 10 (1988): 56–73.

Meikle, Robert B. "Thematic Transformation in the First Movement of Beethoven's *Eroica* Symphony." *Music Review* 32, no. 3 (August 1971): 205–18.

Meyer, Leonard. "Exploiting Limits: Creation, Archetypes, and Style Change." *Daedalus* 109, no. 2 (Spring 1980): 177–205.

Morgan, Robert. "The Theory and Analysis of Tonal Rhythm." *Musical Quarterly* 64, no. 4 (October 1978): 435–73.

Nagy, Gregory. *The Best of the Achaeans: Concepts of the Hero in Archaic Greek Poetry*. Baltimore: Johns Hopkins University Press, 1979.

Nietzsche, Friedrich. *Friedrich Nietzsche Gesammelte Werke*. 23 vols. Munich: Musarion Ausgabe, 1922–29.

Oster, Ernst. "The Dramatic Character of the *Egmont* Overture." *Musicology* 2, no. 3 (1949): 269–85. Reprinted in *Aspects of Schenkerian Theory*, ed. David Beach, 209–22. New Haven: Yale University Press, 1983.

Oulibicheff, Aléxandre. *Beethoven, ses critiques, ses glossateurs.* Paris: Gavelot and Leipzig: F. A. Brockhaus, 1857.

Ratner, Leonard. *Classic Music: Expression, Form, and Style.* New York: Schirmer Books, 1980.

Redfield, James M. *Nature and Culture in the Iliad: The Tragedy of Hector.* Chicago: University of Chicago Press, 1975.

Réti, Rudolph. *Thematic Patterns in Sonatas of Beethoven.* Ed. Deryck Cooke. London: Faber and Faber, 1967.

————. *The Thematic Process in Music.* 1951. Reprint, Westport, Conn.: Greenwood Press, 1978.

Reynolds, Christopher. "The Representational Impulse in Late Beethoven, II: String Quartet in F Major, Op. 135." *Acta Musicologica* 40, no. 1 (1988): 180–94.

Riemann, Hugo. *Die Elemente der musikalischen Aesthetik.* Berlin: W. Spemann, 1900.

————. *Geschichte der Musik seit Beethoven (1800–1900).* Berlin: W. Spemann, 1901.

————. *L. van Beethovens sämtliche Klavier-sonaten: Ästhetische und formal-technische Analyse mit historischen Notizen.* 3 vols. 3d ed. Berlin: Max Hesses Verlag, 1920.

Riezler, Walter. *Beethoven.* Trans. G.D.H. Pidcock. New York: Dutton, 1938.

Rolland, Romain. *Beethoven the Creator. The Great Creative Epochs: I (From the "Eroica" to the "Appassionata").* Trans. Ernest Newman. New York: Garden City Publishing, 1937.

Rosen, Charles. *The Classical Style: Haydn, Mozart, Beethoven.* New York: Norton, 1972.

————. *Sonata Forms.* Rev. ed. New York: Norton, 1988.

Schenker, Heinrich. *Beethoven V. Sinfonie.* Vienna: Universal Edition, 1925.

————. "Beethovens Dritte Sinfonie, in ihrem wahren Inhalt zum erstenmal dargestellt." In Schenker, *Das Meisterwerk in der Musik: Ein Jahrbuch,* vol. 3, 29–101. Munich: Drei Masken Verlag, 1930.

————. *Beethovens Neunte Sinfonie.* Vienna: Universal Edition, 1912.

————. "Fortsetzung der Urlinie-Betrachtungen." In *Das Meisterwerk in der Musik: Ein Jahrbuch,* Vol. 1, 185–200. Munich: Drei Masken Verlag, 1925.

————. "Fortsetzung der Urlinie-Betrachtungen." In *Das Meisterwerk in der Musik: Ein Jahrbuch,* Vol. 2, 11–42. Munich: Drei Masken Verlag, 1926.

————. *Harmony.* Trans. Elizabeth Mann Borgese. Chicago: University of Chicago Press, 1954.

————. *Der Tonwille: Flugblätter zum Zeugnis unwandelbarer Gesetze der Tonkunst einer neuen Jugend dargebracht von Heinrich Schenker.* 10 vols. Vienna: Tonwille-Flugblätterverlag, 1921–24.

Schering, Arnold. *Beethoven und die Dichtung.* Berlin: Junker und Dünnhaupt, 1936.

————. "Die Eroica, eine Homer-Symphonie Beethovens?" *Neues Beethoven Jahrbuch* 5 (1933): 159–77.

————. *Humor, Heldentum, Tragik bei Beethoven: Über einige Grundsymbole der Tonsprache Beethovens.* Strasbourg: Librairie Heitz, 1955.

Schiano, Michael. "Arnold Schoenberg's *Grundgestalt* and Its Influence." Ph.D. dissertation, Brandeis University, 1992.

Schiller, Friedrich. *Schillers Werke*. National Ausgabe. Weimar: Hermann Böhlaus, various dates.

Schlegel, August Wilhelm. *Kritische Schriften*. Ed. Emil Staiger. Zurich: Artemis, 1962.

Schlegel, Friedrich, and August Wilhelm Schlegel, eds. *Athenäum: Eine Zeitschrift von August Wilhelm Schlegel und Friedrich Schlegel*. Berlin: Friedrich Vierweg, 1798.

Schleuning, Peter. "Beethoven in alter Deutung: Der 'neue Weg' mit der 'Sinfonia Eroica.'" *Archiv für Musikwissenschaft* 44, no. 3 (1987): 165–94.

Schmitt, Ulrich. *Revolution im Konzertsaal: Zur Beethoven-Rezeption im 19. Jahrhundert*. Mainz: Schott, 1990.

Schmitz, Arnold. *Das romantische Beethoven-Bild*. Berlin: Dümmler, 1927.

Schrade, Leo. *Beethoven in France: The Growth of an Idea*. New Haven: Yale University Press, 1942.

Sipe, Thomas. "Interpreting Beethoven: History, Aesthetics, and Critical Reception." Ph.D. dissertation, University of Pennsylvania, 1992.

Solie, Ruth. Review of William C. Mickelsen's *Hugo Riemann's Theory of Harmony*. *19th-Century Music* 2, no. 2 (1978): 178–85.

Solomon, Maynard. *Beethoven*. New York: Schirmer Books, 1977.

———. *Beethoven Essays*. Cambridge, Mass.: Harvard University Press, 1988.

———. "Beethoven's Ninth Symphony: A Search for Order." *19th-Century Music* 10 (Summer 1986): 3–23.

Subotnik, Rose Rosengard. *Developing Variations: Style and Ideology in Western Music*. Minneapolis: University of Minnesota Press, 1991.

Sullivan, J.W.N. *Beethoven: His Spiritual Development*. New York: Alfred A. Knopf, 1927.

Taylor, Gary. *Reinventing Shakespeare: A Cultural History from the Restoration to the Present*. Oxford: Oxford University Press, 1989.

Thaler, Lotte. *Organische Form in der Musiktheorie des 19. und beginnenden 20. Jahrhunderts*. Munich: Musikverlag E. Katzbichler, 1984.

Thorslev, Peter L., Jr. *The Byronic Hero: Types and Prototypes*. Minneapolis: University of Minnesota Press, 1962.

Tovey, Donald Francis. *Beethoven*. London: Oxford University Press, 1945.

———. *A Companion to Beethoven's Pianoforte Sonatas*. London: Associated Board of the Royal Schools of Music, 1931.

———. *Essays in Musical Analysis*, vol. 1: *Symphonies*. London: Oxford University Press, 1935.

———. *Essays in Musical Analysis*, vol. 3: *Concertos*. London: Oxford University Press, 1936.

———. *Essays in Musical Analysis*, vol. 4: *Illustrative Music*. London: Oxford University Press, 1937.

———. *Essays in Musical Analysis*, vol. 5: *Vocal Music*. London: Oxford University Press, 1937.

Wagner, Richard. *Beethoven*. Leipzig: E. W. Fritzsch, 1870.

———. *Gesammelte Schriften und Dichtungen*. Leipzig: E. W. Fritzsch, 1871–83.

Waldbauer, Ivan. "Riemann's Periodization Revisited and Revised." *Journal of Music Theory* 33, no. 2 (Fall 1989): 333–91.

Wallace, Robin. *Beethoven's Critics: Aesthetic Dilemmas and Resolutions during the Composer's Lifetime*. Cambridge: Cambridge University Press, 1986.

Webster, James. "The D-Major Interlude in Haydn's 'Farewell Symphony.'" *Studies in Musical Sources and Style: Essays in Honor of Jan LaRue*, ed. Eugene K. Wolf and Edward H. Roesner, 339–80. Madison, Wis.: A-R Editions, 1991.

———. *Haydn's "Farewell" Symphony and the Idea of Classical Style*. Cambridge: Cambridge University Press, 1991.

Wellek, René. *A History of Modern Criticism 1750–1950*, vol. 2: *The Romantic Age*. Cambridge: Cambridge University Press, 1981.

INDEX

SCOTT BURNHAM IS ASSOCIATE PROFESSOR OF MUSIC AT PRINCETON UNIVERSITY